The Econometrics of Sport

NEW HORIZONS IN THE ECONOMICS OF SPORT

Series Editors: Wladimir Andreff, *Department of Economics, University of Paris 1 Panthéon Sorbonne, France* and Marc Lavoie, *Department of Economics, University of Ottawa, Canada*

For decades, the economics of sport was regarded as a hobby for a handful of professional economists who were primarily involved in other areas of research. In recent years, however, the significance of the sports economy as a percentage of GDP has expanded dramatically. This has coincided with an equivalent rise in the volume of economic literature devoted to the study of sport.

This series provides a vehicle for deeper analyses of the demand for sport, cost–benefit analysis of sport, sporting governance, the economics of professional sports and leagues, individual sports, trade in the sporting goods industry, media coverage, sponsoring and numerous related issues. It contributes to the further development of sports economics by welcoming new approaches and highlighting original research in both established and newly emerging sporting activities. The series publishes the best theoretical and empirical work from well-established researchers and academics, as well as from talented newcomers in the field.

Titles in the series include:

The Economics of Sport and the Media
Edited by Claude Jeanrenaud and Stefan Késenne

The Economic Theory of Professional Team Sports
An Analytical Treatment
Stefan Késenne

Economics, Uncertainty and European Football
Trends in Competitive Balance
Loek Groot

The Political Economy of Professional Sport
Jean-François Bourg and Jean-Jacques Gouguet

Contemporary Issues in Sports Economics
Participation and Professional Team Sports
Edited by Wladimir Andreff

The Economics of Sport, Health and Happiness
The Promotion of Well-being through Sporting Activities
Edited by Plácido Rodríguez, Stefan Késenne and Brad R. Humphreys

The Econometrics of Sport
Edited by Plácido Rodríguez, Stefan Késenne and Jaume García

The Econometrics of Sport

Edited by

Plácido Rodríguez

University of Oviedo, Spain

Stefan Késenne

University of Antwerp and Catholic University of Leuven, Belgium

Jaume García

Universitat Pompeu Fabra, Spain

NEW HORIZONS IN THE ECONOMICS OF SPORT

Edward Elgar

Cheltenham, UK • Northampton, MA, USA

Published by
Edward Elgar Publishing Limited
The Lypiatts
15 Lansdown Road
Cheltenham
Glos GL50 2JA
UK

Edward Elgar Publishing, Inc.
William Pratt House
9 Dewey Court
Northampton
Massachusetts 01060
USA

A catalogue record for this book
is available from the British Library

Library of Congress Control Number: 2013932952

This book is available electronically in the ElgarOnline.com
Economics Subject Collection, E-ISBN 978 1 78100 286 5

ISBN 978 1 78100 285 8

Typeset by Servis Filmsetting Ltd, Stockport, Cheshire
Printed and bound in Great Britain by T.J. International Ltd, Padstow

Contents

Contributors

 Gabriel M. Ahlfeldt is a lecturer in Urban Economics and Land Development at the London School of Economics and Political Sciences, UK. His quantitative research covers the fields of applied urban and regional economics. He is interested in the spatial dimension of the urban and regional distribution of economic activity, and the spatial interaction between economic agents at various geographic levels. He has published in several journals, including the *Journal of the Royal Statistical Society A*, *Economics Letters*, *Journal of Economic Geography* and *Regional Science and Urban Economics*.

 José Baños is a Lecturer in Economics at University of Oviedo, Spain. He is also coordinator of the Inter-University Master in Economics (University of Oviedo, University of Cantabria and University of País Vasco). He has published several articles in scientific journals, including *Applied Economics Letters*, *Journal of Cultural Economics*, *International Journal of Transport Economics*, *European Journal of Operational Research*, *Papeles de Economía Española*, *Journal of Productivity Analysis* and *International Journal of Sport Management and Marketing*.

 Robert Baumann is Associate Professor in the Department of Economics at the College of the Holy Cross, Worcester, Massachusetts, USA. His research fields deal with labour economics and sports economics. He has published several papers in specialized journals, including the *Journal of Sports Economics*, the *Southern Economic Journal* and *Urban Studies*.

 David J. Berri is a sports economist and an Associate Professor of Applied Economics at Southern Utah University, USA, known for his sometimes-controversial analysis of NBA basketball. He is a member of the editorial board of the *Journal of Sports Economics*.

 Rodney Fort is Professor of Sport Management at University of Michigan, USA. He is the author of the book *Sports Economics* and co-author, with James Quirk, of the books *Pay Dirt: The Business of Professional Team Sports* and *Hard Ball: The Abuse*

of Power in Pro Team Sports. He was, alongside James Quirk, the first author to publish a paper about sports economics in the *Journal of Economic Literature.* He is co-editor with John Fizel of the books *International Sports Economics Comparisons* and *Economics of College Sports.*

 Bernd Frick is Professor of Organizational and Media Economics in the Department of Management and Vice President of the University of Paderborn, Germany with the responsibility for strategy, finance and international relations. His research interests are in labour and personnel economics, and organizational economics, as well as in sports economics. He has published about fifty refereed papers in peer-reviewed journals and is currently working on a monograph entitled *Calcio, Football, Soccer: The Economics of the World's Greatest Team Sport.*

 Jaume García is Professor of Applied Economics at University Pompeu Fabra in Barcelona, Spain. He has published in numerous journals including the *Journal of Sports Economics*, *European Sport Management Quarterly*, *Applied Economics*, *Health Economics* and the *Oxford Bulletin of Economics and Statistics.* He was President of the Spanish Statistics Institute (INE) from 2008 to 2011.

 William Greene is Professor of Economics, Toyota Motor Corp. Professor of Economics and Faculty Fellow of Entertainment, Media and Technology at Stern School of Business, New York University, USA. He has published numerous papers in specialized journals, including the *Journal of Transport Economics and Policy*, *Journal of Econometrics* and the *American Economic Review.*

 Brad R. Humphreys is Professor in the Department of Economics at the University of Alberta, Canada, where he holds the Chair in the Economics of Gaming. He belongs to several editorial boards and has published articles in the *Southern Economic Journal*, *Applied Economics*, *Journal of Sport Management*, *Journal of Sports Economics* and *Contemporary Economic Policy.*

 Leo Kahane is Professor of Economics at Providence College, USA. His research has been published in the *Atlantic Economic Journal*, *Economica*, *Economic Inquiry*, *Public Choice*, *Applied Economics*, the *American Journal of*

Economics and Sociology and the *Review of Economics and Statistics*. He is the co-founder and editor-in-chief of the *Journal of Sports Economics*. His teaching interests include international trade, sports economics and econometrics.

 Georgios Kavetsos is an economist at the Department of Social Policy at the London School of Economics, UK. There are two main themes to his work. The first looks at individuals' revealed preferences to value regional policy interventions; the second uses subjective wellbeing data to value non-market goods. He is currently conducting research on the intangible benefits of the London 2012 Olympic Games.

 Stefan Késenne is Professor of Economics at University of Antwerp and Leuven, Belgium. He has published in numerous journals, including the *European Economic Review, Journal of Industrial Economics, Scottish Journal of Political Economy, Journal of Sports Economics, International Journal of Sport Finance* and the *European Sports Management Quarterly*. He is the author of the book *The Economic Theory of Professional Team Sport: An Analytical Treatment*.

 Young Hoon Lee is Professor of Economics at Sogang University, South Korea, and has a PhD in Economics from Michigan State University, USA. He is an expert in econometrics and sports economics and has published various papers in specialized journals, including *Journal of Econometrics, Economic Inquiry, Journal of Productivity Analysis* and *Journal of Sports Economics*. He has also been a member of the editorial board of the *International Journal of Sport Finance* since 2006.

 Neil Longley is Professor of Economics at the Isenberg School of Management, University of Massachusetts Amherst, USA. His research interests are sports economics and sport finance. He has published in several journals, including the *Journal of Sports Economics* and the *Atlantic Economic Journal*.

 Victor A. Matheson is a Professor of Economics at the College of the Holy Cross, Worcester, Massachusetts, USA. He is an expert in sports economics, especially, in the analysis of great sports events' impact, public finance and gaming economics. He has collaborated as an expert in magazines, including *Forbes, ESPN Magazine* and *The New York Times*.

Roger G. Noll is Professor of Economics Emeritus at Stanford University and a Senior Fellow at the Stanford Institute for Economic Policy Research, USA, where he directs the Program in Regulatory Policy. He is the author or co-author of 12 books and over 300 articles and reviews. Noll's primary research interests include economics of sports and entertainment, among others.

 Plácido Rodríguez is Professor EU of Economics in the Department of Economics at Oviedo University, Spain. He is co-editor of the books *Sports Economics after Fifty Years: Essays in Honour of Simon Rottenberg, Governance and Competition in Professional Sports Leagues, Threats to Sports and Sports Participation and Social Responsibility and Sustainability in Sports*. He was President of Real Sporting de Gijon Football Club, and is the current Director of the Sports Economics Observatory Foundation and the President of International Association of Sports Economists (IASE).

 Robert Simmons is Senior Lecturer in Economics at the Management School, Lancaster University, UK. An expert in labour economics and sports economics, he has been consultant to the International Labour Organization. He is Editor in Chief of the *International Journal of Sport Finance.*

 Stefan Szymanski is the Stephen J. Galetti Professor of Sport Management in the School of Kinesiology at the University of Michigan, USA. He is the author of numerous books and articles on sports economics. His areas of study are sports management and economics; sport history, culture and society; European sport and the internationalization of sport; international sports federations and the governance of sport.

 John Vrooman is a Lecturer in Economics at Vanderbilt University in Tennessee, USA. He has a PhD in Economics from the University of Texas. He is the author of several papers on competitive balance, ('Competitive balance in monopoly sports leagues') and players' labour market of the baseball league ('Unified theory of capital and labor markets in Major League Baseball').

Foreword

This year's Gijon conference on sports economics focused on econometrics and quantitative analysis of sports outcomes. Given the ready availability of large (massive) quantities of high-quality data that are true measurements of their theoretical counterparts, it is to be expected that econometrics would occupy a large part of the literature on the analysis of sports. That literature has traditionally built on four central themes:

- Competitive balance
- Labor relations
- Attendance and demand, price and income elasticities
- Economic impact of sport on the economic community.

Each of these has been explored in a vast theoretical and applied literature. Correspondingly, each occupies a section in this volume.

The quantitative analyses in that tradition have tended to rely on some familiar econometric methods, primarily linear regression methods and dynamic linear models including applications of panel data methods. However, recent studies have also begun to move into less traditional areas, such as discrete choice modeling (for example, for attempting to measure streaks as in basketball and tennis), multinomial choice (for analyzing outcomes of horse races) and stochastic frontier models (for analysis of player performance). This introduction to the conference notes the four traditional foci of research, and briefly touches on a few of these innovations.

COMPETITIVE BALANCE

Team and league owners and player union representatives are concerned with two major issues when they meet – salaries and the distribution of revenues, and competitive balance. The various leagues and organizations have had different degrees of success in achieving these objectives. The roles of incentives and incentive compatibility are large in these areas. The history of organized sports is punctuated with labor problems and strikes, walkouts and lockouts. In 2011, the National Football League

(US) was able to avoid a strike that would have truncated the 2011–12 season by forging a new player agreement. At the time of writing, the National Basketball Association (NBA) is still working on a solution. In their detailed analysis of the problem of competitive balance, writers disagree on the success of league attempts to achieve competitive balance. Revenue sharing is a device used in several sports to attempt to achieve that end. Whether revenue sharing, at the 'back end' of the revenue generation chain should improve results in the competitiveness at the front end is debatable. In one of the centrepieces of this literature, Szymanski and Kesenne (2004) find a counterintuitive result that revenue sharing leads to lower, not higher, investment in talent, and ultimately works in the wrong direction. Nonetheless, sports leagues have relied heavily on revenue sharing to attempt to further competitive balance. The UK, Brazil and other countries also use a system of promotion and relegation within the vertical divisions of football competition to reward success and penalize the lack of it.

Ultimately, the objective of competitive balance is team value. In the US, Major League Baseball and the National Football League (NFL) have had different degrees of success in sharing revenues, with the latter being much more successful. Recent numbers on team valuations (see www.forbes.com) are telling: the striking feature of these data is not the levels of the team valuations – the NFL is clearly more successful overall – but the variances of the two series (Table 1). The NFL, which is much more aggressive about revenue sharing appears to be much more successful in equating team values. As the analysts at *Forbes Magazine* (the source of these data) note, however, the overall level of NFL team valuations has fallen in 2010/11 for the first time since they began tracking team values in 1998.

ATTENDANCE MODELS, DEMAND AND PRICING

Dozens of authors have analyzed attendance and price and income elasticities for sporting events. García and Rodríguez (2009) provide an extensive survey of demand studies for sporting events. A recurrent theme in this literature is the pricing conundrum. Analysts perenially find estimates of the price elasticity between −1 and 0. The implication would be that local monopolies are pricing suboptimally in the inelastic region of the demand curve, in contradiction to what basic theory would predict. Various theories have been advanced for the finding, some based on the econometric methods and others based on the underlying theory of the model. For the first of these, some authors have suggested that 'fan loyalty' (lagged

Table 1 2010 team values

Rank	NBA team	Current value ($MIL)	Rank	NFL team	Current value ($MIL)
1	New York Yankees	1500	1	Dallas Cowboys	1650
2	New York Mets	912	2	Washington Redskins	1550
3	Boston Red Sox	833	3	New England Patriots	1361
4	Los Angels Dodgers	722	4	New York Giants	1183
5	Chicago Cubs	700	5	Yew York Jets	1170
6	Los Angeles Angels of Anaheim	509	6	Houston Texans	1150
7	Philadelphia Phillies	496	7	Philadelphia Eagles	1123
8	St Louis Cardinals	486	8	Tampa Bay Buccaneers	1085
9	San Francisco Giants	471	9	Chicago Bears	1082
10	Chicago White Sox	450	10	Denver Broncos	1081
11	Atlanta Braves	446	11	Baltimore Ravens	1079
12	Houston Astros	445	12	Carolina Panthers	1049
13	Seattle Mariners	426	13	Cleveland Browns	1032
14	Washington Nationals	406	14	Kansas City Chiefs	1027
15	Texas Rangers	405	15	Indianapolis Colts	1025
16	San Diego Padres	401	16	Pittsburgh Steelers	1020
17	Baltimore Orioles	400	17	Green Bay Packers	1019
18	Cleveland Indians	399	18	Miami Dolphins	1015
19	Arizona Diamondbacks	390	19	Tennessee Titans	1000
20	Colorado Rockies	373	20	Seattle Seahawks	994

Source: www.forbes.com.

variables) will improve the models, while others rely on more elaborate models, such as the Tobit framework as opposed to linear regression.

The analysis of fan demand for tickets is a pursuit in its own right. It can also provide input for further analyses. For example, one of the key ingredients of many studies is the extent to which team success translates to demand for tickets. This, in turn provides grist for analysis of the success of major player acquisitions. The case of Alex Rodriguez provides an intriguing example. When the Texas Rangers hired him with an eye-popping 10-year contract in 2000, it was believed that his presence on the team could be expected to produce eight more wins per year. The analytic challenge at this point is to translate eight more wins per year into a broader measure of success. An attendance model of the form

$$Attendance_{it} = \alpha_i + \beta_1 Wins_{it} + \beta_2 Wins_{i,t-1} + \beta_3 Attendance_{i,t-1} + \ldots + \varepsilon_{it}$$

incorporates the relevant effects and the aforementioned fan loyalty effect. In this model, the impact of additional wins on equilibrium attendance is $\partial E[Equilibrium\ Attendance]/\partial Wins = (\beta_1 + \beta_2/(1 - \beta_3))$. No reasonable values of the model parameters produces the roughly 100 000 fans per win per year for 10 consecutive years that would have been necessary to justify economically the roughly $16 000 000 per year that this acquisition cost the team.

This analysis leaves the pricing conundrum to be considered. Two possibilities have been proposed. In a widely cited study, Marburger (1997) argued that teams should be treated as multiproduct firms – seats in the stands are only one of several products they sell. In this setting, the optimal price vector for the firm could well involve pricing one of the several products in the inelastic region of the demand curve. This model is clearly at work in the pricing of movie tickets at theaters, where the main driver of profits is the concession stand, not the film.

A second possibility noted by Roger Noll in his study in this volume (Chapter 7), is a major specification problem. The face value of a ticket to a sporting event (or any other entertainment event) does not represent the true price of the event. The buyer invests often large amounts of time getting to, at and returning from the event. Any reasonable value of the buyer's time will multiply the cost of the event from the buyer's perspective. Since the elasticity is $\partial \ln Q/\partial \ln P$, the denominator is greatly overestimated if the calculation is done with ticket prices without regard to the value of time. For an example, the value $-.57$ is reported in Lee and Miller (2006) for baseball tickets. We suppose this represents the elasticity at a base price of $20 increasing to $25. For a baseball game that involves three hours in the stadium and an hour of transportation in each direction, if time is valued at $10 per hour, the $5 increase in the ticket represents only a 7 percent change in the ticket price, not a 25 percent increase. This translates into an elasticity estimate of $(25\%/7\%)'(-.57)$ or -2.04. The upshot is that measured elasticities may well be measuring the wrong price, and the direction of the error is against the conundrum.

THE HOT HAND AND PROBABILITY MODELING

The search for a 'hot hand' is another area that has attracted some attention in sports. A model that embodies the hypothesis in various forms is one in which outcomes are autocorrelated. The psychology of the perception of a hot hand in basketball was examined by Gilovich et al. (1985). In spite of their negative finding, authors have continued to search for autocorrelation in sequences of ouctomes. The notion has been incorporated in models of basketball, tennis outcomes by Franc et al. (2001) and, recently, in gambling by Rabin and Vayanos (2010). Results are mixed for performance sports as just noted, and likewise for using multinomial discrete choice modeling for handicapping horse races by Bolton and Chapman (2008).

STOCHASTIC FRONTIER MODELING

We note, finally, the availability of rich, accurate data sets on sports performance provides a natural laboratory for modeling in the frontier framework. Koop (2002, 2004) has applied the stochastic frontier model to several performance measures in baseball. In another contribution to this conference, Lee (2011) has used the approach to study baseball success more broadly.

CONCLUSION

The study of sports in the economy presents a rich arena for application of sharply focused micro economics, macroeconomics and econometrics to team and individual outcomes. This conference volume offers a survey of recent analyses that continues the tradition of empirical and theoretical analysis of the economics and econometrics of sports.

REFERENCES

Bolton, R. and R. Chapman (2008), 'Searching for positive returns at the track: a multinomial logit model for handicapping horse races', in D.B. Hausch, V. Lo and W. Ziemba (eds) *The Efficiency of Racetrack Betting Markets*, Hackensack, NJ: World Scientific.

Franc, J., G. Klaassen and J. Magnus (2001), 'Are points in tennis independent and identically distributed? Evidence from a dynamic binary panel Data Model', *Journal of the American Statistical Association*, **96** (454), 500–509.

García, J. and Rodríguez, P. (2009), 'Sports attendance: a survey of the literature – 1973–2007', *Rivista di Diritto ed Economia dello Sport*, **V** (2), 111–51.

Gilovich, T., R. Vallone and A. Tversky (1985), 'The hot hand in basketball: on the misperception of random sequences', *Cognitive Psychology*, **17** (3), 592–6.

Koop, G. (2002), 'Comparing the performance of baseball players: a multiple output approach', *Journal of the American Statistical Association*, **97**, 710–20.

Koop, G. (2004), 'Modelling the evolution of distributions: an application to Major League Baseball', *Journal of the Royal Statistical Society (Series A)*, **167**, 639–56.

Lee, S., K. Park and P. Miller (2006), 'Ticket pricing Per team – the case of MLB', working paper, Department of Sports Management, University of Minnesota.

Lee, Y. (2011), 'Is the small-ball strategy effective in winning games? A stochastic frontier approach', *Journal of Productivity Analysis*, **35**, 51–9.

Marburger, Daniel R. (ed.) (1997), *Stee-rike Four! What's Wrong with the Business of Baseball?* Westport, CT: Praeger Press.

Rabin, M. and D. Vayanos (2010), 'The gambler's and hot-hand fallacies: theory and application', working paper, Department of Economics, University of California, Berkeley.

Szymanski, S. and S. Kesenne (2004), 'Competitive balance and gate revenue sharing in team sports', *Journal of Industrial Economics*, **52** (1), 165–77.

Preface

This book, *The Econometrics of Sport*, focuses on the empirical analysis of sports economics models using econometric techniques. In the Foreword Professor William Greene points out that this literature has been traditionally built on four central themes: competitive balance; labour relations; attendance and demand, price and income elasticities; and economic impact of sport on the economic community. Each section of this volume is devoted to one of these topics.

The first section is devoted to competitive balance with two papers by John Vrooman, and Rodney Fort and Young Hoon Lee. Vrooman presents a comprehensive study on competitive balance theory and Fort and Lee analyse the effect of the uncertainty of outcome on attendance for the case of Major League Baseball. The second part of the book is divided into four chapters about player's labour markets. In the first two, Stefan Szymanski and Bernd Frick study the relationship between players' wages and team performance for the case of English Premier League and European Football Leagues, respectively. The third chapter by Leo Kahane, Neil Longley and Robert Simmons estimates a salary model to distinguish between the salary returns to major and minor offenses in the National Hockey League and they also examine how the post-2004/05 lockout rule changes have affected salaries. The last paper by David Berri, Brad Humphreys and Robert Simmons is an application of what is known as nano-econometrics in which they estimate the returns to performance for offensive linemen in the National Football League.

Attendance is the topic of the third section with three papers. Roger Noll discusses the most relevant specification issues in demand modelling, Young Hoon Lee estimates variations in fan loyalty between teams and through time using multi-factor models applied to data from the Major Baseball League and Jaume García and Plácido Rodríguez analyse the determinants of football match attendance for two different groups of spectators: occasional spectators and season ticket holders, using data from the Spanish Football League. The last section is devoted to economic impact studies and is composed of three studies. In the first, Robert Baumann and Victor Matheson present an empirical examination of the errors in expost economic impact analysis using data on college athletics in the USA. Gabriel Ahlfeldt and Georgios Kavetsos focus on the impact that professional sports facilities have on prices of proximate properties in Greater London. Finally José Baños and Plácido Rodríguez analyse the expected economic impact for Spain of becoming the organizer of the FIFA World Cup.

PART I

Competitive Balance

1. Two to tango: optimum competitive balance in professional sports leagues

John Vrooman

We need to recognize that the smaller clubs are necessary for competition. After all, 15 clásicos at the Bernabéu and 15 at Camp Nou would be a bit boring wouldn't it?

(Fernando Roig, President of Villarreal CF, Spanish Primera Division)

I INTRODUCTION

According to received theory, the perfect game is a symbiotic contest between equal opponents. The practical economic problem is that professional sports leagues form imperfectly competitive natural cartels where games are played between teams with asymmetric market power. In the realm of pure theory the natural duality of sports leagues seems to imply that dominant teams are really only as strong as their weakest opponents. In the real world, however, the success of unbalanced leagues dominated by a few perennially powerful clubs raises the important empirical question as to whether optimal competitive balance may obtain at less than absolute team equality.

The economics of sports has been preoccupied with two prescient propositions from Rottenberg's classic paper on the baseball players' labor market. The first argument centers on the invariance proposition that free agency for baseball players would yield the same talent distribution as the reserve system (since 1876) that bound a player to one team for life. In its strong form the invariance proposition holds that revenue sharing has no effect on talent distribution and it serves only to deepen player exploitation.

In theory, there are only two ways to beat large-market clubs. The logical way is to increase product market competition by adding more teams to their monopoly markets. The second solution involves the internalization of diseconomies of dominance by the large market clubs themselves.

According to the uncertainty of outcome hypothesis (UOH), fans prefer close competition with quality opponents and large market dominance is ultimately self-defeating. The UOH conveniently implies concave revenue functions and diminishing marginal revenue from winning that dampen the internal objectives of profit-maximizing team owners. The UOH rests on the simplifying assumption that fans prefer balanced competition, when they may in fact prefer dominance.

The theoretical foundations of the economics of sports are found in El Hodiri and Quirk (1971). The modern awakening of sports economics came when Quirk and Fort (1992) published a popular version of Quirk's early model, followed by two separate adaptations of sports league theory to the changing realities of the American sports-scape (Fort and Quirk, 1995; Vrooman, 1995). European theorists (Szymanski, 2003, 2004; Szymanski and Kesenne, 2003) used non-cooperative game theory to show that the invariance proposition does not hold in open markets of European football, and that revenue sharing leads to less competitive balance. Open- and closed-market theories both lead to the same paradox: revenue sharing does increase competitive balance.

The open-market distinction may not make any difference in the end, however, because both open and closed labor market models are based on assumptions that owners are profit maximizers. It is likely team owners are sportsmen who sacrifice profit in order to win (Kesenne, 1996; Vrooman, 1997, 2000, 2007). At the limit, sportsman-owners become win maximizers, who spend to win at all cost. The sportsman is constrained by zero profit rather than maximum profit, and distinctions between closed and open labor markets become academic. If owners are sportsmen, then intuition prevails over paradox and it is easy to show that revenue sharing increases competitive balance.

It can easily be shown that sportsman leagues are less balanced than profit-maximizing (profit-max) leagues (Vrooman, 2007, 2009), but also that win-maximizing (win-max) imbalance is superior to profit-max balance in terms of fan welfare. This is true because fans and win-max owners share the singular objective to win. There is evidence that major sports leagues have become dominated by sportsman-owners. The players' share of revenue has recently exceeded 60 percent in the four major North American (NA) leagues and four of the Big 5 European leagues. Player cost controls have also evolved to be very similar in NA, where all leagues except Major League Baseball (MLB) have imposed salary caps just below 60 percent of league revenue.

Since 1990 the Big 5 European leagues have experienced explosive transformations in their media revenues. In 2010 media revenues were 50 percent or more of total revenues in the English Premier League (EPL),

Italian Serie A, Spanish La Liga and the National Football League (NFL). The media revolution transforms optimal competitive balance in two interrelated ways. First, quasi-public games become less exclusive through increased media coverage. Media expands or globalizes 'home markets' and alters fan preferences more toward home team dominance and less toward competitive balance and quality opposition. Given their local home clubs in ticket/gate leagues, fans can only choose among quality opponents, but in media leagues they can freely choose their home teams, regardless of where they reside.

Second, media revenue sharing in sportsman leagues can alter revenue asymmetries among clubs and thereby change increase competitive balance. In all NA leagues national media revenue is shared equally. In four of the Big 5 European leagues media revenue is split using equal/merit/appearance formulae. Ironically, the brave new world of win-max owners playing in media leagues has negated the two founding propositions of sports economics. First, if competitive balance can be engineered through revenue sharing then the invariance proposition does not hold. Second, if competitive balance is not socially optimal in media revenue leagues, then the UOH does not hold either.

This chapter begins with a restatement of the general theory of sports leagues followed by a comparison of operating rules of the Big 4 NA leagues and Big 5 European football leagues. After addressing empirical questions about the effects of media revolutions throughout the leagues, the argument concludes with a comparison of competitive balance in the world's nine major sports leagues over the last 40 years.

II SPORTS LEAGUE THEORY

A Profit Maximizing Owners

Conventional theory of sports leagues (Fort and Quirk, 1995; Vrooman, 1995) begins with simultaneous maximization of twin profit functions in a simplified two-team league:

$$\pi_1 = R_1[m_1, w_1(t_1, t_2)] - ct_1 \qquad \pi_2 = R_2[m_2, w_2(t_2, t_1)] - ct_2 \qquad (1.1)$$

Revenue R_1 of team 1 is a function of its market size m_1 and its winning percentage w_1, which is determined by a contest success function of the standard logistic probability form $w_1(t_1, t_2) = t_1/(t_1 + t_2)$, first used in a sports context by El-Hodiri and Quirk (1971). The zero-sum nature of an n-team league requires $\Sigma w_i = n/2$ and $\partial w_1/\partial w_2 = \partial w_2/\partial w_1 = -1$. A profit-maximizing owner's objective is to max π_1 with respect to t_1. In contrast, a sportsman owner's goal is to maximize wins w_1 produced through t_1, given $\pi_1 \geq 0$.

At the profit maximum, team 1 sets payroll ct_1 by acquiring talent until the marginal revenue product of talent MRP_1 is equal to the marginal cost of talent c (marginal factor cost), which is assumed to be the same for both teams that share a common talent pool:

$$MRP_1 = MR_1 MP_1 = (\partial R_1/\partial w_1)(\partial w_1/\partial t_1) = c \qquad (1.2)$$

Simultaneous profit maximization (mutual best response) for both teams yields:

$$MRP_1 = (\partial R_1/\partial w_1)(\partial w_1/\partial t_1) = c = MRP_2 \qquad (1.3)$$

The standard logit $w_1 = t_1/(t_1 + t_2)$ yields the marginal product of talent MP_1,

$$MP_1 = \partial w_1/\partial t_1 = (t_2 - t_1 \, \partial t_2/\partial t_1)/(t_1 + t_2)^2 \qquad (1.4)$$

That satisfies $\partial w_1/\partial t_1 > 0$; $\partial^2 w_1/\partial t_1^2 < 0$; $\partial w_1/\partial t_2 < 0$. In league equilibrium, the MRP for both teams is equal to their mutual wage rate c:

$$MRP_1 = MR_1 \, MP_1 = [\partial R_1/\partial w_1] \, [(t_2 - t_1 \, \partial t_2/\partial t_1)/T^2] = MRP_2 = c \qquad (1.5)$$

1 Open and closed leagues

In a closed league an inelastic supply of skilled talent $T^* = t_1 + t_2$ is fixed, and one team's talent gain is another team's zero-sum talent loss $\partial t_1/\partial t_2 = \partial t_2/\partial t_1 = -1$. Substitution into (1.5) yields the closed league equilibrium condition:

$$MR_1 = MR_2 = cT^* \qquad (1.6)$$

By comparison, teams in an open league face an elastic supply of talent at an exogenous wage rate c^*. In an open league team 1 talent acquisition has no effect on the talent of team 2, such that $\partial t_1/\partial t_2 = \partial t_1/\partial t_2 = 0$. Substitution into (1.5) yields the open league solution:

$$MR_1 w_2 = MR_2 w_1 = c^* T \qquad (1.7)$$

2 Asymmetric markets

An asymmetric revenue advantage $m_1 > m_2$ for team 1 can be shown through a model that generalizes profit-max solutions with a parameter $\sigma > 1$. The UOH is the empirical argument that fans prefer close wins instead of blow outs. Fan-preference for competitive balance implies strictly concave revenue functions where $\phi \in [0, 1]$:

$$\pi_1 = \sigma[\phi\, w_1 + (1 - \phi)\, w_1 w_2] - ct_1 \qquad \pi_2 = [\phi\, w_2 + (1 - \phi)\, w_1 w_2] - ct_2$$
$$(1.8)$$

The UOH suggests $\phi = .5$ and the zero-sum constraint $w_2 = 1 - w_1$ simplifies (1.8):

$$\pi_1 = \sigma(w_1 - .5w_1^2) - ct_1 \qquad \pi_2 = w_2 - .5w_2^2 - ct_2 \qquad (1.9)$$

In a closed league from (1.6), simultaneous profit maximization yields:

$$MR_1 = MR_2 = \sigma w_2 = w_1 = cT^* \qquad (1.10)$$

Team 1 dominates a closed league by the imbalance ratio $w_1/w_2 = \sigma$ with respective team win percentages $w_1 = \sigma/(1 + \sigma)$ and $w_2 = 1/(1 + \sigma)$. League payroll is $cT^* = \sigma/(1 + \sigma)$ and respective team payrolls are $ct_1 = w_1 cT^* = \sigma^2/(1 + \sigma)^2$ and $ct_2 = w_2\, cT^* = 1/(1 + \sigma)^2$ The closed-league solution is shown at A in Figure 1.1 for $\sigma = 2$, where $w_1/w_2 = .667/.333$.

By comparison the σ-model open-league solution from (1.7) is:

$$MR_1 w_2 = MR_2 w_1 = \sigma w_2^2 = w_1^2 = c^* T \qquad (1.11)$$

An open league has greater competitive balance $w_1/w_2 = \sigma^2$ for team win percentages $w_1 = \sigma^2/(1 + \sigma^2)$ and $w_2 = 1/(1 + \sigma^2)$. The open league Nash solution at B is compared to the closed league solution at A in Figure 1 for $\sigma = 2$, where $w_1/w_2 = .586/.414$.

3 Invariance proposition

The strong form of the invariance proposition holds that competitive balance in a sports league will be the same with or without revenue sharing. In effect revenue sharing serves only to shift monopsony rent from players to owners. Strong form invariance can be shown with a straight pool-sharing formula $R_1' = \alpha R_1 + (1 - \alpha)(R_1 + R_2)/2$, where each team blends an α-share of its revenue with an equal $(1 - \alpha)$-share of a league revenue pool, where $\alpha \in [0,1]$. The league's zero-sum win con-

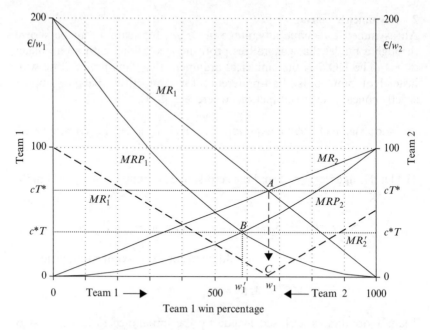

Figure 1.1   Open and closed leagues

straint implies $\partial w_1/\partial t_1 = -\partial w_2/\partial t_1$ and closed league α-sharing from (1.10)
yields the σ solution for $MR_1' = MR_2' = c'T$:

$$\alpha\sigma w_2 + (1 - \alpha)(\sigma w_2 - w_1)/2 = \alpha w_1 - (1 - \alpha)(\sigma w_2 - w_1)/2 \quad (1.12)$$

This results in the same imbalance $w_1/w_2 = \sigma$ as (1.10), regardless of the
level of α-sharing. The second term in (1.12) vanishes for both teams at
equilibrium ($\sigma w_2 = w_1$) and the lower league payroll $c'T = \alpha\sigma w_2 = \alpha w_1$
$= \alpha\sigma/(1 + \sigma)$ reveals the degree of talent exploitation equal to the league
pooled revenue share $(1 - \alpha)$. The perfect syndicate solution ($\alpha = 0$) is
shown at C in Figure 1.1 for $\sigma = 2$, where the invariance proposition still
holds and the cost per unit of talent has been reduced to the reservation
wage.

By comparison the open-league revenue sharing solution from (1.11)
implies:

$$2\alpha(\sigma w_2^2 - w_1^2) + (1 - \alpha)(\sigma w_2 - w_1)(w_1 + w_2) = 0 \quad (1.13)$$

If there is no revenue sharing ($\alpha = 1$) then the second term vanishes and
(1.13) reduces to the Nash open league solution $w_1/w_2 = \sigma^2$ in (1.11), but

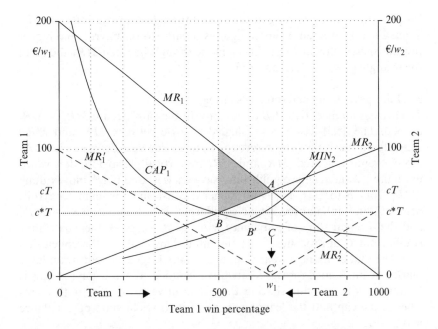

Figure 1.2   Payroll cap and revenue sharing in profit-max league

as the league approaches a perfect syndicate ($\alpha \to 0$) the first term vanishes and the second term approaches the closed league solution $w_1/w_2 = \sigma$ in (1.10). At the revenue-sharing limit ($\alpha = 0$) open and closed league solutions are identical at C in Figure 1.1. Revenue sharing in an open league reduces competitive balance and allows teams to collusively maximize league-cartel revenues.

4   Payroll cap in a profit-max league
A league-wide payroll cap constrains each team's payroll to a constant λ-share of the average club's revenue $cTw_1 = \lambda(R_1 + R_2)/2$. If CAP_1 is defined as an iso-payroll cap constraint (locus of $\lambda(R_1 + R_2)/2$ for all w_1) for team 1, the closed league solution becomes:

$$CAP_1 = MR_2 = \lambda(R_1 + R_2)/2w_1 = cT \qquad (1.14)$$

In order for the cap to constrain team 1, $\lambda \leq 4\sigma^2/[(1 + \sigma)(1 + \sigma + \sigma^2)]$. To achieve absolute balance at $w_1 = w_2$ a cap should be set a $\lambda = 1.33/(1 + \sigma)$. The cap-constrained equilibrium is shown at B in Figure 1.2 for $\sigma = 2$ and $\lambda = .44$. The effect of the payroll cap on team 1's profit is ambiguous, because gains from lower payroll $.5 (c - c^*)T$ are offset by revenue losses from winning fewer games (shaded triangle between MR_1 and cT). Team 2's improvement is unambiguous because lower payroll and higher revenue increase team 2's profits from the triangle between MR_2 and cT to the triangle between MR_2 and $c*T$.

5   Joint payroll cap and revenue sharing

Team 1 has an incentive at B to circumvent the cap because $MR_1 > MR_2$ at .500. The dead-weight loss (shaded triangle between MR_1 and MR_2) suggests mutual gain from a revenue-sharing side deal between clubs. As more revenue is shared, MR_1 and MR_2 are vertically displaced downward in Figure 1.2 and league equilibrium between MR_2' and CAP_1 moves along CAP_1 from B to C. CAP_1 is no longer a constraint for team 1 payrolls below C, and unbalanced league equilibrium is restored at $MR_1' = MR_2'$ and the original state of imbalance $w_1/w_2 = \sigma$. As $\alpha \to 0$ league π-max equilibrium C approaches C' at the limit. This leads to the conclusion that when taken alone a salary cap in a π-max league will constrain large market teams and improve competitive balance. When a payroll cap is combined with revenue sharing the disincentive to win for both teams negates the cap and the league returns to its original state of imbalance $w_1/w_2 = \sigma$.

A payroll minimum is necessary to create competitive balance in a profit-max league with revenue sharing. If the payroll minimum is set at $MIN_2 = \mu(CAP_2$ ($\mu < 1$) in Figure 1.2, league revenue sharing equilibrium would follow the path from B to B' along CAP_1. At B' the league is constrained by $CAP_1 = MIN_2$ at $w_1/w_2 = 1/\mu$ ($w_1 = .600$ for $\mu = .66$ in Figure 1.2). With additional sharing the league moves along $MR_1' = MIN_2$ until team 1 payroll falls to the point where both clubs are symmetrically constrained at .500 by the payroll minimum at $MIN_1 = MIN_2$. (CAP_2 and MIN_1 are not shown in Figure 1.2). This leads to the conclusion that revenue sharing in a profit-max league leads to competitive balance, but only if revenue is shared in combination with a minimum team payroll requirement.

B   Sportsman League

In sportsman leagues, team owners are willing to sacrifice profit for winning. At the limit, a pure sportsman becomes a win maximizer, constrained by zero profit rather than maximum profit, such that $R_1 = ct_1$ and $R_1/w_1 = ct_1/w_1 = cT$, where $t_1 = w_1 T$. The sportsman league win-max solution becomes:

$$AR_1 = AR_2 cT \tag{1.15}$$

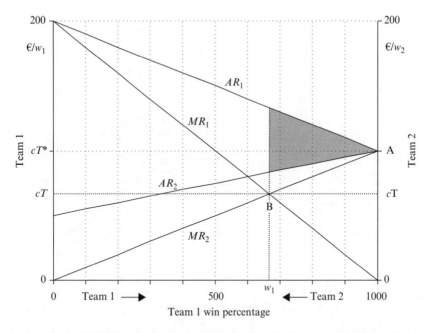

Figure 1.3   Sportsman win-max league

This is true whether the talent markets are open or closed. Substitution of (1.9) into (1.15) yields the pure sportsman σ–model result:

$$AR_1 = AR_2 = \sigma(1 - .5w_1) = (1 - .5w_2) = cT \qquad (1.16)$$

with less balance than either open or closed π–max solution: $w_1/w_2 = (2\sigma - 1)/(2 - \sigma)$; with win percentages $w_1 = (2\sigma - 1)/(1 + \sigma)$ and $w_2 = (2 - \sigma)/(1 + \sigma)$. Team 1's total win-max dominance of team 2 ($w_2 = 0$) is shown at A in Figure 1.3 for $\sigma = 2$. Existence of the league therefore constrains $\sigma \leq 2$ for the UOH assumption $\phi = .5$ in (1.9)

It is easy to see that social welfare (comprised of club profit, player salaries and fan surplus) is maximized by the win-max sportsman where the area under the AR (demand) curves is maximized at $AR_1 = AR_2$. In a win-max league, the sum of player salaries cT^* and fan surplus is maximized and profit is zero. The win-max social optimum is realized because sportsman owners have essentially the same objectives as their fans. This leads to the conclusion that fans prefer more competitive imbalance than that implied by profit-max owners in open or closed leagues, and that interior profit-max optima are inferior with respect to social welfare. (Profit-max welfare loss is the shaded area in Figure 1.3.)

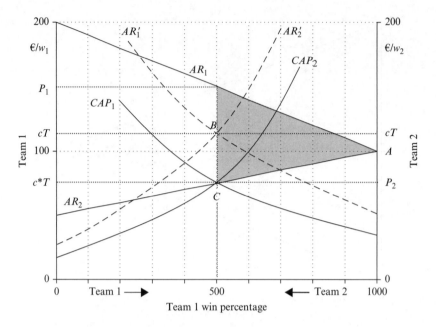

Figure 1.4   Payroll cap and revenue sharing in sportsman league

1   Revenue sharing in win-max league

The question whether the invariance proposition holds in a win-max league can be answered by modifying the pool-sharing formula in (1.12) so that $AR_1' = AR_2' = cT$:

$$\alpha R_1/w_1 + (1 - \alpha)(R_1 + R_2)/2w_1 = \alpha R_2/w_2 + (1 - \alpha)(R_1 + R_2)/2w_2 = cT \tag{1.17}$$

If there is no revenue sharing ($\alpha = 1$) then the second term vanishes for each team and $AR_1 = AR_2 = cT$ as in (1.16). In a pure syndicate ($\alpha = 0$) revenues and payrolls become the same for each team $(R_1 + R_2)/2$, which implies that the league is competitively balanced at $w_1 = w_2 = .500$. A pure sportsman syndicate is shown at B in Figure 1.4.

In a win-max syndicate league payroll is equal to total revenue, which is divided equally between clubs $cT/2$. The σ-solution yields pure syndicate revenue and payroll of $cT = .375(1 + \sigma)$ or €112.5 million for $\sigma = 2$ in Figure 1.4. Both clubs have zero profits because all revenue is paid to the players to maximize wins. League payroll increases with revenue sharing toward the league total revenue maximum. Maximum revenue at $\sigma w_2 = w_1$ requires $\alpha = [\sigma^4 + \sigma^3 - (\sigma + 1)]/[\sigma^4 + \sigma^3 - (3\sigma + 1)]$. If $\sigma = 2$ for example, then $\alpha = .64$ would yield an internal league revenue maximum for a sportsman league. The most interesting conclusion is that revenue sharing in the singular pursuit of competitive balance leads to a net loss in social welfare (the shaded area between AR curves).

2 Payroll cap in win-max league

To see the equalizing effects of a separate payroll cap in a win-maximizing league reconsider the cap solution from (1.13) revised for a sportsman league $CAP_1 = AR_2 = c*T$.

$$\lambda(R_1 + R_2)/2w_1 = R_2/w_2 = \lambda [.5 + \sigma w_1 - .5(\sigma + 1) w_1^2]/2w_1 = (1 - .5w_2) \tag{1.18}$$

Competitive balance at $w_1 = w_2 = .500$ requires a payroll cap $\lambda = 2/(1 + \sigma)$. A payroll cap of $\lambda = .67$ for $\sigma = 2$ is shown in Figure 1.4 at C where $CAP_1 = AR_2$. Under the iso-payroll cap, payroll for each team is $c*T/2 = R_1/\sigma = R_2$ at $w_1 = w_2$. Team 1's profit rate is $1/\sigma R_1$ (50 percent of €75 million for $\sigma = 2$) and team 2's profit is zero, because it spends all of its revenue on its €37.5 million payroll. If $\sigma = 2$ then league payroll of $75 million is 67 percent of league revenue of €112.5 million. League revenue maximum obtains if the payroll cap set at $\lambda = 4\sigma^2/(1 + \sigma)(1 + \sigma + \sigma^2)$. If $\sigma = 2$, for example, then $\lambda = .76$ payroll cap yields the revenue maximum $(\sigma w_2 = w_1)$ in a sportsman league (€116.7 million for $\sigma = 2$). Once again, however, the payroll cap constraint leads to a net reduction in social welfare.

3 Joint payroll cap and revenue sharing

The combined implementation of a payroll cap ($\lambda = .67$) and equal revenue sharing ($\alpha = 0$) virtually clones equality in team revenues $cT/2$ at B, team payrolls $c*T/2$ at C, and profits $(c - c*) T/2$ in Figure 1.4. Each team has the same revenue, payroll and profit, and total payroll capped at two-thirds of league revenue. These results lead to opposite conclusions for π-max and win-max leagues. In π-max leagues revenue sharing does not increase competitive balance, but it does increase talent exploitation. Players are paid less than their marginal revenue product by the amount of revenue that is shared.

In contrast, win-max leagues initially have greater competitive imbalance than profit-max leagues, but revenue sharing in sportsman leagues can potentially increase competitive balance and lead to higher revenue and greater payroll toward the league maximum. This is because sportsmen owners pay players their average revenue product to maximize wins. Unfortunately these player gains come at the expense of inferior fan welfare (shaded net loss between the AR curves in Figure 1.4).

C   Optimal Competitive Balance

1   Fan preference

UOH appeals to our intuition and yields well-behaved and tractably concave revenue functions (downward sloping *MR* curves), but the simplifying assumption that fans prefer balanced competition over dynasties remains an important empirical question. The more general issues of fan-preference for competitive balance and fan-welfare optimization can be addressed by relaxing the limiting assumption that $\phi = .5$ in (1.9). The zero-sum constraint simplifies (1.8) in more general terms of ϕ:

$$\pi_1 = \sigma(w_1 - (1 - \phi)w_1^2) - ct_1 \qquad \pi_2 = w_2 - (1 - \phi)w_2^2 - ct_2 \qquad (1.19)$$

In a closed profit-max league ($\partial t_1/\partial t_2 = \partial t_2/\partial t_1 = -1$) simultaneous profit max of (1.19):

$$MR_1 = \sigma[1 - 2(1 - \phi)\, w_1] = MR_2 = 1 - 2(1 - \phi)\, w_2 = cT^* \qquad (1.20)$$

yields the closed-league competitive balance $w_1/w_2 = (\sigma + 1 - 2\phi)/(\sigma + 1 - 2\sigma\phi)$ where:

$$w_1 = [\sigma + 1 - 2\phi]/[2(\sigma + 1)(1 - \phi)] \qquad w_2 = [\sigma + 1 - 2\sigma\phi]/[2(\sigma + 1)(1 - \phi)] \qquad (1.21)$$

Substitution of (1.21) into (1.20) sets league payroll $cT^* = 2\sigma\phi/(\sigma + 1)$ Existence of the league requires $w_2 \geq 0$, which constrains $0 \leq \phi \leq [(\sigma + 1)/2\,\sigma]$ for $\sigma \geq 1$.

In a win-max sportsman league, simultaneous win maximization of (1.19):

$$AR_1 = \sigma[1 - (1 - \phi)w_1] = AR_2 = 1 - (1 - \phi)\, w_2 = cT^* \qquad (1.22)$$

yields the win-max-league competitive balance solution $w_1/w_2 = (\sigma - \phi)/(1 - \sigma\phi)$ where:

$$w_1 = (\sigma - \phi)/(\sigma + 1)(1 - \phi) \qquad w_2 = (1 - \sigma\phi)/(\sigma + 1)(1 - \phi) \qquad (1.23)$$

Substitution of (1.23) into (1.22) sets league payroll $cT^* = \sigma(\phi + 1)/(\sigma + 1)$ Existence of the league requires $w_2 \geq 0$, which constrains $0 \leq \phi \leq 1/\sigma$ for $\sigma \geq 1$.

2   Ticket and media leagues

Fort and Quirk (2007) suggest that the length of seasons in professional sports leagues determines the relative importance of competitive balance in fan preferences. If the season is relatively short like the 8 home-games in the NFL, then fans base their preferences more on the quality of the home team than the quality of the visitor. If the season is relatively long like the 81 home games in MLB, then fans are more selective about the quality of the opponent. The shorter NFL season increases the attractiveness of season-tickets, while the longer MLB season increases the appeal of single-game tickets.[1]

A broader distinction can be made between leagues that rely on gate (ticket) revenue (MLB, National Basketball Association [NBA], National Hockey League [NHL] and Bundesliga) and those leagues that rely more heavily on media revenue (NFL, and more recently EPL, La Liga Serie A and Ligue 1). The gate-media distinction closely follows the intuition that individual team quality is better suited for media leagues, while the quality of the opposition (competitive balance) is more important in gate (ticket revenue) leagues. This distinction also advances the hypothesis that fan preference for competitive balance is inversely related to increased media coverage of league games across leagues over time. Media revolutions in sports leagues expand local 'home' markets and result in the wider global appeal of dominant teams.

Comparative analysis of competitive balance in ticket leagues and media leagues can be accomplished by setting the ϕ fan-preference parameter approximately equal to the media share of total revenue in each league over time. For example, substitution of $\phi = 0$ for extreme ticket leagues into equation (1.21) yields the profit-max solution $w_1/w_2 = 1$ and a win-max equilibrium $w_1/w_2 = \sigma$ Fan preference for competitive balance in a ticket league is shown at profit max $MR_{T1} = MR_{T2}$ (point *C*) and win-max $AR_{T1} = AR_{T2}$ (point *B*) in Figure 1.5. Profit for both teams is the area under their respective *MR* curves. Profit-max payroll is zero in a ticket-league because fan preference for absolute balance negates the incentive to win for either team. The ticket-league win-max solution from (1.23) at *B* is also the social welfare optimum. The welfare loss of profit-max competitive balance for the ticket league at *C* is the shaded triangle between AR_{T1} and AR_{T2}.

Substitution of $\phi = .5$ for media leagues into equation (1.21) yields the familiar profit-max solution $w_1/w_2 = \sigma$ at *B* and a win-max equilibrium from (1.23) at *C* where $w_1 = 1$ Fan preferences for Team 1's increased dominance in media leagues is shown at both the profit max solution $MR_{M1} = MR_{M2}$ (point *B* in Figure 1.5) and win-max solution $AR_{M1} = AR_{M2}$ (point *A* in Figure 1.5). Media-league profit for each team is the area between their respective *MR* curves and payroll cT. The media-league

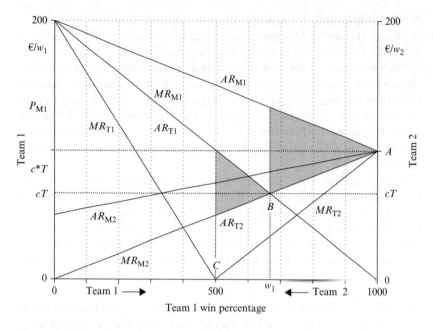

Figure 1.5   Media and optimum balance

win-max solution at point A is also the social welfare optimum, and the
welfare loss of profit-max for the media league at B is the shaded triangle
between AR_{M1} and AR_{M2}. When ticket leagues evolve into media leagues,
fan preferences, profit maxima and welfare optima all shift toward less
competitive balance and greater dominance for large market teams. The
first conclusion is that social welfare is optimized at a greater competitive imbalance than required by profit maximum in either open or closed
leagues, regardless if the leagues are driven by ticket or media revenue
streams.[2] The second conclusion is that welfare is optimized at even
greater imbalance in leagues that depend more heavily on media revenue.

III   EMPIRICAL QUESTIONS

A   Win-Max Media Revolution

A comparison of league-wide revenues and player cost structures for the
Big 4 NA sports leagues and the Big 5 European football leagues is shown
in Table 1.1. Player cost–revenue ratios of 60 percent in all NA leagues
suggest that these leagues are win-max sportsman leagues. Three of the

Table 1.1   Media revolution in professional sports leagues (€millions)

	Revenues 2009				Revenues 1997			
	Total	Gate	Media	Payroll	Total	Gate	Media	Payroll
National Football League	5673	.188	.466	.571	1650	.291	.553	.674
Major League Baseball	4174	.381	.253	.554	1307	.390	.382	.537
National Basketball Assoc.	2693	.301	.244	.579	1178	.406	.370	.469
National Hockey League	1995	.422	.053	.534	778	.605	.150	.512
English Premier League	2326	.286	.488	.670	685	.420	.209	.471
German Bundesliga	1575	.230	.310	.510	444	.322	.250	.502
Spanish La Liga	1501	.281	.414	.626	524	.280	.424	.439
Italian Serie A	1494	.131	.597	.732	551	.374	.361	.575
French Ligue 1	1048	.143	.550	.689	293	.218	.324	.608

Note: €1 = $1.413 (30 June 2009).

four NA leagues (the exception being MLB) are controlled by salary caps. Major League Baseball is interesting because the players' share of revenues is similar to the other NA leagues (at just below 60 percent) without exogenous league controls.[3] In absence of player cost controls in 4 of the Big 5 Euro leagues the players' share of revenue has rapidly grown to 70 percent since the *Bosman* verdict in 1995–96. The exception is Bundesliga which is audit-controlled by strict licensing requirements. This player cost squeeze serves as additional evidence that the Big 5 European leagues are also controlled by win-max sportsmen.[4]

The media revenue revolution in the Big 4 NA leagues occurred over 40 years after the Sports Broadcasting Act of 1961, which exempted collective negotiation of television rights from antitrust violation.[5] As a result of legislated antitrust exemption, the NFL television cartel has become the most media-dominated NA league. National media generates over half of total NFL revenues, and local media revenue is insignificant. Local/regional television comprises about half of media revenues in the other three leagues. Since 1990 all NA leagues have gone through counter-revolutions in venue revenue derived from a proliferation of exclusive luxury-seat venues. As a result television revenue reliance of all 4 NA leagues has been reduced. Only the NFL can still be considered a media league, and the other three NA leagues are driven primarily by local revenue. As a result, fan preference for imbalance in the NFL should be much higher than for the other local-revenue leagues.

The media revenue revolution is shown in Table 1.1 for the Big 5 European leagues.[6] English Premier League broadcast revenues grew from 9 percent of total revenue in 1992 to 12 percent at the time of Bosman, and then exploded to 45 percent by 2004. All Big 5 leagues except Bundesliga have become media-dominated leagues. Theory suggests that fans' preference for competitive imbalance is directly proportional to the importance of media revenue. Fans should therefore prefer unbalanced competition in NFL, EPL, La Liga, Ligue 1 and Serie A, and prefer balanced leagues in MLB, NBA, NHL and Bundesliga.

B   Revenue Sharing and Payroll Caps

1   North American Big 4

Revenue sharing and payroll cap arrangements of the Big 4 American leagues are compared in Table 1.2. National media revenue is shared equally in all Big 4 leagues. The major equity issue in NA leagues is the sharing of local revenues. Local media revenues in the NFL are insignificant and 34 percent of gate revenue is pooled and split evenly among the clubs.[7] The NFL's current problem is that unshared local venue revenue has grown from 10 percent to 23 percent of total revenue because of the venue revolution. Nonetheless the NFL is the most socialistic league with 53 percent of its revenue shared.

In MLB after the 1994–95 player strike 20 percent of all local revenues (media, gate and venue) were shared until 2002 CBA when 34 percent was shared, and currently after the 2006 CBA when 31 percent of local revenue is shared.[8] Local television rights on regional MLB sports networks are significant and overall they comprise about 16 percent of total revenue. New York Yankees' local annual revenue from team-owned YES Network is estimated at €115 million, compared to smaller markets at €10 million media revenue. These estimates put the amount of revenue shared in MLB at about 42 percent.

Local revenue sharing in the NBA and the NHL is relatively insignificant and so the amount of revenue shared is roughly equal to the national television money in the NBA, and a modest revenue transfer

Table 1.2   North American revenue-sharing and payroll cap rules

	NFL	MLB	NBA	NHL
Revenue sharing				
National media	100%	100%	100%	100%
Local media	0%	31%	0%	0%
Gate	34%	31%	0%	0%
Venue	0%	31%	0%	0%
Payroll cap				
Maximum	57%	–	57%	57%
Minimum % of max	90%	–	75%	–$16m

Notes:
NFL local media is insignificant comprises about one-half of media revenue in other NA leagues.
NFL allows 15 percent deduction for game-day expenses before 40 percent visiting teams share, so effective tax rate is .85 × .40 = .34.
MLB allows a deduction for stadium expenses including depreciation before the 31 percent visitors share is calculated. MLB visitor share was 20 percent before 2002, 34 percent from 2002 to 2006 and 31 percent after 2006 CBA.
NFL cap can be temporarily avoided through signing bonuses prorated over the length of contracts.
NBA payroll cap is considered a soft cap because it can be exceeded to resign own free agents.
MLB imposes a competitive balance tax for payrolls above a threshold which usually only applies to the New York Yankees.
Payroll cap base in all leagues excludes revenues unrelated and is subject to deductions over time for team venue expenses.
NFL hard payroll cap began in 1994, NBA soft cap in 1984 and NHL hard cap after the 2004–05 lockout.
NHL does have a modest sharing system where top clubs subsidize bottom clubs to make the payroll minimum.

from the top ten revenue clubs to the bottom ten revenue clubs so they can afford the salary cap minimum. Estimates put the amount of revenue sharing in the NBA at about 25 percent and in the NHL at about 12 percent.

The NFL and the NHL both have hard salary caps in that they cannot be exceeded in the long run.[9] Both maximum payrolls are set at about 57 percent of total revenues. The NFL has a minimum payroll set at 90 percent of the maximum, and the NHL minimum payroll is set at about €11.43 million below the maximum before each season.[10] Major League Baseball has implemented a luxury tax rather than a hard team-salary cap in each CBA after the 1994–95 strike. The 'competitive balance tax' (CBT) is a tax on team payrolls over a threshold set so high that the tax is effectively a New York Yankee tax.[11]

Table 1.3 Big 5 European media revenue-sharing rules (percentages)

	Equal	Merit	Facility	Market
English Premier League	50	25	25	–
German Bundesliga	50	50	–	–
French Ligue 1	50	30	20	–
Italian Serie A	40	30	–	30
Spanish La Liga	40	60	–	–

Notes:
Bundesliga merit is 75 percent based on previous three seasons and 25 percent on current season.
Ligue 1 merit and facility shares (number of appearances) based on five previous seasons and current season.
Ligue 1 changed the shares before 2004–05 season to improve the chances of French clubs in Europe. Before 2004–05 Ligue 1 shares were 83 percent equal, 10 percent merit for current season and 7 percent for appearances over the four previous and current seasons.
Starting in 2010–11 Serie A merit share: 10 percent club history, 15 percent last 5 years and 5 percent current season. No sharing before 2010.
La Liga proposals after 2014 season: big clubs: Barcelona and Real Madrid 34 percent; Valencia and Atletico 11 percent and the rest of the league 55 percent. Alternative formula proposed by Villareal and Sevilla would be 40 percent equal and 60 percent merit.

The NBA has a 'soft cap' in that it can be exceeded for a variety of exceptions including resigning a team's own free agent. Since the soft cap began in 1984, the overt strategy of the NBA has been to promote team continuity, competitive imbalance and dynasties to maximize national television rights fees. This NBA dynasty strategy is basically a corollary of the theory advanced above. There is a direct relationship between fan preferences for competitive imbalance and national/global television coverage. The ideal goal of revenue sharing and payroll caps in win-max sportsman leagues is to allow the optimal competitive balance consistent with those consumer preferences.

2 European Big 5

Media revenue-sharing arrangements of the Big 5 European leagues are compared in Table 1.3. Since its media-motivated breakaway from the Football Association in 1992 the EPL has shared collectively negotiated broadcast rights according to the formula: fifty percent for solidarity, 25 percent for merit (standings) and 25 percent for facility fee (appearances). A one-half parachute television share is given to relegated teams for two years, and international media revenues are shared equally. As media revenues have soared, the EPL's redistribution formula has become the model for the rest of the Big 5 leagues.

The German Bundesliga divides collectively negotiated television revenue 50 percent equally, 37.5 percent based on merit over the last three years and 12.5 percent based on current standings. Before 2005, the French Ligue 1 split 83 percent of its collectively marketed television revenue equally for solidarity, 10 percent for merit and 7 percent based on appearances. Beginning in 2005, however, Ligue 1 reduced the solidarity share and increased the merit share to 50 percent each, with 30 percent merit based on league finish (25 percent current season and 5 percent last five seasons) and 20 percent based on appearances (15 percent current and 5 percent last five seasons). Increased merit sharing under Charte 2002 des clubs de football was justified on the premise that Ligue 1 clubs faced a disadvantage in European competition because of solidarity sharing.

Italian Serie A returned to collective selling of television rights for 2010–11 (individual rights had been allowed since 1999) and clubs now distribute fees: 40 percent solidarity, 30 percent performance (10 percent history, 15 percent last 5 years and 5 percent for current season) and 30 percent according to fan base (5 percent home market and 25 percent estimated number of 'supporters').

The Spanish La Liga will also negotiate as a collective for 2014–15, and the distribution formula is currently under negotiation. Real Madrid and Barcelona have agreed to take 34 percent of La Liga's television revenue (under individual selling both receive about one-half), leaving 11 percent for Atlético Madrid and Valencia and 45 percent to be split among the remaining 16 clubs.[12] A rival proposal by Sevilla and Villarreal would divide 40 percent equally among the clubs and 60 percent based on merit and fan base (similar to Serie A).

Salary caps and cost controls are much discussed but rarely used in Europe's premier leagues. The Big 5 leagues briefly considered a salary cap proposed (G-14) for the 2005–06 season that would have capped club payrolls at 70 percent of that clubs revenue, but the cap was never applied. More recently the Union of European Football Association (UEFA) has developed a financial fair play plan (FFP) with a 'break even rule' whereby clubs will only be allowed to enter European competition if their revenues are greater than or equal to their costs.

Based on information from the 2011–12 and 2012–13 seasons, initial action can be taken during the 2013–14 season with the first possible exclusions from UEFA competition taking place in 2014–15.[13] While the ostensible targets are high wages and transfer fees, the main impact of G-14 payroll caps and FFP cost controls will be felt by lower-revenue clubs. Ironically, FFP targets 'sugar-daddy' owners of large market teams, but the primary effect will be to constrain small market clubs and reduce competitive balance.

C   Global Preference

1   Champions effect

In the wake of the European media explosion since 1990, UEFA was forced to make a series of revolutionary changes in Champions League format that have since distorted competitive balance throughout domestic European football. The constant threat of a breakaway European Super League in 1990 forced UEFA to change its knockout format from the European Champions Cup (since 1955) to include a group stage in 1991–92 and ironically change its name to 'Champions League'. UEFA pre-empted two more threats in 1997–98 by allowing second place team to qualify for the the UEFA Champions League (UCL) in the eight top national leagues. Then in 1999–2000 four teams in the top three leagues could qualify. Successive super-league breakaway threats reveal the underlying tendency toward the unification of European football. Instead of a legitimate super-league, UEFA has created a de facto meta-league within the UCL format that distorts domestic competition throughout Europe.

Total media revenue distributed to the 32 teams in the group stages of the Champions League had grown to €746.4 million in 2009–10.[14] In terms of total media revenue this places the UEFA Champions League third behind the EPL (€1134 million) and Serie A (€892 million), ahead of La Liga (€621 million), Ligue 1 (€576 million) and the Bundesliga (€489 million). The distribution of UCL media revenues is shown in Table 1.4 for the top 12 media clubs in Europe for 2009–10. It is clear that the addition of UCL media rights complicates the revenue-sharing arrangements of the Big 5 European leagues. This list is topped by La Liga's two traditional media giants, followed by Serie A's Big 3, EPL's Big 4, Bundesliga's exception Bayern Munich and, finally, two perennial Ligue 1 contenders, Lyon and OM.[15]

Table 1.4 also reveals the nature of media in the Big 5 leagues. The two Spanish giants garner about 45.2 percent of La Liga domestic media without UEFA, and 56.4 percent of media revenue including UEFA. UCL media is roughly 20 percent of total media for Barcelona and Real Madrid. The Big 3 from Serie A derive 60 percent of their revenue from media and UCL's share of their media is normally below 20 percent The exception was UCL champion Inter Milan whose prize share was 35.7 percent of their media revenue. The Big 4 EPL clubs derive about 40 percent of their revenue from media and about one-third of that comes from UEFA. UCL runner up Bayern Munich received only a quarter of its revenue from media and over half of that came from UEFA. Lyon and OM derive over half of their revenue from media and about a quarter of that comes from the Champions League. The exception in 2010 was UCL semi-finalist Lyon whose prize share was 37.5 percent of their media revenue total.

Table 1.4   Top 12 European club media rights 2009–10 (€m)

Club 2009–10	Media	UEFA	UEFA (%)	Revenue	Media (%)
Barcelona	178.1	39.5	22.2	398.1	44.7
Real Madrid	158.7	27.2	17.1	438.6	36.2
AC Milan	141.1	24.1	17.1	235.8	59.8
Internazionale Milano	137.9	49.2	35.7	224.8	61.3
Juventus	132.5	21.8	16.5	205.0	64.6
Manchester United	128.0	46.4	36.3	349.8	36.6
Arsenal	105.7	33.8	32.0	274.1	38.6
Chelsea	105.0	32.6	31.0	255.9	41.0
Liverpool	97.1	29.4	30.3	225.3	43.1
Bayern Munich	83.4	45.3	54.3	323.0	25.8
Olympique Lyonnais	78.4	29.4	37.5	142.1	55.2
Olympique Marseille	70.8	17.3	24.4	141.1	50.2

Note: Media revenue includes UEFA.

Source: Deloitte Sports Business Group.

2   Extended fan base

It is well known that the UEFA Champions League creates significant media revenue imbalances among clubs and distorts competition through-out European domestic leagues. What we have previously failed to realize or acknowledge is that UEFA also expands the global fan bases of these perennially dominant teams. Whether fan globalization occurs through Champions League or ultimately from a formal unification of European football, it creates unbalanced competition abhorred by purists but vastly preferred by global fans.

The results of a survey by SPORT+MARKT comparing national and European fan bases for 2010 is shown in Table 1.5 for the top 20 clubs.[16] The European fan bases are obviously related to a team's success in European competition (compare with Table 1.4) and a club's home base is related to its success in domestic competition. The most interesting result, however, concerns La Liga's Barcelona and Real Madrid. Real Madrid is more popular in Spain with 36 percent of the fans (6.8 million) compared with Barcelona with 29 percent of domestic Spanish fans (5.5 million). Almost two-thirds of the fans in Spain prefer one of the participants in El Clasico (any match between Barca and Real Madrid).

El Clasico is viewed by over 14.6 million Spaniards with a 75 percent share, and worldwide it may have more viewers than Champions League final or the Super Bowl.[17] On the broader European football stage 57.8

Table 1.5   European and domestic fan bases 2010 (millions)

European fan base	Fans	Domestic fan base	Fans	Share (%)
FC Barcelona	57.8	FC Dynamo Kyiv	5.3	47
Real Madrid CF	31.3	AFC Ajax	4.3	39
Manchester United FC	30.6	Galatasaray SK	5.9	39
Chelsea FC	21.4	Real Madrid CF	6.8	36
FC Bayern München	20.7	Olympique Marseille	6.6	36
Arsenal FC	20.3	Fenerbahce SK	5.2	35
AC Milan	18.4	FC Bayern München	10	29
FC Internazionale	17.5	FC Barcelona	5.5	29
Liverpool FC	16.4	FC Zenit St. Petersburg	12.4	27
Juventus FC	13.1	Juventus FC	5.5	24
FC Zenit St. Petersburg	12.6	Olympique Lyon	4.4	24
CSKA Moscow	10.5	CSKA Moscow	10.5	23
FC Spartak Moscow	9.0	FC Spartak Moscow	8.6	19
Olympique Marseille	7.8	Manchester United FC	4.7	18
AFC Ajax	7.1	AC Milan	4.1	18
Galatasaray SK	6.8	Liverpool FC	4.4	17
Olympique Lyon	6.6	FC Internazionale	3.1	17
Fenerbahce SK	6.1	Arsenal FC	3.9	12
AS Roma	6.0	AS Roma	1.6	7
FC Dynamo Kyiv	5.3	Chelsea FC	1.6	6

Notes:
European fans include domestic fans.
Barcelona had 41.4 million European fans in 2005–06 compared with Real Madrid with 48.6 million.

Source: SPORT + MARKT.

million fans back Barcelona, while 31.3 million prefer Real Madrid. This leads to the conclusion that increased media expands or globalizes fan preferences for dominant teams and in quasi-public way, media coverage increases the socially optimal level of competitive imbalance (dominance).

D   Competitive Balance

This section explores the relationship between media revenue and competitive balance in the Big 4 NA leagues and the Big 5 European leagues. The dynamics of competitive balance can be captured by an auto-regressive β-estimate (beta balance) of winning percentages w_{ijt} for team i in league j from season $t - 1$ to season t:

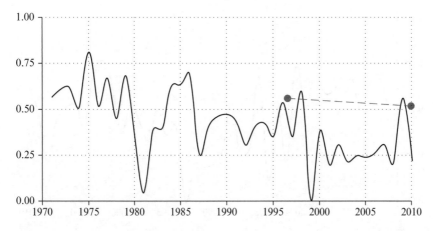

Figure 1.6 National Football League

$$w_{ijt} = \alpha + \beta w_{ijt-1} + \varepsilon_{ijt} \qquad (1.24)$$

$\beta \in [0,1]$. If $\alpha = .500$ and $\beta = 0$ then (1.24) becomes $w_{ijt} = .500$, and each season is a random walk and every team has an equal chance to win. At the other extreme, if $\alpha = 0$ and $\beta = 1$, then (1.24) reduces to $w_{ijt} = w_{ijt-1}$ then season outcomes are predetermined.

Beta balance coefficients are shown in Figures 1.6–1.14 over the period 1970–2010 for each of the nine leagues (solid lines) along with the media revenue ratios (dashed lines) from Table 1.1 for 1997 and 2009. The feeling is that the percentage of media revenue should roughly approximate fan preference for imbalance, and that a comparison with league betas should indicate the relative efficiency of revenue sharing and payroll caps in the optimization of fan welfare. It is assumed that all leagues are sportsman leagues.

As shown in Figure 1.6, the NFL has the lowest betas (greatest competitive balance) of all leagues and it has effectively become a random league after 1998. This is due to both cost controls and revenue sharing (Figure 1.4). The hard salary cap that was imposed in 1994 became effective after a four-year lag (equal to the length of average contract).[18] Equally shared NFL television rights fees more than doubled from \$1.1 billion per year (1994–97) to \$2.6 billion annually (1998–2005) and \$3.73 billion (2006–11). The problem with the NFL is that a random league has been engineered from both the revenue and cost side, when in fact the major national media presence suggests that fans would instead prefer greater imbalance. In this case the NFL has imposed suboptimal random mediocrity in the name of competitive balance.

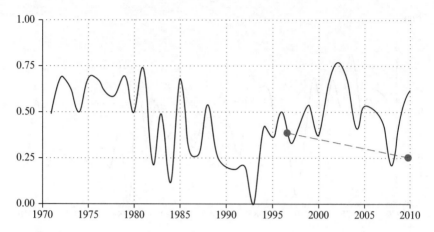

Figure 1.7   Major League Baseball

Since the players' strike (1994–95) beta balance (β = 5) in MLB has been consistent with the decline in national media (Figure 1.7). Major League Baseball revenue dropped from €260 annually (1990–93) to €150 (1994–95); €232 million (1996–2000); €400 million (2001–05) and €575 million (2007–13). Increased reliance on gate revenue has shifted fan preference toward greater competitive balance, and modest revenue sharing in the absence of a salary cap has allowed competition to approach the welfare optimum. Random competition (β = 0) before the strike (1990–93) reflects inferior mediocrity/parity similar to the current NFL.

Competitive imbalance (β > .5) engineered by the NBA since 1984 (Figure 1.8) is consistent with the intent of the soft salary cap and minor revenue sharing tactics designed to maintain dynasties preferred by national television audiences. Given the recent decline in the relative importance of national television rights in the NBA, the NBA is proposing a hard salary cap in current Collective Bargaining Agreement negotiations. This implies that the NBA switching competitive balance strategy and is efficiently seeking increased balance preferred by local fans derived from increased importance of local gate and venue revenue.

Competitive balance in the NHL has gradually declined over the last 40 years (Figure 1.9). The hard salary cap imposed after the 2004–05 owners' lock-out has effectively balanced the league at (β ≈ .5). Given the insignificance of national television revenue (6 percent including Canada and US) and the relative importance of gate and venue revenues, the NHL should seek even greater balance and superior fan welfare through increased revenue sharing.

Competitive balance in the EPL has decreased markedly since 1998, the

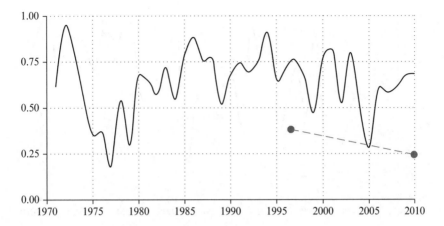

Figure 1.8   National Basketball Association

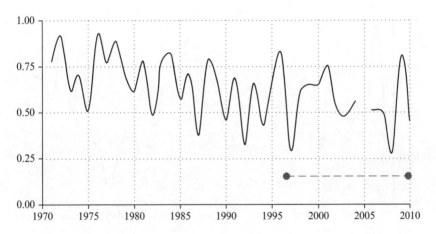

Figure 1.9   National Hockey League

first year of multiple teams placed in Champions League (champion effect) (Figure 1.10). This is also the first season of the major television contract of the EPL media explosion. Annual television rights increased from €75.7 million, in 1992–97 to €313.3 million in 1998–2001; €815.6 million in 2002–04; €704.8 in 2005–07; and €1243.1 in 2008–10. As a result of the media explosion, the increased dominance of the Big 4 is consistent with fan preferences and welfare also shifting toward imbalance. The difference between the EPL and NFL (as a media league) is the absence of salary cap and the 50/25/25 revenue sharing formula, both of which allow EPL competitive balance to approach the social optimum. In contrast, revenue

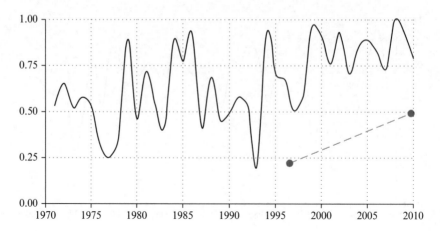

Figure 1.10   English Premier League

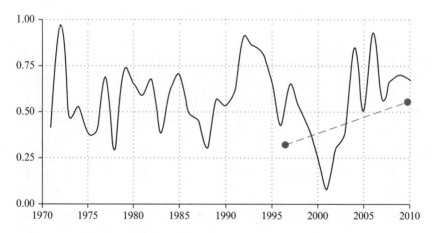

Figure 1.11   French Ligue 1

sharing and cost constraints have trapped the NFL in socially inefficient mediocrity.

French Ligue 1 has been considered the European exception because of its unique competitive balance between large and small markets. The problem with intra-league balance in the midst of unbalanced leagues is that French clubs were at a disadvantage in European competition. Beginning in 2005–06, Ligue 1 reduced its solidarity share and adopted a 50:30:20 formula that sacrificed intra-league balance to improve inter-league chances (Figure 1.11). The new formula became effective when Ligue 1 annual television rights exploded from

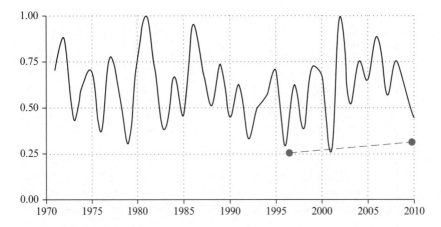

Figure 1.12   German Bundesliga

€335 million in 2000–05 to €600 million in 2006–08; and €668 million in 2009–12.

Bundesliga (Figure 1.12) has become the new European exception. Bundesliga has the least media revenues and the most competitive balance of the Big 5 leagues. Given equal importance of gate, venue and media revenues, Bundesliga should have the greatest fan preference for competitive balance. In 2009–10 only 31 percent (€489 million) of Bundesliga's €1575 million revenue came from media, compared with 23 percent from gate, 31 percent from venue sponsorships and 15 percent merchandizing. Strict licensing controls and 50+1 ownership rules have created a balanced league consistent with fan preference.

Until recently Italian Serie A (Figure 1.13) has relied most heavily on media revenue (60 percent) and has been the least balanced of all Big 5 leagues ($\beta = .8$). Media coverage should increase fan preference for imbalance (Big 3 dominance). Ironically, individual negotiation of media rights and unequal distribution of media revenues 1999–2010 have created an unbalanced league that is superior in terms of fan welfare. Fan welfare is a function of media, but competitive balance is a function of media revenue distribution. The 40/30/30 formula from 2010–11 should bring balance closer to the welfare optimum.

Since 2006 La Liga (Figure 1.14) has lost its competitive balance ($\beta = .6$ before 2005) with the dominance of Real Madrid and Barcelona. Unequal media revenue distribution yields a suboptimal dominance for a league with 41 percent media share in 2009–10. Barcelona and Real Madrid individually negotiated contracts for 45.2 percent of €597.1 million La Liga media revenue in 2009–10, and 47.2 percent of €712.6 million league

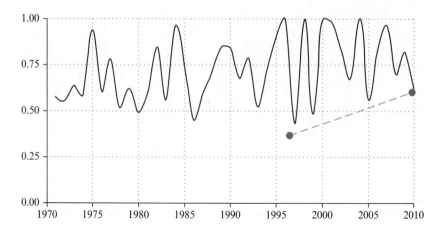

Figure 1.13   Italian Serie A

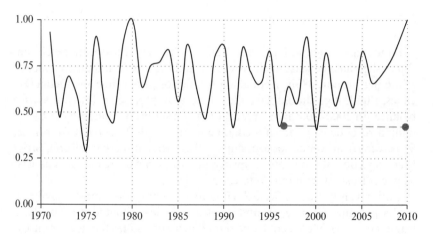

Figure 1.14   Spanish La Liga

revenue after UCL prize distributions. This supports the efficiency argument for collective television rights with an egalitarian 40/60 sharing formula similar to that adopted by Serie A in 2010–11.

IV   CONCLUSION

The core theory of sports economics is based on the simplifying hypothesis (UOH) that fans prefer balanced competition between evenly matched opponents. In fact, optimal competitive balance remains an empirical question complicated by the real-world success of unbalanced leagues dominated by a few perennially powerful clubs. The core theorem (invariance proposition) traditionally holds that revenue sharing and salary caps are welfare inferior in profit-max leagues because they only shift the surplus from players to owners and ultimately have no impact on competitive balance. In the real world, sporting owners are more interested in maximizing wins than profits, and revenue sharing and salary caps can efficiently adjust competitive balance toward a social optimum

There is convincing evidence that all major sports leagues have become dominated by sportsman win-max owners whose objectives are to win at all cost. Players' shares of revenues have recently exceeded 60 percent in the Big 4 NA leagues, and have approached 70 percent in four of the Big 5 European football leagues. Revenue-sharing regimes are different among NA leagues, but player cost controls are very similar. Salary caps have been imposed in all NA leagues, except MLB, just below 60 percent of league revenue.

In the Big 5 European leagues there are currently no salary caps but break-even licensing requirements are effective cost controls in Bundesliga and UEFA. In the near future all Big 5 European leagues will sell television rights collectively with revenue redistribution formulas set to insure some degree of solidarity. If there is an optimal competitive balance and if revenue-sharing and salary caps be used adjust relative balance, optimum combinations of cost caps and revenue-sharing regimes can be used to maximize social welfare.

Since 1990 all sports leagues have been rapidly transformed by increased media coverage and exploding media rights fees. Media revenues comprise 50 percent or more of total revenues in the EPL, Italian Serie A, Spanish La Liga and the NFL. It is argued here that media coverage expands or globalizes home markets and shifts fan preferences more toward home-team dominance and less toward quality opposition and competitive balance. In media leagues fans can freely choose their 'home' teams regardless of where they reside. They can simultaneously support competitive balance for their local club and have a preference for the dominance of their global club. For example, SPORT+MARKT 2010 estimates that Real Madrid has 6.8 million fans for 36 percent of the domestic Spanish market, compared with Barcelona with 5.5 million fans for 29 percent of the local market. The opposite is true throughout Europe however, where FC Barcelona has 57.8 million fans compared with Real Madrid with 31.3 million fans.

These arguments imply that revenue sharing and payroll caps are tools to find optimal competitive balance consistent with media coverage and fan preference, but also that overly aggressive controls in the singular pursuit of parity could lead to suboptimal competitive balance and medi-ocrity. In NA for example, the welfare inferiority of parity/mediocrity in the NFL is a matter of fan preference but in Europe, the inferiority of intra-league parity can become a matter of inter-league survival. In 2004–05 French Ligue 1 reduced its egalitarian sharing formula from 83/10/7 (equal/merit/appearances) to 50/30/20 to improve the competitive chances of domestic French clubs in Europe.

Equal solidarity/merit (50/50) sharing has moved competitive balance toward an optimum in the EPL, Bundesliga and Ligue 1 consistent with media coverage and fan preference for more imbalance. The recent pros-pects of 40/60 equal/merit (market size) sharing of collectively negotiated television rights in Serie A and La Liga (proposed) are steps toward increased social welfare (profits + wages + fan welfare) in these two his-torically excellent and yet unbalanced leagues. North American leagues (NFL) should re-examine misguided obsession with absolute parity. Socially optimal competitive balance lies between dynastic distortions from large market monopoly power and competitive mediocrity from overcompensating constraints that serve to tear apart excellent and efficient teams.

NOTES

1. Fort and Quirk (2010a, 2010b) concluded that socially optimal competitive balance remains an empirical question in both single game (MLB) and season ticket (NFL) leagues.
2. Open-league competitive balance solutions: $w_1/w_2 = 1$ for $\phi = 0$; $w_1/w_2 = \sqrt{\sigma}$ for $\phi = .5$ and $w_1/w_2 = \sigma$ for $\phi = 1$. The open-league profit-max solution is unconstrained because $w_2 \geq 0$ for $0 \leq \phi \leq 1$ and $\sigma \geq 1$. Dietl and Lang (2008) and Dietl et al. (2009) use a nonlinear demand distribution from Falconieri et al. (2004) and fan preference function from Vrooman (2009) to show that welfare is maximized at greater competitive imbal-ance $w_1/w_2 = \sigma$ than the internal profit maximum $w_1/w_2 = \sigma^2$.
3. Major League Baseball has an ineffective competitive balance (luxury) tax that applies to clubs over a high payroll threshold (New York Yankees). Major League Baseball player development expenses are counted separately from payroll, and on average player development expenses (a multi-tiered minor league system is subsidized by the parent MLB club) usually amount to about 10 percent of revenues. National Football League and NBA player development expenses are insignificant because training costs are shifted to the amateur National Collegiate Athletic Association (NCAA) college where players acquire general playing skills as undergraduates. The 2005 NHL Collective Bargaining Agreement (CBA) rolled back all player contracts by 24 percent to lower the player-share from 75 percent before the 2004–05 lockout to 57 percent by 2005.
4. Bundesliga also has a 50+1 rule that requires that the majority of a club be owned by the fans. Fan ownership also implies that Bundesliga is controlled by ownership groups whose sole objective is winning at all cost.
5. See Vrooman (2009) for discussion of revenue revolutions in NA leagues and Vrooman (2007) for Big 5 European leagues.

6. The exception is Bundesliga, resulting from financial collapse of KirchMedia in 2002. Original Kirch rights of €1.53 billion 2001–04 were replaced with €290 million for 2002–04 and €295 million and €300 million for 2005–06.
7. Before 2002 each 34 percent visitor's share was derived from games in which teams actually played. After 2002 realignment shares were pooled and split evenly so that all teams received the same visiting teams share
8. In both NFL and MLB clubs can deduct private stadium costs from revenues before the tax rate is applied. In this way large market clubs like the New York Yankees and Mets and the New York Giants and Jets can shield stadium expenses from revenue sharing and effectively shift visitor share of stadium costs to the rest of the league.
9. The NFL cap was part of the 1994 CBA compromise whereby NFL players received free agency after four years of service, and the NHL cap was imposed after the 2004–05 NHL lock-out.
10. The NFL cap can be temporarily avoided by signing bonuses that are prorated over the length of the contract which averages about four years in the NFL. Current team payroll including bonuses can exceed the cap now but are amortized forward to restrict payroll below the cap by an equivalent amount in the future (dead cap space).
11. The Yankees have been taxed each season since the CBT began in 2003 and they have paid over 90 percent of the total tax. Luxury tax rate is 22.5 percent of payroll over €121 million in 2010, €127 million in 2011; tax rate escalates to 30 percent and 40 percent for the second and third breach. The tax is paid in addition to revenue sharing.
12. Nine percent shared with Segunda division and each of three relegated clubs would receive €9 million parachute.
13. Money invested in stadiums and player development does not count in expenditures for FFP. Sportsman owners are allowed to contribute up to a maximum of €45 million for the 2013–14 and 2014–15 seasons together and €30 million for 2015–16, 2016–17 and 2017–18 combined.
14. The champion effect occurs when post-season tournaments introduce a convexity to strictly concave regular season revenue functions (Vrooman, 2007). This creates multiple league equilibria and polarizes competion in domestic leagues. The champion effect depends on the relative size and certainty of the post-season prize. The most likely conditions for the champion effect are found in MLB and UEFA leagues.
15. The 2009–10 Champions League results: champion Inter Milan; runner-up Bayern Munich; semi-finalists: Barcelona and Lyon.
16. SPORT+MARKT is conducting a similar fan base survey being used in the Serie A revenue sharing formula.
17. About 109 million people watched Barcelona beat Manchester United in the 2009 UCL final, while 106 million (68 percent share) watched the New Orleans Saints defeat the Indianapolis Colts in Super Bowl XLIV in 2010.
18. The NFL hard cap can be temporarily avoided by prorating large upfront bonuses over the length of NFL contracts. Unfortunately the amortized bonus continues to count against future salary caps and create what is called dead cap space. In the cap's first season, 1994, the average NFL contract increased from three to four years.

REFERENCES

Dietl, H. and Lang, M. (2008), 'The effect of gate revenue sharing on social welfare', *Contemporary Economic Policy*, **26** (3), 448–59.
Dietl, H., Lang, M. and Werner, S. (2009), 'Social welfare in sports leagues with profit-maximizing and/or win-maximizing clubs', *Southern Economic Journal*, **76** (2), 375–96.

El Hodiri, M. and Quirk, J. (1971), 'An economic model of a professional sports league', *Journal of Political Economy*, **79**, 1302–19.

Falconeiri, S., Palomino, F. and Sakovics, J. (2004), 'Collective versus individual sale of television rights in league sports', *Journal of the European Economics Association*, **2** (5), 833–62.

Fort, R. and Quirk, J. (1995), 'Cross-subsidization, incentives, and outcomes in professional team sports leagues', *Journal of Economic Literature*, September, 1265–99.

Fort, R. and Quirk, J. (2007), 'The competitive talent market model: rational expectations in pro sports leagues', *Scottish Journal of Political Economy*, **54**, 374–87.

Fort, R. and Quirk, J. (2010a), 'Optimal competitive balance in a season-ticket league', *Economic Inquiry*, **49** (2), 464–73.

Fort, R. and Quirk, J. (2010b), 'Optimal competitive balance in single-game ticket sports leagues', *Journal of Sports Economics*, **11** (December), 587–601.

Kesenne, S. (1996), 'League management in professional team sports with win maximizing clubs', *European Journal for Sports Management*, **2**, 14–22.

Quirk, J. and R. Fort (1992), *Pay Dirt: The Business of Professional Team Sports*, Princeton, NJ: Princeton University Press.

Szymanski, S. (2003), 'The economic design of sporting contests', *Journal of Economic Literature*, **41**, 1137–87.

Szymanski, S. (2004), 'Professional team sports are only a game: Walrasian fixed-supply conjecture model, contest Nash equilibrium and the invariance principle', *Journal of Sports Economics*, **5**, 111–26.

Szymanski, S. and Kesenne, S. (2003), 'Competitive balance and gate revenue sharing in team sports', *Journal of Industrial Economics*, **52** (1), 165–77.

Vrooman, J. (1995), 'General theory of professional sports leagues', *Southern Economic Journal*, **61** (4), 971–90.

Vrooman, J. (1997), 'Unified theory of capital and labor markets in Major League Baseball', '*Southern Economic Journal*, **63** (3), 594–619.

Vrooman, J. (2000), 'The economics of American sports leagues', *Scottish Journal of Political Economy*, **47** (4), 594–619.

Vrooman, J. (2007), 'Theory of the beautiful game: the unification of European football', *Scottish Journal of Political Economy*, **54** (3), 314–54.

Vrooman, J. (2009), 'Theory of the perfect game: competitive balance in monopoly sports leagues', *Review of Industrial Organization*, **34** (1), 5–44.

2. Major League Baseball attendance time series: league policy lessons

Rodney Fort and Young Hoon Lee

I INTRODUCTION

In this chapter, we offer policy observations based on the impact of competitive balance and the behavior of structural break points in Major League Baseball's (MLB's) attendance time series. First, game uncertainty and dynasties (that is, winning consecutive championships) do not matter for attendance but playoff uncertainty does. However, the impact of playoff uncertainty is economically unimportant. Second, structural breaks occur proximate only to post-World War II racial integration, expansion in the early 1960s, expansion and the introduction of division play in 1969, and for the commonly acknowledged hitting power escalation of the late 1980s. No structural breaks coincide with other expansion episodes or the explosion of cable television in the 1980s.

Past work on attendance time series in MLB have focused on the impact of strikes (Schmidt and Berri, 2002, 2004), econometric time series issues (Fort and Lee, 2006) and the role of outcome uncertainty (Lee and Fort, 2008). None of these are explicitly aimed at extracting policy lessons as we do in this chapter for each of the episodes just identified.

The statistical analysis behind these observations is not original to this chapter, appearing also in our other published work on attendance (Lee and Fort, 2008). In our opinion, the additional policy observations offered here are valuable enough to stand on the same earlier statistical analysis, that is, we would do the same analysis in order to address our policy issues.

Some readers will be left wanting more than we provide here. We have no doubt that actually assessing the explanations and policy implications we offer will prove insightful. However, everything cannot be done in one go and we leave that additional research to subsequent analysis.

The chapter proceeds as follows. We briefly present our earlier statistical findings in section II. The policy observations are in section III. The chapter concludes with a summary of the implications for policy and suggestions for future work in section IV.

II STATISTICAL FINDINGS

We base our policy conclusions on the following statistical results from our previous work (Lee and Fort, 2008). The unit of observation was MLB attendance at the annual league level as opposed to cross-section analysis of individual team attendance or the analysis of game day attendance. We have no doubt that other levels of aggregation also prove informative – aggregated and disaggregated analyses are complementary. However, league-level aggregation does have two things to recommend it. First, Rottenberg's (1956) original discussion concerned just why attendance, as a measure of economic health, is a league-level concern. Second, all three types of outcome uncertainty should matter in aggregate – game-level uncertainty, playoff level uncertainty and uncertainty across consecutive seasons.

Briefly, to derive the results, we applied the methods of Perron (1989) and Bai and Perron (1998, 2003), henceforth the BP method, to pin down the break points in the average annual per-game attendance in each of the American League (AL) and the National League (NL). The technique is now tried and true in the sports economics literature applied to both competitive balance (Lee and Fort, 2005; Fort and Lee, 2007) and attendance (Lee and Fort, 2008), and we do not reprise it here. Moreover, the unit root test method with endogenous structural breaks helps identify stationary periods in the attendance time series. This method also has the advantage of allowing elasticity calculations that is lost using the method common to non-stationary time series, taking first differences of the dependent variable (Fort and Lee, 2006).

In framing the actual model, we took account of the following. First, Lee and Fort (2005) detect break points in the competitive balance time series but none of these coincide with the break points discovered by Lee and Fort (2008) in the attendance time series. So, we utilized a one-step procedure, including measures of game-level uncertainty, playoff uncertainty, and consecutive season uncertainty in the break point analysis since they may be one of the determinants of the attendance break points in the first place. Second, to account for scale effects due to expansion in the number of teams, we measured attendance on a league average per game basis. The AL and NL were analyzed separately since measures of competitive balance are generated from separate league play for nearly the entire sample.

Finally, Schmidt and Berri (2002, 2004) and Coates and Harrison (2005) found that strikes and lockouts might have short-term effects on the attendance time series. Dummy variable techniques cannot be used in the BP method. In some cases, dummy variables could equal zero or one for all observations in sub-samples used to estimate break points via the BP method. So we account for work stoppages using the mean difference of league average attendance per game between strike years and regular seasons as the dependent variable during strike years.

We applied the BP method, allowing both levels and trends to change (Perron, 1989), for the AL and NL over the period 1901–2003. The results with breaks were from the following attendance regression:

$$LAPG_t = z_t\beta_i + x_t\gamma + \varepsilon_t, t = T_{i-1} + 1,\ldots,T_i, i = 1,\ldots,m + 1 \quad (2.1)$$

In equation (2.1), $LAPG_t$ was league average attendance per game (adjusted for strikes), $t = 1901$–2003. z_t was a $(q \times 1)$ dimensional covariate with coefficients β_i subject to change over time, essentially the constant and a trend. x_t was a $(p \times 1)$ covariate comprised of our outcome uncertainty variables (discussed presently). Subscript i indexed the ith regime, and the indices $(T_1,\ldots,T_m)$ were treated as the unknown break points. For example, we found that there were three breaks in the NL (1918, 1945 and 1967) but in this case $i = 1,\ldots, 4$: (1901, 1918), (1919, 1945), (1946, 1967), (1968, 2003).

Equation (2.1) is a partial structural change model since the parameter vector γ is not subject to change. When $p = 0$, this model is a pure structural change model where all the coefficients are subject to change. Perron's GAUSS code was used to estimate the break points using equation (2.1).

Our extensive exploration of outcome uncertainty variables led to the following choices (again, fully described in Lee and Fort, 2008). For game-level uncertainty, we arrived at the winning percentage 'tail likelihood' measure first used by Fort and Quirk (1995). An increase in tail likelihood indicates a reduction in outcome uncertainty at the game level. For playoff uncertainty, we used the average difference across a given league in winning percentages between first- and second-place finishers. This measure, of course, required adaptation to two- and three-division play for 1969–93 and 1994 on, respectively. As this variable increases, playoff uncertainty declines since division races are less likely to be tight. Finally, for consecutive season uncertainty, we used the correlation of winning percentage between this season and the last three seasons first suggested by Butler (1995). If this correlation increases, the same teams dominate over time and consecutive season uncertainty decreases. Descriptive statistics for all variables are in Table 2.1.

The estimation results from the BP model from Lee and Fort (2008) are summarized in Table 2.2. That other work goes into great detail on the impact of outcome uncertainty and we do not do so here. But it is

Table 2.1   Descriptive statistics, 1901–2003

Variable	Min.	Max.	Median	Mean	Std dev.
AL					
LAPG	3067	30366	12313	13270	7859
GU	0.0003	1.621	0.068	0.167	0.239
PU	0.004	0.128	0.042	0.046	0.031
CSU	−0.197	0.942	0.618	0.564	0.245
NL					
LAPG	2701	32532	13928	13836	8420
GU	0.0001	2.421	0.091	0.211	0.350
PU	0.006	0.198	0.034	0.043	0.032
CSU	−0.536	0.958	0.614	0.533	0.320

worth noting for our following policy assessment that only playoff-level uncertainty had any statistically detectable impact on the attendance time series. However, while statistically significant, the economic impact was very small.

Since they have received little attention in the literature, we emphasize our findings on dynasties as well. For example, in our 'interesting' 1946–1962 period for the AL, the New York Yankees won 13 of 17 AL pennants, with a streak of 4 consecutive pennants (1955–58) sandwiched between two streaks of 5 consecutive pennants (1949–53; 1960–64). However, we found no evidence at all that consecutive season uncertainty mattered for annual per-game attendance in either the AL or the NL. Of course, for a strongly held prior belief, a lack of statistical significance either rejects the belief or begs for more data and/or better treatments of the data. Since there are no other MLB data (literally) for our aggregate form of analysis, perhaps better treatments will follow ours and find otherwise. We hold off on the policy implications of these findings until a later section.

Most important for framing our presentation of policy lessons, we found four break points in the AL – 1918, 1945, 1962 and 1987 – and three for the NL – 1918, 1945 and 1967. Their contribution to the statistical explanation of league attendance per game is detailed in Table 2.2. However, it is easier to discuss these break points using the fitted values of the dependent variable in Figures 2.1 and 2.2 for the AL and the NL, respectively (the break points are also clearly identified by vertical lines). Using the coefficient estimates on the trend variables to interpret changes before and after the break points is straightforward. But it is not so easy to see what happens with the coefficient estimates of intercepts. For example,

Table 2.2   *Generalized least squares attendance estimation results, AL and NL*

Regime	Variables	AL	NL
(1901, 1918)	Intercept	6.094*	7.002*
		(7.92)	(6.50)
	Trend slope	−0.064	−0.153***
		(−0.85)	(−1.63)
(1919, 1945)	Intercept	8.101*	7.131*
		(8.00)	(6.16)
	Trend slope	−0.001	0.026
		(−0.04)	(0.07)
(1946, 1962)	Intercept	25.201*	
		(7.91)	
	Trend slope	−0.204*	
		(−3.23)	
(1963, 1987)	Intercept	−20.431*	
		(−6.22)	
	Trend slope	0.518*	
		(14.57)	
(1988, 2003)	Intercept	18.850*	
		(2.85)	
	Trend slope	0.101	
		(1.41)	
(1946, 1967)			9.115*
			(3.32)
			0.117**
			(2.33)
(1968, 2003)			−12.878*
			(−6.22)
			0.447*
			(17.74)
	GU (TL)	−0.036	0.189
		(−0.52)	(−0.61)
	PU (WINDIFF)	−7.586***	−17.940*
		(−1.73)	(−3.08)
	CSU (CORR)	−0.555	−0.421
		(−0.84)	(−0.80)
	R-squared	0.977	0.971

Notes:
*   Significant at the 99 percent critical level.
**   Significant at the 95 percent critical level.
***   Significant at the 90 percent critical level.

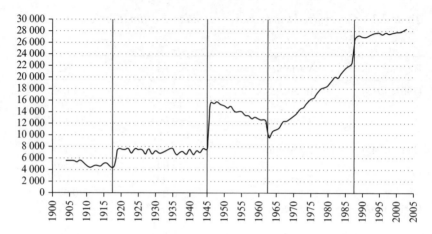

Figure 2.1   Fitted LAPG, AL

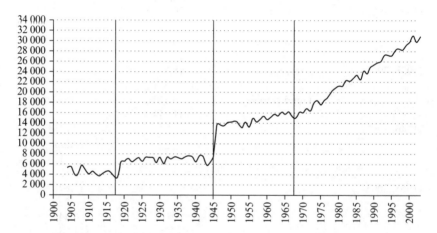

Figure 2.2   Fitted LAPG, NL

the intercept estimates are single-season values for the first season in the
sample, 1901, but not when a season occurs during a break point.

Until 1918, the Figures 2.1 and 2.2 show that attendance were stable
in the two leagues, between 4000 and 5000 per game. After a significant
upward jump to 7000 per game in both leagues, coinciding with the end of
World War I, attendance again remained stable from 1919 to 1945. The
shift up at the end of World War II approximately doubled attendance per
game in each league but, unlike preceding upward shifts, attendance was
anything but stable in either league following this break point.

In the AL, there are three distinct post-World War II periods separated by break points in 1962 and 1987. After the clear shift up at the post-World War II break point, AL attendance per game actually declined up to 1962! This is the only prolonged decline observed over the entire sample period in either league. The AL decline was truly precipitous at the 1962 break point, after which attendance rebounded at the highest rate of increase in the sample for either league. American League attendance then jumped again significantly in 1987, from about 22000 to about 27000 per game, and leveled off thereafter.

In the NL, there are two distinct post-World War II periods separated by the single break point in 1967. After its post-World War II jump, and in contrast to the AL decline, NL attendance gently increased to its 1967 break point. The NL enjoyed a trend increase only, and no associated shift, at its final detected break point in 1967. National League attendance per game has continued its increase at a higher rate since 1967. The last upward shift for the AL in 1987 did overtake attendance in the NL at that time, but the leveling off after that in the AL allowed the continued increase in the NL to bring that league to attendance dominance over the last five years in the sample.

III   LEAGUE POLICY OBSERVATIONS

First and foremost, the only type of competitive balance that matters for aggregate annual league attendance is playoff uncertainty. Thus, access to the playoffs impacts attendance in a statistically significant way. But our other work also shows that it does not matter much economically. Revenue changes due to pretty dramatic increases in playoff access are small. While there remains some small amount of disagreement about whether particular policy elements like the draft, free agency, revenue sharing and taxes on payroll spending actually can improve balance to begin with, our results show that those disagreements may be moot. Subject to the power of our particular test, fans simply do not respond at the gate to changes in game uncertainty, or to the presence of dynasties, and their response to playoff certainty is economically unimportant. We grant that the power of our test may simply miss these other policy interventions.

By and large, some league policy issues do stand out in the structural changes in Figures 2.1 and 2.2. First, there is the post-World War II racial integration period for the AL and the NL. Second, there is league expansion in 1961 (AL) and 1962 (NL). Third, there is another expansion and the introduction of division play in 1969 (both leagues). Finally, there is the escalation of hitting power in the 1980s in the AL.

In our earlier work on competitive balance (Lee and Fort, 2005), we suggested that attitudes toward race might have been different in AL and NL cities over the post-World War II period. That same suggestion lends insight into the negative trend revealed in the AL, compared with the positive trend in the NL, following the post-World War II break point in attendance. From the attendance perspective, an operational hypothesis would be that racial attitudes were different in cities not shared by the AL and the NL. Racial attitudes in jointly occupied cities are the same for teams in either league so the marginal difference must be in cities solely occupied by one league or the other.

Excluding the Twin Cities and Houston that only had teams for one and two years, respectively, over 1946–62, the AL solely occupied Baltimore, Cleveland, Detroit, Kansas City and Washington, and the NL solely occupied Cincinnati, Los Angeles, Milwaukee, Pittsburgh and San Francisco. If fans in cities in the AL list were relatively cooler to integration compared with fans in cities in the NL list, attendance could fall in the former and rise in the latter. Interestingly, Baltimore and Kansas City involved team moves (the St. Louis Browns to Baltimore and the Philadelphia Athletics to Kansas City) that resulted in increased attendance. Further, both Baltimore and Kansas City were previous strongholds for African American baseball prior to the demise of that league. Thus, racial attitude difference would have had to be very strong in Cleveland, Detroit and Washington. We also simply note the East-Central composition of the AL teams and the West-Central composition of the NL teams. Further, since both leagues enjoyed strong attendance increases after 1962, it required the extraordinary jump in 1987 for the AL to catch up to the NL fully 25 years after its declining attendance episode.

Other coincidental evidence based on possibly different racial attitudes is found in the relative speed of integration in the two leagues, shown in Table 2.3 and Figure 2.3. While the two leagues integrated initially at about the same rate (1946–1953), the eventual integration of the AL proceeded more slowly. Indeed, the NL was completely integrated for nearly three full seasons before Pumpsie Green joined the Red Sox most of the way through the 1959 season to complete the integration of the AL. Expansion teams added shortly thereafter were all integrated from their inception. Of course, this is only story-telling and the fact that the Boston Braves of the NL integrated early on, while the Boston Red Sox of the AL were the last to integrate, remains to be explained.

It is tempting to incorporate the Yankee dominance of the post-World War II period, described above, into the explanation. And what a nice episode it would make for Rottenberg's outcome uncertainty hypothesis (that is, fans detest competitive imbalance) if it were not for the fact that

Table 2.3   Chronology of MLB integration

Player	Team	Date
Jackie Robinson	Brooklyn Dodgers, NL	15 April 1947
Larry Doby	Cleveland Indians, AL	5 July 1947
Hank Thompson	St. Louis Browns, AL	17 July 1947
Roy Campanella	Brooklyn Dodgers, NL	20 April 1948
Monte Irvin, Hank Thompson	New York Giants, NL	8 July 1949
Sam Jethroe	Boston Braves, NL	18 April 1950
Minnie Miñoso	Chicago White Sox, AL	1 May 1951
Bob Trice	Philadelphia Athletics, AL	13 Sept. 1953
Ernie Banks	Chicago Cubs, NL	17 Sept. 1953
Curt Roberts	Pittsburgh Pirates, NL	13 April 1954
Tom Alston	St. Louis Cardinals, NL	13 April 1954
Nino Escalera, Chuck Harmon	Cincinnati Reds, NL	17 April 1954
Carlos Paula	Washington Senators, AL	6 Sept. 1954
Elston Howard	New York Yankees, AL	14 April 1955
John Kennedy	Philadelphia Phillies, NL	22 April 1957
Ozzie Virgil, Sr	Detroit Tigers, AL	6 June 1958
Pumpsie Green	Boston Red Sox, AL	21 July 1959

Source: Wikipedia (2009).

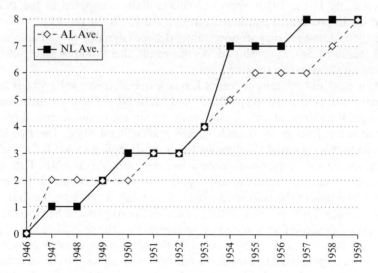

Figure 2.3   Number of integrated teams, AL versus NL, 1946–49

Table 2.4   Playoff uncertainty by decade, AL and NL

Decade	AL Ave.	NL Ave.	Ave. Diff.	Ave. % Diff.
1900s	0.027	0.082	−0.054	−48.2
1910s	0.051	0.062	−0.010	−14.6
1920s	0.050	0.032	0.019	152.8
1930s	0.072	0.029	0.043	204.2
1940s	0.045	0.043	0.002	128.1
1950s	0.040	0.038	0.002	128.5
1960s	0.047	0.030	0.018	155.1
1970s	0.043	0.040	0.003	61.7
1980s	0.035	0.038	−0.003	65.7
1990s	0.045	0.038	0.008	41.2
1990a	0.039	0.035	0.005	62.7
1990b	0.051	0.039	0.012	38.0
2000s	0.042	0.044	−0.002	119.3
1901–2003	0.046	0.043	0.003	90.0

our model produces no statistically significant impact for dynasty occurrences (more about this at the end of the section).

Neither is it the fact that reductions in playoff uncertainty are responsible for this decline in the AL. Table 2.4 shows that our measure of playoff uncertainty in the 1940s improved substantially compared to the 1930s and the improvement continued through the 1950s for the AL. Not until the 1960s do we see playoff uncertainty decline (signaled by an increase in our measure). Since fans should like this result, this would be an offsetting effect on the negative trend in Figure 2.1.

Our next observation concerns league expansion in 1961 (Angels and Senators II, AL) and 1962 (Colt.45s and Mets, NL). There are three items of note. First, this expansion was clearly a response to the invention of the Continental League by Branch Rickey and William Shea. The two had designed this potential third major league and applied to MLB for inclusion, spurring the expansion response by the existing AL and NL. Thus it is not surprising that a fundamental impact on attendance occurred. The negative direction of the shift is consistent with weak teams entering that are not as much fun to watch and that describes the Angels and Senators II in the AL. Our second item of interest reinforces that the shift would be negative. At the same time as the expansion, the perennially weak Washington Senators I also moved to Minnesota and proved a hapless bunch for a time. Our final item of interest is that while there was a break point for the AL in 1963, there was no proximate break in the NL. This suggests something different about the expansion to Houston and back to the New York market.

Third, there is another expansion and the introduction of division play in 1969 (Pilots and Royals in the AL, Padres and Expos in the NL) corresponding to the break point in 1968 for the NL. One difference between the two leagues in this case is the location experiment to Canada and additional satisfaction for far western fans in San Diego. Also, in the AL, the Pilots only lasted one season in Seattle and the Royals were a replacement for the recently departed Athletics (to Oakland in 1965).

Finally, turning to the 1987 break point for the AL only, Table 2.4 shows that playoff uncertainty had never been better in this league (except for the very distant history of the decade of the 1900s) and we also can identify a possible structural issue that remains important to present. This is the period characteristic of the new age of hitter power (as opposed to statistically measured 'power hitting'), exemplified by the 'Bash Brothers' of the Oakland A's (Jose Canseco and Mark McGwire). Of course, this also marks the beginning of a period retroactively cast under the shadow of performance enhancing drugs (PEDs).

Beginning a set of interesting results for expansions other than those in the 1960s covered above, the 1977 expansion causes no stir (Mariners and Blue Jays in the AL). We go ahead and note out of order that subsequent expansions in 1994 (Rockies and Marlins in the NL) and 1998 (Devil Rays and Diamondbacks in the NL) have no associated break either. Perhaps the interesting conclusion is that there is nothing really novel about these expansions. The Mariners replaced the Pilots, there was already baseball in Canada, and baseball was not new in any of the rest of the locations. Florida had enjoyed MLB presence in spring training forever and the west was, by now, quite used to MLB presence.

Neither do we find any break point coinciding with the explosion of regional cable television through the early 1990s. Unlike the impacts of the original introduction of division play in 1969, we find the path of attendance unaffected by the extension to three divisions following expansion of the NL in 1994. The results from Lee (2009) suggest this could be due to the fact that playoff uncertainty is capturing part of these impacts and that is consistent with our data here. For example, in Table 2.4 and Figure 2.4, the 1960s showed a significant divergence in our measure for the AL (worse) and the NL (better). However, they converged to be similar for the 1970s and 1980s but in a curiously asymmetric way; there was an improvement in the AL but not in the NL. The reason for this asymmetric response to the same type of move to playoffs remains one line of future research, but converge they did, so this helps with the difference between the original institution of division play and the later three-division approach.

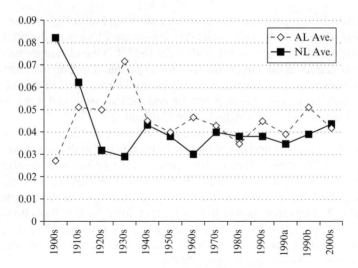

Figure 2.4   Playoff uncertainty by decade, AL and NL

IV   IMPLICATIONS AND SUGGESTIONS FOR FUTURE WORK

Overall, the implications are clear. In terms of competitive balance and attendance, game uncertainty does not matter for aggregate league attendance per game. Playoff uncertainty matters but economically it matters very little. We also find no evidence that fans either abhor or adore dynasties.

This suggests that claims by owners and the commissioner that fans are better off with improved balance are overblown. Our results also dispel claims by proponents of the draft that fans like the fairness of it, whether it impacts balance or not. For critics of free agency, our results suggest that any lack of team continuity or the high salaries earned as free agents do not discourage fans in their attendance decisions. This is important since, without fail, this type of debate about competitive balance arises every time players and owners sit down to tweak the game in the name of balance at collective bargaining junctures.

Of course, this also raises the question of just what it is that owners are hoping to gain from their balance argument. More in-depth research on the actual distributional consequences of the draft, free agency, revenue sharing and payroll taxes should shed light on this. The consequences will be found in the reallocation of revenues between owners and players, some owners and others, and some players and others.

The next policy implication from our work is that the economic success (in terms of attendance) of increasing the racial variety of players put in front of fans depends on the fans. The emerging story is that NL fans were more amenable to integration than AL fans in some important cities. Perhaps this explains the pattern of Asian player location as their presence grows in MLB. Interestingly, Hispanic players appear to be much more widely distributed. Once again, to our knowledge, the distribution of players by race and the relationships between MLB and international leagues remain pretty much wide-open research areas.

Finally, our work indicates that the structure of the game itself, in terms of the number of teams and where they are located, and the form of the determination of the final champion, matters in fan attendance consideration. In addition, this happens in a nuanced way. The 1961 AL expansion resulted in what most people would expect – weak teams and decreased fan interest. After that, it appears that expansion increases attention when it is carefully managed! The 1969 expansion in the NL was into 'undiscovered territory' – the US far west of San Diego and the first expansion into Canada in Montreal. Expansion in the same year in the AL, as well as later expansions, was not associated with detectable structural change in balance. The creation of playoffs might also matter, but in its initial incarnation rather than in subsequent alterations.

This suggests two things. First, future expansions need some novelty characteristic in order to impact aggregate league attendance per game. Second, recent discussion in MLB about expanding the playoffs even further cannot be about the impact in some indirect way on regular season attendance. As for future research, it is pretty clear to us (as we also noted in our previous work) that little about the impacts of expansion is very well understood.

The implications concerning the hitting power explosion in the 1980s are more speculative. The shift up in attendance, followed by a leveling of attendance in the AL, is consistent with AL fans first identifying with more exciting hitting power and then finding the source of that excitement distasteful after learning that players were using PEDs. Further, the dramatic shift upward for the AL at this point could help explain MLB's reluctance to intervene strenuously on behalf of clean play at that time (and possibly today). The league should be expected to weigh the preference of some fans and observers for 'clean play' against the observed fact of a large AL attendance jump. Future research in this area would continue to quantify both the impact of PEDs on performance and the subsequent impact on revenues (following DiNardo and Winfree, 2010).

Again, these are only occurrences that coincide at this historical juncture and only further analysis will settle the question. Ours is only one piece of what might be a complicated puzzle; cross-section time series analysis may discover otherwise in the disaggregate or it could be the case that fans in some locations feel differently than fans in other locations. For example, the impact of many league policies may have been of short duration, without a structural impact on the attendance time series, but interesting nonetheless.

Our finding that successive wins do not matter for aggregate attendance suggests that other work may wish to revisit the assumption that attendance increases with consecutive season uncertainty (Humphreys, 2002; Hadley et al., 2005).

Finally, our findings hold for one North American league and there are three others as well as worldwide leagues.

ACKNOWLEDGEMENT

This work was supported by a National Research Foundation Grant funded by the Korean Government (MEST) (KRF-2009-220-B00008).

REFERENCES

Bai, J. and Perron, P. (1998), 'Estimating and testing lineal models with multiple structural changes', *Econometrica*, **66**, 47–78.

Bai, J. and Perron, P. (2003), 'Computation and analysis of multiple structural change models', *Journal of Applied Econometrics*, **18**, 1–22.

Butler, M.R. (1995), 'Competitive balance in Major League Baseball', *American Economist*, **39**, 46–52.

Coates, D. and Harrison, T. (2005), 'Baseball strikes and the demand for attendance', *Journal of Sports Economics*, **6**, 282–302.

DiNardo, J. and Winfree, J. (2010), 'The law of genius and home runs refuted', *Economic Inquiry*, **48**, 51–64.

Fort, R. and Lee, Y.H. (2006), 'Stationarity and MLB attendance analysis', *Journal of Sports Economics*, **7**, 408–15.

Fort, R. and Lee, Y.H. (2007), 'Structural change, competitive balance, and the rest of the major leagues', *Economic Inquiry*, **45**(3), 519–32.

Fort, R. and Quirk, J. (1995), 'Cross-subsidization, incentives, and outcomes in professional team sports leagues', *Journal of Economic Literature*, **23**, 1265–99.

Hadley, L., Ciecka, J. and Krautmann, A. (2005), 'Competitive balance in the aftermath of the 1994 players' strike', *Journal of Sports Economics*, **6**, 379–89.

Humphreys, B.R. (2002), 'Alternative measures of competitive balance in sports leagues', *Journal of Sports Economics*, **3**, 133–48.

Lee, Y.H. (2009), 'The impact of postseason restructuring on the competitive balance and fan demand in Major League Baseball', *Journal of Sports Economics*, **10**, 219–35.

Lee, Y.H. and Fort, R. (2005), 'Structural change in baseball's competitive balance: the Great Depression, team location, and racial integration', *Economic Inquiry*, **43**, 158–69.

Lee, Y.H. and Fort, R. (2008), 'Fan demand and the uncertainty of outcome hypothesis in baseball', *Review of Industrial Organization*, **33**, 281–95.

Perron, P. (1989), 'The Great Crash, the oil price shock, and the unit root hypothesis', *Econometrica*, **57**, 1361–401.

Rottenberg, S. (1956), 'The baseball players' labor market', *Journal of Political Economy*, **64**, 242–58.

Schmidt, M.B. and Berri, D.J. (2002), 'The impact of the 1981 and 1994–1995 strikes on Major League Baseball attendance: a time-series analysis', *Applied Economics*, **34**, 471–8.

Schmidt, M.B. and Berri, D.J. (2004), 'The impact of labor strikes on consumer demand: an application to professional sports', *American Economic Review*, **94**, 334–47.

Wikipedia (2009), 'List of first black Major League Baseball players by team and date', available at: http://en.wikipedia.org/wiki/List_of_first_black_Major_League_Baseball_players_by_team_and_date (accessed 26 May 2009).

PART II

Player's Labour Markets

3. Wages, transfers and the variation of team performance in the English Premier League*

Stefan Szymanski

1 INTRODUCTION

In the world of football, transfer fees are investments in intangible fixed assets – the cost of acquiring the player registration which ties the player to the club for the life of his contract. The contract also specifies a wage payment schedule over the life of the contract. This chapter uses a database of player transfer fees and wage payments to measure the relationship between expenditures and team performance.

The standard formal model of a sports league is a contest in which teams compete for a share of success (win percentage, points or league rank) by investing in playing talent. This structure was adopted in the first formal models produced by El Hodiri and Quirk (1971) and Quirk and El Hodiri (1974), and subsequently extended by Atkinson et al. (1988) Fort and Quirk (1995), Vrooman (1995), Késenne (2000), Szymanski and Késenne (2004) and Dietl and Lang (2008).

The precise mechanism by which the expenditure of owners translates into playing success has been debated in the literature, but the basic story must go something like this:

1. Team owners hire playing talent in a market subject to competition between teams.
2. Competition should ensure that the price paid for a player (contractual wages and any acquisition costs) should reflect their expected productivity (and in a perfectly competitive market their marginal revenue product).

Arguably, this market conforms to several of the assumptions deemed essential to perfectly competitive outcomes – there are many buyers and sellers, and a good deal of public information is typically available about the expected productivity of players – the observation of player productivity is what spectator sport is all about.

An empirical implication of the standard model is that the aggregate expenditure on players should be closely correlated with the playing performance of teams. However, the wide array of restraints adopted in American sports leagues conspire to conceal this relationship. Most obviously, the hard salary cap adopted in the National Football League (NFL) has ensured that the variation in aggregate player spending by teams is negligible, and hence aggregate wage spending cannot account for the variation in team performance.

However, in the world of football (soccer), there are considerably fewer restraints on the operation of the labour market. Teams bargain freely for the services of players and there is considerable mobility both within and between leagues, nationally and internationally. There is considerable evidence of a high correlation between aggregate player spending and the league performance of teams (for example, García del Barrio and Szymanski, 2009; Forrest and Simmons, 2002; Szymanski, 2003; Szymanski and Smith, 1997).

However, some questions still remain about this relationship. First, it may be objected that the direction of causation in fact runs from success to player spending because successful teams reward their players with bonuses and the like. Hall et al. (2002) tested for Granger causality and found evidence that causation runs from wages to success for data drawn from English league football, but the power of the test may not be that great. Second, while wages can account for most of the in-league performance in the soccer world, large sums are spent on player transfers and no satisfactory explanation of the relationship between transfer fees and wages and between transfer fees and league performance has been advanced.

2   DATA

Data on player wages for English football clubs is relatively easily available. As documented by Szymanski and Smith (1997), English football clubs have traditionally operated as limited companies, and under English law limited companies must file annual accounts with a public body (Companies House) and these accounts are available for inspection by the public for a small fee. The accounts must disclose the total cost of employing staff, and while a football club has more staff than just the players, the wages of the players account for by far the largest share of total staff costs. Unlike the USA, there is no source for individual salary data.

Data on transfer fees is harder to obtain. Historically, clubs tended to report transfer fees paid and received in a given year. In general clubs did not capitalize transfer expenditures but simply wrote them off in the year of acquisition. In 1998 an accounting standard, FRS10, was introduced recommending that intangible assets (such as player registrations) should be amortized over their contractual life, and most clubs now follow this policy.

The major problem with transfer fees is constructing a valuation relevant to the season in question. It can reasonably be assumed that almost all wage payments in a given season relate to player services provided in that season. Thus while there has been considerable wage inflation in football, the wage spending of a team relative to the average wage spending of every other team is stationary. There is no easy way to construct a current value of player acquisitions – that is, the equivalent expenditure on transfer fees in current money that would be required to assemble the current squad of players – using only accounting information.

Transfer fees are widely reported in the sporting press. These announcements are not audited figures like the staff costs in company accounts, and estimates can vary widely. However, Tomkins et al. (2010) report on the construction of a transfer fee database for Premier League football players going back to 1992/93, and creator of that database, Graeme Riley, kindly agreed to let me use his data.

His approach is to aggregate the total fees paid for all players in the Premier League in a given season to construct a price index. This index is then used to convert the transfer fee valuation of a player to current prices (he calls this the Current Transfer Purchase Price, or CTPP). Thus a CTTP can be identified for each player currently playing for a club. This figure can then be used as a form of capital value of the playing squad.

The transfer also includes information on the number of playing appearances in a season by each squad member. Presumably a player is most valuable to his team when he is on the pitch, and hence a more accurate measure of current player value could be obtained by weighting each player's CTTP by the proportion of games in which they played during the season. Aggregating across all players in the team, this is used to produce a squad valuation which Riley calls £XI, that is, the current valuation for the players appearing on the pitch.

Table 3.1 shows that the total number of players on the books of Premier League clubs has remained fairly constant at around 550 (about 26 per club) while the sum of starting appearances is defined by the number of teams in the league, which was reduced from 22 to 20 in the 1995/96 season. Teams can acquire players in three ways – by transfer (where a fee is paid although which in about 20 per cent of cases the fee is zero), by placing a trainee on a permanent contract (that is, 'home grown'

Table 3.1   Player origins

Season	Number of players	Sum of appearances (starting XI)	% of appearances by players for whom a transfer fee was paid	% of appearances by trainees	% of appearances by players on loan
1992–93	562	10 164	76.1	23.5	0.4
1993–94	564	10 164	78.5	21.2	0.3
1994–95	554	10 164	77.2	21.8	1.0
1995–96	517	8 360	79.2	20.3	0.5
1996–97	522	8 360	80.6	18.6	0.8
1997–98	549	8 360	80.1	19.6	0.3
1998–99	560	8 360	79.4	20.1	0.5
1999–2000	549	8 360	79.7	19.6	0.8
2000–01	560	8 360	81.5	17.6	0.9
2001–02	541	8 360	81.7	16.0	2.3
2002–03	538	8 360	79.2	17.2	3.5
2003–04	531	8 360	80.0	15.0	5.0
2004–05	532	8 360	84.6	13.2	2.2
2005–06	553	8 360	82.1	13.5	4.4
2006–07	551	8 360	80.3	16.0	3.7
2007–08	554	8 360	86.2	10.8	3.0
2008–09	563	8 360	84.1	11.9	4.0
2009–10	565	8 360	86.6	9.0	4.4

talent) or by borrowing a player from another team (loan). The percentage of players acquired by transfer has increased from around 75 per cent to over 85 per cent, matched by a decrease in the production of trainees. This period also coincides with a large increase in the purchasing power of Premier League clubs which has produced a large influx of players from abroad, and this may explain the fall in the production of trainees. There is also a noticeable increase in the use of loan players.

Table 3.2 illustrates the large increase in spending by clubs since the creation of the Premier League. Note that the data used here only runs until the 2008/09 season since the accounts for 2009/10 season were not available at the time of writing. Three observations are missing because accounts were not filed, yielding a total of 343 observations over 17 seasons. The share of wage spending in the total has increased from just over 50 per cent to as much as 75 per cent of total player spending. This may be a consequence of the Bosman judgment in 1995 which abolished the system whereby clubs could impose a transfer fee on the movement of player even if he was out of contract.

Table 3.2   Total player expenditure

Season	Wage costs £m	Sum of transfer fee expenditure £m
1993–94	117	88
1994–95	142	125
1995–96	164	174
1996–97	218	169
1997–98	297	201
1998–99	392	266
1999–2000	478	242
2000–01	566	335
2001–02	681	377
2002–03	759	246
2003–04	801	288
2004–05	768	321
2005–06	849	310
2006–07	950	373
2007–08	1201	590
2008–09	1328	690

3   MODEL AND RESULTS

The basic model in the sports economics literature suggests that playing talent produces success. If the player market functions efficiently then expensive teams will do better than less expensive teams, whether we measure expense through player wages or through transfer fee expenditure. Given the rapid inflation in player wages and transfer fees, we can express these relative to the average in a given season. Table 3.3 shows a simple correlation matrix for these relative values and league rank. The correlation is highest for relative wages. The Relative £XI figure, which weights the CTPP player values for the number of appearances in a season, is also highly correlated with league rank and even more so with relative wages.

This is surprising for a number of reasons. First, we know that the transfer fee figures are not official figures and reports can vary widely. Second, transfer fee figures do not take account of home-grown talent, which might be expected to contribute significantly. Third, even if transfer fees are an accurate reflection of expected productivity at the time the player is transferred, over time a player's value is likely to change for better or for worse. The data suggests that newspaper estimates of transfer fees are not only unbiased estimates, but are fairly accurate.

Table 3.3　Correlation matrix

	League rank	Relative wages	Relative £XI
Relative wages	−0.756		
Relative £XI	−0.719	0.874	
Relative CTTP	−0.662	0.887	0.973

Table 3.4 reports the results of the regression model. A number of other variables were added to the basic model (model 1). In model 2 both the average and the variance of age of the squad significantly affect outcomes – younger squads do better as do squads where there is more variance in age, suggesting that a blend of youth and experience is more likely to be successful. As in earlier research (for example, Szymanski and Smith, 1997) the smaller the number of players used in the season, the better the likely outcome, which may reflect the influence of injuries and the benefits of playing a settled team. Longer tenure of the team manager is also associated with better performance. The relative share of home-grown and loan players are not significant. This is perhaps most surprising for the measures based on transfer fee values, since these do not incorporate any valuation for these types of player.

Model 3 included dummies for team managers. There were 109 different managers in the Premier League over the period, giving an average tenure of three seasons, but this is highly skewed by a small number of outliers such as Sir Alex Ferguson at Manchester United who was manager for all seasons in the database and Arsene Wenger at Arsenal who was manager for all but four seasons in the data.

Only 12 of the manager dummies were statistically significant at the 5 per cent level. The effect of including these variables is to reduce the size of the coefficient on resources, but it is still highly significant.

4　CONCLUSIONS

This chapter shows that, suitably adjusted, transfer fees paid can capture the variation of team performance in the English Premier League. Transfer fees do not fit the performance data as closely as wage audited wage expenditure, but the two measures are highly correlated.

This suggests a number of interesting conclusions. First, the value of a player does not seem to change much over his career, at least on average. Second, transfer fees and wage payments must be roughly

Table 3.4   Regression results

	Relative wage model		Relative £XI model		Relative CTTP model	
	Coefficient	SE	Coefficient	SE	Coefficient	SE
Model 1 (Resources only)						
Constant	3.391	0.066	2.918	0.051	2.894	0.057
Resources	−1.264	0.059	−0.790	0.041	−0.764	0.047
Adj R-squared	0.570		0.516		0.436	
Model 2 (Resources with squad characteristics)						
Intercept	1.520	0.750	0.492	0.796	1.306	0.838
Resources	−0.886	0.102	−0.679	0.042	−0.656	0.044
Average age	0.068	0.026	0.060	0.028	0.047	0.029
Variance of age	−1.153	0.201	−1.058	0.216	−1.064	0.224
Players used	0.032	0.009	0.049	0.010	0.049	0.010
Manager tenure	−0.029	0.008	−0.039	0.008	−0.044	0.008
Trainees relative to Average	−0.154	0.909	−1.321	0.963	−1.459	0.999
Loans relative to average	0.169	0.269	0.152	0.290	0.170	0.301
Adj R-squared	0.692		0.652		0.615	
Model 3 (Resources with squad characteristics and manager dummies)						
Constant	0.807	0.573	0.198	0.587	0.144	0.599
Resources	−0.739	0.065	−0.441	0.045	−0.418	0.047
Average age	0.065	0.022	0.065	0.023	0.065	0.023
Variance of age	−1.017	0.164	−0.832	0.170	−0.959	0.174

Table 3.4 (continued)

	Relative wage model		Relative £XI model		Relative CTTP model	
	Coefficient	SE	Coefficient	SE	Coefficient	SE
Model 3 (Resources with squad characteristics and manager dummies)						
Players used	0.043	0.007	0.050	0.008	0.055	0.008
Alex Ferguson	−1.198	0.116	−1.326	0.119	−1.435	0.117
Arsene Wenger	−1.065	0.118	−1.178	0.121	−1.239	0.122
Harry Redknapp	−0.240	0.114	−0.282	0.118	−0.266	0.121
David Moyes	−0.397	0.146	−0.314	0.152	−0.318	0.155
Kevin Keegan	−0.386	0.148	−0.388	0.155	−0.431	0.157
Gerrard Houllier	−0.511	0.179	−0.660	0.185	−0.692	0.188
Kenny Dalglish	−0.609	0.174	−0.444	0.185	−0.436	0.190
Rafael Benitez	−0.702	0.178	−0.822	0.183	−0.829	0.187
Bobby Robson	−0.322	0.173	0.039	0.187	−0.094	0.188
Steve McClaren	−0.388	0.174	−0.276	0.181	−0.293	0.184
Jose Mourinho	−0.759	0.226	−0.629	0.252	−0.754	0.255
Martin Jol	−0.545	0.223	−0.358	0.233	−0.372	0.238
Adj R-squared	0.774		0.755		0.745	

Note: SE = Standard error.

60

proportional to each other for each player, even though wage payments have increased significantly relative to transfer fees since the start of the Premier League.

More generally, these results confirm the standard view adopted in the literature that playing resources determine playing outcomes, and show that the market for players, in English Premier League football at least, seems to operate relatively efficiently.

NOTE

*   This chapter could not have been written without access to the transfer fee database of Graeme Riley, which is explored in great detail in the recent book *Pay as You Play* (by Paul Tomkins, Graeme Riley and Gary Fulcher), Gprf Publishing (2010). I am also grateful to Graeme for answering many tedious questions about the construction of the database.

REFERENCES

Atkinson, S., Stanley, L. and Tschirhart, J. (1988), 'Revenue sharing as an incentive in an agency problem: an example from the National Football League', *RAND Journal of Economics*, **19**, 27–43.

Dietl, H. and Lang, M. (2008), 'The effect of gate revenue-sharing on social welfare', *Contemporary Economic Policy*, **26**, 448–59.

El-Hodiri, M. and Quirk, J. (1971), 'An economic model of a professional sports league', *Journal of Political Economy*, **79**, 1302–19.

Forrest, David and Robert Simmons. (2002), 'Team salaries and playing success in sports: a comparative perspective,' *Zeitschrift für Betriebswirtschaft*, **72**, 4.

Fort, R. and Quirk, J. (1995), 'Cross-subsidization, incentives, and outcomes in professional team sports leagues', *Journal of Economic Literature*, **33**, 1265–99.

García del Barrio, P. and Szymanski, S. (2009), 'Goal! Profit maximization and win maximization in football leagues', *Review of Industrial Organization*, **34**, 45–68.

Hall, S., Szymanski, S. and Zimbalist, A.S. (2002), 'Testing causality between team performance and payroll: the cases of Major League Baseball and English soccer', *Journal of Sports Economics*, **3** (May), 149–68.

Késenne, S. (2000), 'Revenue sharing and competitive balance in professional team sports', *Journal of Sports Economics*, **1**, 56–65.

Quirk, J. and M. El Hodiri (1974), 'The economic theory of a professional sports league', in R. Noll (ed.), *Government and the Sports Business*, Washington, DC: Brookings Institution, pp. 33–80.

Szymanski, S. (2003), 'The economic design of sporting contests', *Journal of Economic Literature*, **41**, 1137–87.

Szymanski, S. and Késenne, S. (2004), 'Competitive balance and gate revenue sharing in team sports', *Journal of Industrial Economics*, **52**, 165–77.

Szymanski, Stefan and Ron Smith (1997), 'The English football industry, profit, performance and industrial structure,' *International Review of Applied Economics*, **11**(1), 135–53

Tomkins, P., G. Riley and G. Fulcher (2010), *Pay as You Play: The True Price of Success in the Premier League Era*, Leicester: GPRF Publishing.

Vrooman, J. (1995), 'A general theory of professional sports leagues', *Southern Economic Journal*, **61**, 971–90.

4. Team wage bills and sporting performance: evidence from (major and minor) European football leagues

Bernd Frick

THE (ECONOMIC?) RATIONALITY OF INVESTING IN PLAYER QUALITY

In their recent bestselling book, Berri and Schmidt (2010, p. 13–14) argue that in most US major leagues the variation in team wage bills can explain only a rather small fraction (less than 10 percent) of the variation in wins. Using data from the National Basketball Association and in the National Football League, they conclude that 'simple statistical analysis demonstrates that it takes more than money to find success in sports'.[1]

The reasons for such a weak pay–performance relationship can, of course, be manifold. First, player performance may be difficult to predict (managers make mistakes when assessing talent before signing them to long-term contracts) and, second, talented players may not be willing to cooperate with other equally talented players (envy is said to reduce cooperative behavior if teammates are known to earn higher salaries). Third, and perhaps most important, institutional restrictions on player mobility, such as salary caps, luxury taxes, draft and free agency rules, may create a monopsonistic labor market destroying the relationship between wage bills and on-field performance in professional team sports (see, for example, Simmons and Forrest, 2004).

Clearly, as in any other industry, high-quality inputs (for example, particularly talented players and exceptional head coaches) are required to produce a particular output (for example, winning a championship, ensuring a win percentage figure of more than 0.5 or simply avoiding relegation) in professional team sports. However, since the team sports industry is characterized by two important 'peculiarities' or 'idiosyncrasies' that clearly distinguish it from other sectors ('joint production' (see, for example, Neale, 1964) and the 'rat race' character of the production process (see, for example, Akerlof, 1976)) it may well be that the close pay–performance relationship that most (sports) economists expect to find does not exist.

Others, however, have emphasized that it is exactly these peculiarities that often lead to 'overinvestment' (see, for example, Dietl and Franck, 2007) because, first, managers typically assume a rather close correlation between talent investment and their teams' win probability because otherwise the between-season 'war for talent' would be difficult to explain. Second, the existence of an additional exogenous prize (such as the qualification for a supranational cup competition) as well as a system of promotion and relegation create additional incentives for 'excessive' wage spending and, finally, the quite substantial revenue differentials across the league hierarchy increase the individual clubs' readiness for investments.

In the absence of labor and product market regulation, the interplay of the above three factors may, therefore, result in considerable financial trouble of some (perhaps most) clubs (see, for example, Deloitte 2010):

- Premier League clubs' net debt at the end of the 2008/09 season increased to £3.3 billion, with Chelsea and Manchester United being responsible for more than £1.4 billion.
- At the end of the same season, the clubs in the German first and second Bundesliga reported accumulated liabilities of some €600 million. However, more than 50 percent of that amount goes to three clubs (Schalke 04, 1860 Munich and Hertha BSC Berlin).
- Over the period 1996/97–2008/09, the 20 clubs in the Italian Serie A have produced combined operating losses every single year. In the French Ligue 1 the situation is not as dramatic, but is similar. Here, the 20 clubs manage to avoid operating losses at least once in a while.
- At the beginning of the 2011/12 season, the clubs from the Spanish Primera Division owed their players salaries over €50 million for the last season. More than half of the first and second division clubs are threatened by insolvency, which has been declared already by a number of clubs, among them established teams such as Real Zaragoza, Betis Sevilla, RCD Mallorca, FC Malaga, Real Sociedad San Sebastian, Sporting de Gijon and UD Levante. The combined debt of the 40 clubs in the first and second divisions has recently increased to more than €4 billion.

However, I do not address in this chapter the question of whether these developments are a necessary or already a sufficient condition for regulatory activities (see, for example, Canes, 1974). Instead, I first review the literature on the pay–performance relationship in European football and identify several shortcomings of the existing literature. Second, I present some new evidence based on two different data sets that I have compiled over a number of years. Since the information on the teams' wage bills comes from a single source, it is for the first time possible to study the pay–performance relationship in European football from a comparative perspective. My estimates show a close correlation between sporting success and relative wage expenditures as well as a high explanatory power of the regressions. Both findings suggest, first, the emergence of a single European labor market following the Bosman ruling of the European Court of Justice in 1995[2] and, second, that due to the abolition of restrictions on player mobility this market is now functioning well.

WHAT DOES THE AVAILABLE LITERATURE SHOW?

In a series of widely quoted studies, Stefan Szymanski and his co-authors have demonstrated a remarkably close correlation between wage expenditures and final league position in English professional football over a long period of time. The first study (Szymanski and Smith, 1997) uses data of 48 clubs over the period 1974–89 and concludes that 'the performance and the wage bill of a club are very highly correlated' suggesting that 'the market is competitive' (p. 138). Second, Szymanski and Kuypers (1999) find that differences in wage expenditures of 69 English clubs in the season 1996/97 explain 78 percent of the observable variation in league position. Moreover, wage expenditures also explain the performance of 40 clubs over an extended period of time (1978–97) to a large extent ($R^2 = 0.92$). The authors therefore conclude that the players' labor market is quite efficient: 'That is to say, while an expensive team will not always beat a less expensive one, over the long term and on average the relationship between wage spending and league performance is quite close' (p. 192). Third, Kuper and Symanski (2009) find that wage expenditure relative to the average explains 89 percent of the variation in average league position for Premier League and Championship teams in the years 1998–2007.[3]

Frick (2005) finds that in the German Bundesliga over the period 1981/82–2002/03 (22 consecutive seasons with 398 team-year observations) higher relative player salaries raise performance significantly, but at a decreasing rate. According to the estimates, the turning point (about 2.5 times the average team wage bill) is inside the sample range. An increase in player salaries beyond that point is detrimental to team performance in the sense that it reduces the number of points per season. The small number of cases in the range where negative returns to wage expenditures are encountered (n = 4–6 in the different models) seems to suggest that managers are usually well aware of the negative effects of increasing wages. Relative head coach salary, in turn, has a statistically significant and strictly linear impact on team performance (inclusion of a quadratic term renders the linear as well as the quadratic term insignificant). Moreover, it appears that the pay–performance relationship is getting closer over time (the coefficient of the respective interaction term, however, is significant only at the 10 percent level). Using the same data, Frick and Simmons (2008) calculate the additional expenses required in the Bundesliga to move up one position in the league: teams finishing second would have to increase their relative wage bill from 1.47 to 2.65 to win the championship, while teams finishing fourth would have to increase their salary expenditures from 1.33 to 1.83 to qualify for the Champions League, certainly the most lucrative international cup competition in professional football. At the lower end of the table the required additional expenses are more modest: teams finishing sixteenth would have to increase their wage bill from 0.71 of the average to 0.98 to move up one position, thus avoiding relegation.

Simmons and Forrest (2004) find that teams in England (1977/78–2000/01), Germany (1981/82–1995/96) and Italy (1987/88–1998/99) enhance their sporting performance by increasing spending on wages relative to their competitors, but at a decreasing rate in England and Italy (not in Germany). At a relative wage of 1 (.5), the marginal effect of a .1 standard deviation increase in relative wage is statistically significant and economically relevant in all three leagues with respect to attaining a top-six place (to avoiding relegation). In a companion paper Forrest and Simmons (2002) use data from the Serie A in Italy in the seasons 1995–96 and 2001–02 and find that the wage elasticity at the sample mean of points ratio and wage bill in 1995–96 is 0.4 and 0.2 in 2001–02 suggesting that the move towards free agency that followed the 'Bosman ruling' lowered this elasticity. In the German Bundesliga in the seasons 1998–99 and 1999–2000 this elasticity was found to be far lower at 0.1. For England, the wage elasticity of points ratio is 0.433 (close to the value obtained for Serie A in 1995–96) during the period 1977–78 to 1998–99 in the first season, but declines thereafter first by 0.003 and later by 0.005 per season.

García del Barrio and Szymanski (2009) use an unbalanced panel of teams in the Spanish Primera Division over the period 1994–2004 to estimate the impact of relative wage bills on league position and find that it is statistically highly significant and fairly similar to the one found using data from the English Premier League over the same period of time. This consonance in their findings leads the authors to conclude that 'performance generates revenue, and wages generate performance. Beyond these two relationships, there is relatively little scope for clubs or managers to influence outcomes' (p. 57).

Summarizing the evidence, it appears that in European football – as opposed to US team sports – the impact of relative wage bills on sporting performance is quite strong and that – again in contrast to the evidence available for the major leagues – the explanatory power of the regression models is quite high.[4]

WHAT IS (STILL) MISSING?

Although the literature on the pay–performance relationship in professional football has been growing rapidly over the last couple of years, at least two questions still remain:

- Empirical analyses across divisions and over time are only available for English football, but not for any other top league in Europe. I, therefore, use a new data set from Germany that includes the first three divisions over an extended period of time. The observation period (2002/03–2010/11) includes a recent organizational reform – the implementation of a single third division, which until 2007/08 existed in the form of a northern and a southern league – that allows estimation of an identical regression model for the pre- and the post-reform period.
- Comparative analyses using a larger number of European leagues and/or covering a longer period of time have not yet been conducted. I, therefore, use data from 13 European countries and three different seasons (2006/07, 2008/09 and 2010/11) to study the pay–performance relationship at a supranational level. The estimates reveal that this relationship is very similar across leagues of different playing strength, which leads me to conclude that since the mid-1990s a single European labor market for football players has emerged.

In line with the previous literature I estimate two regression models of rank at the end of the season upon log of team value, expressed relative to the average of all teams' log value in a particular season (one estimation uses the data that are available for the first three divisions in Germany (Table 4.1) and one estimation uses the data that is available for the 13 European first divisions (Table 4.2)).

DATA AND DESCRIPTIVE FINDINGS

The data used in the estimations below comes from www.transfermarkt. de and has been collected since the start of the 2002/03 season. Data for

Table 4.1   Average team values in German professional football prior to and after implementation of league reform (2002/03–2010/11)

	Mean team value	Standard deviation	Coefficient of variation	N of observations
Before league reform				
Division 1	60.4	44.8	74.3	54
Division 2	9.5	5.3	55.0	54
Division 3	2.8	1.2	42.4	110
Total	18.7	32.9	175.5	218
F-value			125.4***	
After league reform				
Division 1	88.4	58.3	65.9	54
Division 2	16.2	6.7	51.7	54
Division 3	4.9	1.2	23.6	60
Total	35.4	49.5	140.0	168
F-value			102.7***	

Germany is available for six seasons (2002–03, 2003–04, 2006–07, 2008–09, 2009–10 and 2010–11), three seasons before and three seasons after a particular organizational reform. Moreover, data for 13 leagues (first divisions) across Europe is available for three seasons (2006–07, 2008–09, and 2010–11). However, since player salaries usually remain confidential and are not disclosed, I use the individual players' market values at the start of the respective season as a proxy for their productivity (and, therefore, their remuneration). These market values are then aggregated to proxy the respective clubs' wage bills.[5]

It appears from Table 4.1 that in the pre-reform period the difference in the market values of first, second and third division teams was far higher than in the post-reform period, suggesting that over time the discrepancy in revenue potentials has declined. This is surprising insofar as most commentators (see for example, Dietl and Franck, 2007) expect that discrepancy to increase. Moreover, the coefficient of variation in the market values of the teams in each of the three leagues declined, too.[6] This, in turn, suggests an increasing homogeneity in the revenue potentials not only across the league hierarchy, but also within the different tiers of German professional football.

A slightly different picture emerges from Table 4.2: across Europe, the differences in the market values of the teams in the respective 13 top divisions have remained more or less constant over the period 2006/07–2010/11.

A closer look, however, reveals that the coefficient of variation of the

Table 4.2   *The development of team values across Europe,*
                2006/07–2010/11

Country	2006/07	2008/09	Δ 2007–2009	2010/11	Δ 2009–2011
England	120.5	144.3	+19.8	167.2	+15.9
Spain	103.1	122.5	+18.8	128.1	+4.6
Italy	86.4	113.4	+31.3	120.3	+6.1
Germany	68.4	78.3	+14.5	95.5	+22.0
France	59.6	65.3	+9.6	72.4	+10.9
Turkey	38.5	40.5	+5.2	45.5	+12.3
Portugal	29.7	30.8	+3.7	42.2	+37.0
Holland	28.8	32.1	+11.5	33.3	+3.7
Greece	21.0	27.1	+28.6	29.7	+9.6
Belgium	19.9	19.6	−1.5	26.3	+34.2
Scotland	18.6	21.1	+13.4	19.6	−7.1
Austria	15.4	13.6	−11.7	13.7	+0.8
Switzerland	12.8	14.8	+15.6	16.2	+9.5
Average	53.3	62.2	+16.7	70.1	+12.7
F-test	8.26***	9.23***		8.63***	

teams' market values varies considerably between the leagues, that is, the level of economic imbalance is rather high in Portugal, Scotland and – to a lesser extent – in Spain,[7] while it is rather low in Austria, Switzerland and – again to a lesser extent – in Germany. Moreover, the coefficient of variation declines in some leagues (such as England, Italy, Holland and Portugal), while increasing in others (such as Turkey, Greece and Switzerland).[8]

PAY AND PERFORMANCE IN GERMAN PROFESSIONAL FOOTBALL

Until the 2007/08 season the German Bundesliga consisted of two top divisions with 18 clubs each. The bottom three clubs from division 1 were relegated to division 2 at the end of the season and were replaced by the top three teams from that lower division. Division 3 (by that time a semi-professional league only) consisted of a northern and a southern branch with 18 or 19 clubs each, of which the two top teams were promoted to division 2, out of which four teams were relegated at the end of the season. Since the start of the 2008/09 season, the league consists of three divisions with 56 professional clubs, of which 18 are playing in division 1, 18 in division 2 and 20 in division 3. Now the two top teams from division 2 get promoted and the two worst teams from division 1 get relegated. The teams ranked sixteenth in division 1 and third in division 2 face each other in a promotion–relegation contest where each team plays once at home and once away. This also happens between the team ranked sixteenth in division 2 and third in division 3. Moreover, the four worst-performing teams in division 3 are replaced by the champions of the four (semi-professional) regional leagues that exist one step further down in the league hierarchy.

The estimated models are of the following general form:

$$FLP_{ij} = \alpha_0 + \alpha_1 RWB_{ij} + \alpha_2 LR + \varepsilon \qquad (4.1)$$

$$FLP_{ij} = \alpha_0 + \alpha_1 RWB_{ij} + \alpha_2 LR + \alpha_3 RWB_{ij} * LR + \varepsilon \qquad (4.2)$$

where

FLP: final league position of team i in season j (team ranked first in division 2 is assigned league position 19 and team ranked first in division 3 is assigned rank 37 because division 1 and division 2 play with 18 teams each). The dependent variable (log of final league position) was calculated as follows: log(position/(57-position)).
RWB: log of wage bill of team i in season j relative to league average in that season.
LR: dummy for league reform (0 = before; 1 = after reform).
RWB * LR: interaction term to capture possible changes in the pay–performance relationship due to the reform of the league system.

Table 4.3 displays the result of four different regressions: an estimation of the impact of relative wage expenditures on league position over the whole period (2002/03–2010/11) and separately in the pre- and the post-reform period (2002/03–2006/07 versus 2008/09–2010/11) (model 1) as well as a second model that includes – apart from the reform dummy – an interaction term to capture possible changes in the relationship that are due to the organizational reform of the league. It appears that the impact of relative wage expenditures on final league position is statistically significant and economically highly relevant in the pre- as well as the post-reform period. However, a Chow-test (Chow, 1960) reveals that the coefficients differ significantly from each other, indicating that the league reform (that is, the merger of the northern and the southern branch of the third division) induced a quite substantial change in the relationship ($F = 15.47, p < 001$).[9]

Thus, the pay–performance relationship remains statistically highly significant after the reform, but is now marginally weaker. This, in turn, is due to the declining variance in team wage bills within each league as well as across the three different leagues.[10] Moreover, the 2010/11 season was

Table 4.3   Wage expenditures and league position in Germany

	Coefficient	Std. error	t
Period 2002/03–2010/11 (6 seasons)			
RWB	−18.506	0.444	−41.69***
LR	−0.300	0.070	−4.31***
Constant	18.807	0.446	42.14***
Observations		386	
F-value		878.4	
R2 * 100		82.0	
Period 2002/03–2005/06 (3 seasons)			
RWB	−17.332	0.512	−33.85***
Constant	17.632	0.514	34.32***
Observations		218	
F-value		1145.9	
R2 * 100		84.1	
Period 2008/09–2010/11 (3 seasons)			
RWB	−20.457	0.779	−26.27***
Constant	20.457	0.781	26.20***
Observations		168	
F-value		690.2	
R2 * 100		80.5	
Period 2002/03–2010/11 (6 seasons)			
RWB	−17.332	0.554	−31.29***
LR	2.824	0.906	3.12***
RWB * LR	−3.125	0.904	−4.46***
Constant	17.632	0.556	31.72***
Observations		386	
F-value		606.4	
R2 * 100		82.5	

an unusual one insofar as a number of small market teams (FSV Mainz, SC Freiburg, Hannover 96, 1. FC Kaiserslautern and 1. FC Nürnberg) all performed exceptionally well, 'destroying' to a certain extent the well-established relationship between wage bills and league position (Figures 4A.1–4A.3 in the appendix reinforce this impression).

THE PAY–PERFORMANCE RELATIONSHIP IN EUROPE

Although the impact of team wage bills on final league position has been documented in a number of papers, truly comparative evidence is not yet available, because the data used in the various papers quoted above come from different sources, implying that the results cannot really be compared. To overcome this problem I have assembled a data set covering three seasons and 13 European leagues (the composition of the sample is described in Table 4A.3 in the appendix). Before estimating the model, I calculate the different clubs final position in Europe by dividing their league position in their home country by the weights displayed in Table 4A.3 (these have been derived from the UEFA rankings of the respective season). This means for example that the champion in Scotland in 2006/07 is assigned league position 2.5 (1/0.4) while the team ranked tenth in Switzerland in that season is assigned league position 32.3 (10/0.31). Thus, the dependent variable position varies from 1 (the team winning the championship in the league with the highest UEFA ranking in a particular season) to 56.25 (the team finishing eighteenth in Belgium in 2008).

The estimated model is of the following general form:

$$FLP_{ij} = \alpha_0 + \alpha_1 RWB_{ij} + \alpha_2 \Sigma CD_{ij} + \varepsilon \qquad (4.3)$$

where

FLP: final league position of team i in season j given the playing strength of the team's national league. Log of final league position was calculated as follows: log(position/(57.25-position)).
RWB: log of wage bill of team i in season j relative to European average in that season.
CD: vector of country dummies (reference country is England).

It appears from Table 4.4 that the impact of wage expenditure on weighted league position is statistically significant and that the explanatory power of the model is again quite high (65 percent).[11] While this may sound surprising to those familiar with the results obtained with data from the US major leagues, it is indicative of the fact that the labor market for football players is quite efficient since there are only few, if any, restrictions on player mobility.[12]

Summarizing, even across a rather heterogeneous sample of European leagues, the variation in team performance can to a large extent be explained by variation in wage expenditures:[13] the more the individual clubs spend on player salaries, the better is their performance on the pitch.[14]

Table 4.4   Wage expenditures and league position in Europe

	Coefficient	Std error	t
RWB	−3.708	0.120	−31.02***
England		Reference league	
Spain	−0.281	0.102	−2.74***
Italy	−0.146	0.103	−1.42+
France	−0.278	0.105	−2.66***
Germany	−0.273	0.106	−2.56**
Turkey	−0.243	0.112	−2.17**
Netherlands	−0.921	0.117	−7.87***
Greece	−0.823	0.122	−6.73***
Portugal	−1.273	0.122	−10.43***
Belgium	−0.798	1.223	−6.50***
Scotland	−1.556	0.138	−11.28***
Austria	−1.306	0.145	−9.02***
Suisse	−1.613	0.144	−11.18***
Constant	2.452	0.173	14.21***
Observations		646	
F-value		95.1	
R2 * 100		65.5	

CONCLUSIONS AND IMPLICATIONS FOR FURTHER RESEARCH

The findings reported in this chapter suggest that in the absence of labor market restrictions the relationship between team wage bills and team performance, measured by either win percentage or final league position, is quite strong in German as well as in European football.

These results notwithstanding, at least two important questions have not been answered in this chapter. First, many leagues increase or decrease over time the number of teams admitted to their top divisions. It is not at all clear whether these changes have any effect on the economic and/or competitive (im-)balance of these leagues. This is clearly a question that needs to be addressed in future research. A perhaps even more important question is whether the financial fair play regulations that UEFA will implement in the near future is likely to reduce the observable differences in team wage bills. The consequences of such regulatory reform (similar to the salary caps used in most of the US major leagues) need to be studied very carefully.

NOTES

1.   Berri and Schmidt (2010) are, of course, not the first skeptics questioning the (presumably) close relationship between a team's wage bill and its winning percentage (see, for example, Zimbalist, 1992, p. 96; 2000, p. 95; Scully, 1995, p. 94). Other prominent examples are Buchanan and Slottje (1996, p. 144) arguing that 'teams that pay the most are not necessarily the teams that win the most', and Sanderson and Siegfried (1997, p. 10) emphasizing that 'the relationship between payroll and team performance is a loose one'.

2.   The impact of the Bosman ruling on player development and mobility, player salaries and contract duration has been analyzed in a number of papers (see, for example, Antonioni and Cubbin, 2000; Frick 2007, 2009; Feess et al., 2004; Simmons, 1997; Tervio, 2006).

3.   Apart from this close relationship the authors emphasize that 'soccer is not merely a small business. It's also a bad one' Kuper and Szymanski, 2009, (p. 78) and 'the most obvious reason soccer is such an incompetent business is that soccer clubs tend to hire incompetent staff' (p. 84).

4.   These findings, in turn, may suggest that in a world without labor market restrictions the 'rich' clubs (large market teams) are able to buy success in the form of championship titles by signing star players from all over the world, while the 'poor' clubs (small market teams) can either try to avoid relegation by signing talented players at affordable prices that the top clubs are not interested in or by entering into a 'rat race' with the rich clubs (with the predictable consequences for their own and their opponents financial viability). Whether these different behaviors are to be observed in reality, is an empirical question that has not yet been answered.

5.   The market values of individual players have indeed been shown to be very good proxies for player salaries (see, for example, Frick; 2011; Torgler et al., 2006). Moreover, the clubs' revenues and their rosters' market value are highly correlated at r > 0.90 (Deloitte, 2011).

6.   These intertemporal changes in the differences in team values within leagues and between leagues can, in principle, be used to test the hypothesis that exogenous interventions are required to maintain (or restore) a particular level of competitive balance.

7.   Not surprisingly, these three leagues have each been dominated for decades by two large market teams.

8.   The detailed statistics are, of course, available from the author upon request.

9.   The LM test statistic (1.66, $p > .10$) suggests that the OLS estimation is to be preferred over the random effects model.

10.   Using the clubs' predicted (instead of the observed) position it is possible to identify underperforming as well as overachieving teams. Overachievers are very often promoted clubs in their first season (due to their cheap squad) or the second teams of first division clubs (in case their top players are not requested by the first team). Underperformers are usually relegated clubs in the first season in the next lower league (due to their expensive squad) or the second teams of first division clubs (in case their top players have to be delegated). Moreover, some clubs both underperform and overachieve within a short period of time (for example, Borussia Dortmund) while some clubs repeat overachievement (for example, SC Freiburg and VfL Bochum) as well as underperformance (see, for example, Bayern Munich).

11.   The LM test statistic (4.23, $p < .05$) suggests to prefer the random effects model over the OLS estimation. The coefficients, however, are very similar to the ones reported in Table 4.4. The detailed results are available from the author upon request (a fixed effects model would not have been feasible because the league dummies are time invariant).

12.   Moreover, these findings are consistent with the evidence presented by Frick (2007) and Flores et al. (2010) that player mobility has increased considerably in European football since the mid-1990s.

13. However, country-by-country estimations reveal that the pay–performance relationship varies to a certain extent between the 13 different leagues. The detailed results are available from the author upon request.
14. The question, whether the causality runs from payroll to performance or the other way round has recently been answered by Hall et al. (2002) showing that Granger causality from higher payrolls to better performance cannot be rejected.

REFERENCES

Akerlof, G. (1976), 'The Economics of caste and the rat race and other woeful tales', *Quarterly Journal of Economics*, **90**, 599–617.

Antonioni, P. and J. Cubbin (2000), 'The Bosman ruling and the emergence of a single market in soccer talent', *European Journal of Law and Economics*, **9**, 157–73.

Berri, D.J. and M.B. Schmidt (2010), *Stumbling on Wins: Two Economists Expose the Pitfalls on the Road to Victory in Professional Sports*, Upper Saddle River, NJ: FT Press.

Buchanan, M.J. and D.J. Slottje (1996), *Pay and Performance in the NBA*, Greenwich, CT: JAI Press.

Canes, M.E. (1974), 'The social benefits of restrictions on team quality', in R. Noll (ed.), *Government and the Sport Business*, Washington: Brookings Institution, pp. 81–113.

Chow, G.C. (1960), 'Tests of equality between sets of coefficients in two linear regressions', *Econometrica*, **28**, 591–605.

Deloitte (2010), *National Interest: Annual Review of Football Finance*, Manchester: Sports Business Group.

Deloitte (2011), *The Untouchables: Football Money League*, Manchester: Sports Business Group.

Dietl, H. and E. Franck (2007), 'How do the peculiarities of German football governance affect the abilities of clubs to create and capture value?', in P. Rodríguez, S. Késenne and J. García (eds), *Governance and Competition in Professional Sports Leagues*, Oviedo: Ediciones de la Universidad de Oviedo, pp. 87–107.

Feess, E., B. Frick and G. Muehlheusser (2004), 'Legal restrictions on outside trade clauses – theory and evidence from German soccer', IZA Discussion Paper No. 1180, Bonn.

Flores, R., D. Forrest and J.D. Tena (2010), 'Impact on competitive balance from allowing foreign players in a sports league: evidence from European soccer', *Kyklos*, **63**, 546–57.

Forrest, D. and R. Simmons (2002), 'Team salaries and playing success: a comparative perspective', *Zeitschrift für Betriebswirtschaft, Ergänzungsheft 4*, **72**, 221–37.

Frick, B. (2005), '". . . und Geld schießt eben doch Tore": Die Voraussetzungen sportlichen und wirtschaftlichen Erfolges in der Fußball-Bundesliga', *Sportwissenschaft*, **35**, 250–70.

Frick, B. (2007), The Football Players' Labour Market: Empirical Evidence from the Major European Leagues. *Scottish Journal of Political Economy*, **54**, pp. 422–446.

Frick, B. (2009), 'Globalization and factor mobility: the impact of the "Bosman-Ruling" on player migration in professional football', *Journal of Sports Economics*, **10**, 88–106.

Frick, B. (2011), 'Performance, salaries and contract length: empirical evidence from German soccer', *International Journal of Sport Finance*, **6**, 87–118.

Frick, B. and R. Simmons (2008), 'The impact of managerial quality on organizational performance: evidence from German soccer', *Managerial and Decision Economics*, **29**, 593–600.

García del Barrio, P. and S. Szymanski (2009), 'Goal! Profit maximization versus win maximization in soccer', *Review of Industrial Organization*, **34**, 45–68.

Hall, S., S. Szymanski and A.S. Zimbalist (2002), 'Testing causality between team performance and payroll: the cases of Major League Baseball and English soccer', *Journal of Sports Economics*, **3**, 149–68.

Kuper, S. and S. Szymanski (2009), *Soccernomics*, New York: Nation Books.

Neale, W.C. (1964), 'The peculiar economics of professional team sports', *Quarterly Journal of Economics*, 78, 1–14.

Sanderson, A.R. and J.J. Siegfried (1997), 'The implications of athlete freedom to contract: lessons from North America', *Economic Affairs*, **17**, 7–12.

Scully, G.W. (1995), *The Market Structure of Sports*, Chicago, IL: University of Chicago Press.

Simmons, R. (1997), 'Implications of the Bosman ruling for football transfer markets', *Economic Affairs*, **17**, 13–18.

Simmons, R. and D. Forrest (2004), 'Buying success: team performance and wage bills in U.S. and European sports leagues', in R. Fort and J. Fizel (eds), *International Sports Economics Comparisons*, Westport, CT: Praeger, 123–40.

Szymanski, S. and T. Kuypers (1999), *Winners & Losers: The Business Strategy of Football*, London: Viking.

Szymanski, S. and R. Smith (1997), 'The English football industry: profit, performance and industrial structure', *International Review of Applied Economics*, **11**, 135–53.

Tervio, M. (2006), 'Transfer fee regulation and player development', *Journal of the European Economic Association*, **4**, 957–87.

Torgler, B., S. Schmidt and B. Frey (2006), 'Relative income position and performance: an empirical panel analysis', FEEM Discussion Paper No. 39, Milano.

Zimbalist, A. (1992), *Baseball and Billions*, New York: Basic Books.

Zimbalist, A. (2000), 'Economic issues in the 1998–1999 NBA lockout and the problem of competitive balance in professional sports', in W.S. Kern (ed.), *The Economics of Sports*, Kalamazoo, MI: W.E. Upjohn Institute for Employment Research, pp. 93–113.

APPENDIX

Table 4A.1   Descriptive statistics (data for Germany)

Variable	Mean	Standard deviation	Min.	Max.
log(FLP)	0.170	1.600	−4.025	4.025
RWB	1.000	0.078	0.852	1.215
LR	0.435	–	0	1

Table 4A.2   Descriptive statistics (data for Europe)

Variable	Mean	Standard deviation	Min.	Max.
log(FLP)	−1.018	1.164	−4.030	4.030
RWB	1.000	0.277	0.393	1.704
England	0.093	–	0	1
Spain	0.093	–	0	1
Italy	0.093	–	0	1
Germany	0.084	–	0	1
France	0.093	–	0	1
Turkey	0.084	–	0	1
Holland	0.084	–	0	1
Greece	0.074	–	0	1
Portugal	0.074	–	0	1
Belgium	0.080	–	0	1
Scotland	0.056	–	0	1
Austria	0.046	–	0	1
Switzerland	0.046	–	0	1

Table 4A.3   Composition of the sample of European leagues

Country (No. of clubs)	UEFA Ranking 2006/07	Weight 2006/07	UEFA Ranking 2008/09	Weight 2008/09	UEFA Ranking 2010/11	Weight 2010/11
Spain (20)	76.89	1.00	74.27	0.93	78.90	0.94
England (20)	68.54	0.89	79.50	1.00	84.36	1.00
Italy (20)	66.09	0.86	62.91	0.79	60.55	0.72
France (20)	53.66	0.70	50.17	0.63	53.68	0.64
Germany (18)	44.36	0.58	56.70	0.71	68.60	0.81
Portugal (16)	42.75	0.56	34.46	0.46	47.20	0.56
Netherlands (18)	39.38	0.51	39.13	0.49	39.96	0.47
Scotland (12)	30.50	0.40	27.85	0.35	25.14	0.30
Belgium (18/16)	29.08	0.38	25.33	0.32	27.00	0.32
Turkey (18)	26.64	0.35	32.23	0.41	35.05	0.42
Greece (16)	25.50	0.33	28.17	0.35	34.17	0.41
Switzerland (10)	23.85	0.31	25.25	0.32	24.90	0.30
Austria (10)	18.50	0.24	17.83	0.22	20.70	0.25

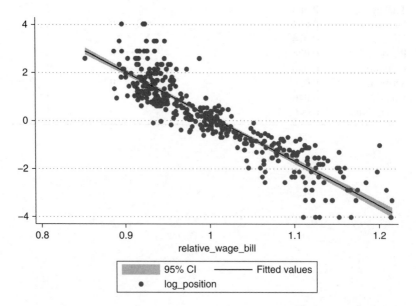

Figure 4A.1   Relative team wage bill and league position in the German Bundesliga, 2002/03–2010/11 (n = 6 seasons)

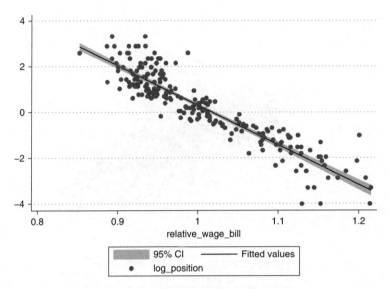

Figure 4A.2   Relative team wage bill and league position in the German Bundesliga, 2002/03–2005/06 (n = 3 seasons before league reform)

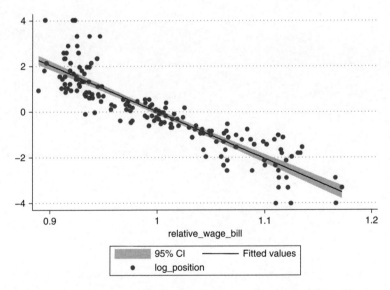

Figure 4A.3   Relative team wage bill and league position in the German Bundesliga, 2007/08–2010/11 (n = 3 seasons after league reform)

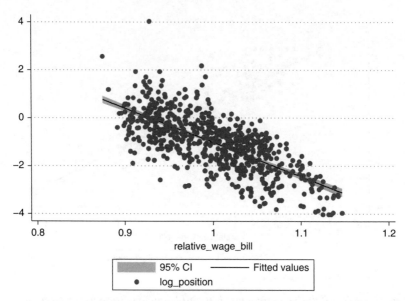

*Figure 4A.4   Relative team wage bill and league position in 13 European
              leagues, 2006/07, 2008/09 and 2010/11 (n = 3 seasons)*

5. Returns to thuggery in the National Hockey League: the effects of increased enforcement

Leo Kahane, Neil Longley and Robert Simmons

I INTRODUCTION

The roles that fighting and violence play within the National Hockey League (NHL) have been the focus of numerous studies within the economics literature. The interest in the topic is rooted in the fact that the NHL is the only professional team sport in North America (and perhaps the world) that does not automatically eject players who fight during a game. This is connected to the common perception that the NHL condones, and possible tacitly encourages, a certain level of fighting and violence in order to better sell its game to fans. However, there is also an opposite perception that fans like free-flowing offensive hockey culminating in goals scored, and on-ice fighting may prevent such exciting attacking play.

If players who fight or commit lesser infractions help their teams win – by preventing the opposition from scoring, by intimidating the opposition or by protecting their own team's offensive players – then this contribution to wins should ultimately be rewarded in salary compensation. In this chapter, we pose two questions relating to the NHL labor market. First, are players rewarded for violent behavior? We are able to separate offenses committed into major (such as fighting) and minor (such as tripping) categories. We then estimate a salary model to distinguish between the salary returns to major and minor offenses. Second, the NHL implemented rule changes after the 2004–05 lockout season specifically designed to enhance offensive play. These rule changes covered both major and minor offenses and were supported by on-ice enforcement by referees, together with a system of player and team fines for certain categories of infractions. Our second question is, then, to what extent did the post-lockout rule changes affect the salary returns to committing major and minor offenses, relative to the more lenient pre-lockout regime? In this respect, our analysis has parallels with the literature on the economics of crime. In that literature, scholars have addressed the questions of whether tougher sentences for criminal conviction and greater police enforcement of laws singly or jointly deter criminal activity. If NHL players suffer salary losses from committing greater on-ice infractions of major and minor types, then the NHL's tougher post-lockout policy towards violence and illegal activity has a stronger chance of being successful.

II FIGHTING AND AGGRESSION IN THE NHL AND POST-LOCKOUT RULE CHANGES

Violence and fighting have been a part of NHL hockey ever since the formation of the League in 1917. In the early years of the NHL, the game was often barbaric, with many incidents of players being seriously injured. One of the most infamous of these occurred in 1933, when Boston's Eddie Shore attacked Toronto's Ace Bailey from behind, injuring Bailey to the point where he lay near death for many weeks after the incident. While Bailey ultimately survived, his playing career was over. Similar incidents of extreme violence have occurred throughout the history of the NHL, with players sometimes even being charged with criminal offences for their on-ice behavior. More recent examples include the attack on Vancouver's Donald Brashear by Boston's Marty McSorley in 2000, and the attack on Colorado's Steve Moore by Vancouver's Todd Bertuzzi in 2004, an attack which resulted in Moore sustaining career-ending injuries. Both incidents resulted in criminal charges being filed against the attackers, with McSorley being convicted, and Bertuzzi pleading guilty and then being given a conditional discharge.

While the McSorley and Bertuzzi incidents have been the most recent examples of extreme violence, the level of violence in the NHL actually peaked during the 1970s. During that era, 'bench-clearing brawls' – where *all* players on the ice were simultaneously engaged in a fight with an opponent, and where players on the bench would jump onto the ice to join the fighting – were commonplace. Such brawling behavior – immortalized in the 1977 Hollywood movie *Slap Shot* that starred Paul Newman – created significant image problems for the NHL, and the league began to crack down on such behaviors.

Over the past three decades, brawling has all but been eliminated from the game. However, fighting still very much remains part of the game – it is just that now these fights are largely contained to isolated one-on-one encounters, rather than simultaneously involving all players. The league's current perspective on fighting could be viewed as ambivalent. On the one hand, the league has sought to eliminate the out-of-control mêlées that were common during the brawling era. However, the NHL has not banned fighting per se – while players that fight are given a 5-minute major penalty, rather than a 2-minute minor penalty, players are not ejected from the game, as they would be if they fought in any other North American professional sport league.

There is also a parallel issue to the fighting discussion. The NHL has for a long time valued players who exhibit 'toughness' and 'grit' – they tend to exhibit a strong physical presence and play aggressively. These players are not necessarily fighters or 'goons' – while they may occasionally fight, they have roles that are much broader. Generally, they are expected to engage in physical battles (often along the boards) to help win puck possession for their team, and/or to help prevent a scoring threat of the opposition. These players, by the nature of their style, often incur a lot of minor penalties – for infractions such as holding, hooking, slashing, interference, and so on.

In the years leading up to the 2004–05 lockout, the style of play in the NHL had gradually become more plodding and defensive oriented. The average number of goals per game declined from a high of 8.03 in 1982–83 to 5.14 in 2003–04, a decrease of 36 percent over the two decades. A common explanation for this decline was that highly skilled, offensive-oriented players were being unduly obstructed by the 'clutch and grab' techniques of lesser-skilled players. As a result, when the lockout ended in the summer of 2005, the NHL decided to implement a wide range of changes to the game that were intended to create more offensive oppor-tunities.[1] The 'red line' was removed, thus allowing for longer passes; goalies were prevented from playing the puck in the corners, and so on. Perhaps the most important change was that referees were instructed to have a 'zero tolerance' policy on obstruction infractions such as interfer-ence, hooking and holding. The rules themselves did not actually change, only the manner in which the rules were interpreted and enforced – in essence, many of the types of attempts to impede the opponent that would have been 'let go' by referees prior to the lockout would now result in a 2-minute minor penalty.

Figure 5.1 shows the effects of such increased enforcement. The average number of minor penalties per team, per season, spiked from 405.9 in 2003–04 to 522.8 in 2005–06. As importantly, however, subsequent seasons saw steady decreases in minor penalties from this 2005–06 high, to the point where the numbers of penalties actually dropped well below the pre-lockout levels. If one assumes that the level of referee enforcement stayed constant across seasons after the lockout, then it would seem that teams and players ultimately made some adjustments to this new environ-ment. Part of this adjustment is simply due to all players being more aware

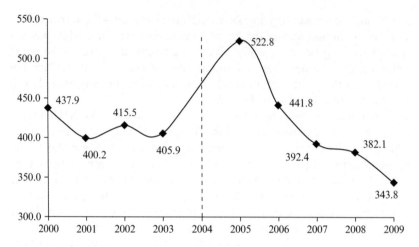

Figure 5.1   Number of minor penalties by season (average per team)

as to which on-ice actions are acceptable, and which are not. However, there is also a second factor at work. To the extent that the number of minor penalties a player incurs is not completely discretionary on his part, but is rather a broad proxy for his style of play and/or skill level – that is, the more penalties, the more defensive his style of play and/or the lower his offensive skills – then the increased enforcement of the obstruction rules makes certain types of players less valuable to their teams than they were before the lockout. Thus, teams may make roster adjustments to reduce the number of physically oriented players on the team (that is, those more prone to be affected by the increased enforcement) and simultaneously increase the number of offensively skilled players on the team.

In addition to the rule changes regarding obstruction, the NHL also made adjustments to the rules on fighting. After the lockout, any player instigating a fight during the last 5 minutes of a game is ejected from the game and receives an additional one-game suspension, and the team's coach is fined $10 000. The suspension and fine double for each successive incident. These changes were enacted to reduce the propensity of teams that were clearly not going win the game, and hence had 'nothing to lose', from resorting to overt intimidation tactics near the end of the game. Figure 5.2 shows that while fighting did decline in the first season immediately after the lockout, it has steadily increased since then, to the point where in 2010–11 it was near pre-lockout levels.

Simultaneous to all of these rule changes, the economic structure of the NHL also changed radically after the lockout. Prior to the lockout,

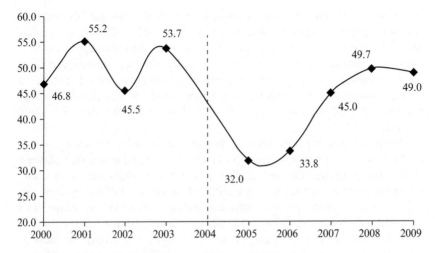

Figure 5.2   Number of major penalties by season (average per team)

no salary cap existed in the league, nor were there any limitations on the salaries of individual players. The new Collective Bargaining Agreement (CBA) that ended the lockout resulted in both the implementation of a hard salary cap (and floor) for team payroll, and a limitation on the maximum that any individual player could be paid. For the first season after the lockout, 2005–06, the cap ceiling was set at $39, with floor of $21.5 million. Compare this with 2003–04, the last year before the lockout, where actual team payrolls ranged from $23 million to $78 million. Thus, the introduction of the salary cap had the effect of greatly reducing the variance in payrolls across teams in the League.

III   PREVIOUS RESEARCH

Numerous early studies of the NHL attempted to investigate the possible link between violence and consumer demand. Stewart et al. (1992) used data from the 1981 to 1983 seasons, and modeled attendance as a function of violence, where violence was measured in the aggregated form as the sum of minor, major and misconduct penalties. They found violence had two opposing effects – it increased demand directly by appealing to fans desire for 'blood lust', but simultaneously decreased a team's chances of winning, which, in turn, decreased demand. In a relatively similar study, Jones et al. (1993) examine the 1983–84 season and find that violence, again measured in the aggregate as the sum of all types of penalties, increased attendance for franchises in both Canada and the US, but that the more extreme types of violence (majors and misconducts) are associated with increased attendance only for US cities, perhaps suggesting that American fans have a greater desire for violence than Canadians fans. This latter hypothesis, that there were pronounced effects in the US compared to Canada, was given further support from Jones et al.'s (1996) findings for the 1989–90 season, and Paul's (2003) findings for the 1999–2000 season.

Given this consistent finding of a positive relationship between violence and attendance, a natural extension has been to examine whether player's that possess higher degrees of fighting/violence 'skills' are financially compensated for such skills. In a study by Jones et al. (1997) they first classify players as either 'grunts' (physical-oriented, more violent players) or non-grunts. Using data from 1989–90, they then estimate separate salary models for each, and test for equality of coefficients across the models. They find the salary determination process is different for grunts and non-grunts, but overall, grunts did not receive any type of salary premium. Using penalty minutes as proxy for violent behavior, the authors find for forwards that there is a positive and significant effect of penalty minutes on salary. The authors' sample comprises 250 forwards and 138 defensemen and can be criticized for being on the low side, thus inhibiting successful inference.

A follow-up study by Jones, Nadeau and Walsh (1999) used the same season's data, 1989–90, and focussed on testing for ethnic salary discrimination against French Canadians.[2] In this study, the authors identify players hired for their physical presence as opposed to skill as 'goons'. The authors' model includes a goon dummy, penalty minutes and an interaction term between goons and penalty minutes. For forwards, they find that being a goon raises salary, controlling for penalty minutes. Having more penalty minutes also raises salary significantly, conditional on goon status. But increasing penalty minutes for a goon significantly reduces player salary. The interaction term offsets the positive impact of being a physically aggressive player. Unlike the 1997 study by the same authors, this study found a positive, significant effect of penalty minutes on salary for defensemen. But as in the 1997 paper, defensive goons do not have a significant salary premium.

In an NHL salary study, Vincent and Eastman (2009) estimate a standard salary model using quantile regression and look at forwards and defensemen separately. They have cross-section data from the 2003–04 season. Player aggression is modelled by penalty minutes per game. For forwards at the median or above in the salary distribution – but not for those below the median – the authors find that increased penalty minutes are significantly associated with higher salary. Conversely, there is no significant effect of penalty minutes on salaries for defensemen. Sample sizes are small (for example, just 218 defensemen), however, and this may mitigate against finding significant effects. Also, as this is a cross section, the authors cannot control for unobserved heterogeneity.

Haisken-DeNew and Vorell (2008) is the paper in the literature that is closest to our study. They examine the 1996–2007 seasons and find that teams that engaged in more fights had a greater probability of advancing to the championship finals. They have data on numbers of fights by players, and also numbers of fights won. In a salary model for all players, the authors find that penalty minutes have a positive and significant coefficient in ordinary least squares (OLS) estimation with fixed effects. But breaking down by position, it appears that the only position to exhibit a significant positive effect of penalty minutes on salary is centers (who are the key goal scorers). The authors find that wing players – but not other positions – receive a substantial salary premium for the number of fights engaged in. The estimated effect is nearly US$11 000 per fight. Moreover, the per-fight salary premium is even bigger (US$18 000) for wing players who win their fights. The authors argue that wing players get into fights to protect the star forwards. The salary premia, first for fighting and then for winning fights, is then a suitable incentive to perform well in this protective role.

Haisken-DeNew and Vorell seem to take a workplace-safety perspective on the issue of NHL violence, and argue that a 'fight fine' would reduce or eliminate the incentive to fight, and thus reduce the possibility of career-ending injuries that might result from such fights. Our analysis differs from Haisken-DeNew and Vorell in a number of ways. First, the Haisken-DeNew and Vorell paper has no controls for the pre- and post-lockout periods. In our analysis, we compare how (if at all) the returns to skills/thuggery have changed after the lockout to see if the attempts to reduce fighting have had any effect. Second, Haisken-DeNew and Vorell do not consider how the post-lockout regime entailed more severe enforcement of minor penalties. As noted earlier, among the post-lockout changes was a 'zero tolerance' policy on interference, holding/obstruction and hooking. This increased enforcement could affect returns to skills of toughness and aggression. Also, Haisken-DeNew and Vorell (2008) only consider fighting, whereas majors may include other penalties (for example, boarding, charging, spearing).

The issue of aggression in the NHL has found its way into the literature on the economics of crime. These studies have often focused on the NHL's decision to experiment with using two referees (instead of one) in certain games during the 1998–99 and 1999–2000 seasons. These studies view the addition of a second referee as in increase in 'policing' activity. The net effects of such increased policing are a priori indeterminate, since there are two opposing forces at work. Increased policing leads to greater monitoring, and hence more arrests, but also introduces a deterrent element, thus causing fewer crimes to be committed in the first place. It becomes an empirical question as to which of these effects dominate. In that regard, Heckelman and Yates (2003) found evidence of a strong monitoring effect, but no deterrent effect. They attribute the lack of deterrent effect to the fact that many infractions occur in the heat of battle, and may be reactive or retaliatory – analogous to a crime of passion – rather than being a rationally planned act.[3]

While this chapter draws elements from each of these streams in the literature, it most closely follows the economics of crime approach in that it examines the effects of an increased enforcement of rules. While the work of Levitt (2002) and Heckelman and Yates (2003) examines one type of structural change in enforcement – the addition of a second referee – we examine a more recent attempt by the NHL to better enforce its rules.

IV   MODEL AND DATA

In order to consider the returns to violence/aggressive play in the NHL we model player salaries as a function of various measures of playing skill and experience and include measures of a player's record of committing major and minor penalties.[4] The basic model we employ is the following:

$$Ln\ (Real\ Salary)_{it} = \alpha_o + \beta_1 X_{it} + \beta_2 V_{it} + \beta_3 D_t + \beta_4(D_t \cdot X_{it}) + \beta_5(D_t \cdot V_{it})$$
$$+ \mu_i + \gamma_t + e_{it} \tag{5.1}$$

where X_{it} is a vector containing measures of player skills and experience, and V_{it} contains measures on penalties committed (both major and minor penalties). Given that player salaries are determined prior to the start of a season, the measures appearing in X_{it} and V_{it} are career per-game averages up to, but not including the current season. The variable D_t is a dummy variable that takes the value of 1 if the observation is from a season following the 2004–05 lockout, 0 if from a pre-lockout season. The variable μ_i is a player individual effect and γ_t is a vector of season dummies. Lastly, e_{it} is the stochastic error term.

As for measures of player skills appearing in X_{it}, we employ two variables. The first is a player's career points per game which is included to capture a player's offensive abilities.[5] Other things equal, we expect that players with greater offensive skills will earn greater salaries and thus we expect a positive coefficient to this variable. Our second measure is a player's career plus-minus statistic. Skaters in the NHL (that is, non-goalkeepers) essentially have two functions: to help with scoring goals for their team and to help in preventing goals from being scored by their opponents. While career points per game is a good measure of the former, it does not capture a player's contributions to preventing opponents from scoring. The plus-minus statistic is employed by the NHL to try and capture this 'two-way' play (both scoring and the prevention of being scored upon) of skaters and is computed as follows: a player is awarded a $+1$ if they are on the ice during a game when their team scores an even strength goal, they are awarded a -1 if their team gives up an even strength goal. All else equal, we expect a positive coefficient for this variable.

Regarding experience, we include in X_{it} both career games played and its square. The assumption here is that career games played may capture other skills gained through experience that are not represented by a player's points and plus-minus statistics. We expect that the coefficient to career games will be positive. The squared term allows for diminishing returns to experience in which case we expect a negative coefficient to this variable.

In order to control for a player's history in committing penalties we employ two measures in the vector V_{it}. The first is a player's career minor penalties committed per game. Minor penalties are generally called for less violent acts that do not result in injury to opposing players. Thus, for example, such acts as tripping, holding or hooking (using one's hockey stick to impede the progress of an opponent) result in a minor penalty if detected by the referees. The cost to a team from a player receiving a minor penalty is that his team will have to play short-handed during the penalty (typically 2 minutes) and thus leading to a greater risk of being scored upon. In this respect, one may expect a player with a history of committing many minor penalties to be paid less, other things equal. On the other hand, having a high career minor penalty per game statistic may indicate that a player plays aggressively and, in doing so, is penalized more frequently. To the extent that aggressive play is helpful to team success, we may expect that aggressive players would earn greater salaries, all else equal. Given these two opposing forces, the net effect of aggressive play for a team (and hence for a player's salary) would depend on the frequency with which the player is called for a minor penalty. As noted earlier, prior to the 2004–05 lockout many of these acts did not result in penalties as enforcement was generally more lax during this period. Following the lockout, however, the NHL put a greater emphasis on calling such penalties. Indeed, as we saw earlier in Figure 5.1, the number of minor penalties per season (averaged across teams) peaks in the 2005–06 season which followed the lockout, then declines monotonically over subsequent seasons. The pattern in Figure 5.1 is consistent with the theory that an aggressive style of play may have benefitted teams more (or at least cost them less) in the pre-lockout period (when they were more likely to get away with such behavior) than after the lockout. Based on the above, the expected sign for the coefficient to career minor penalties is ambiguous. However, we expect the coefficient to the interaction of minor penalties with the lockout dummy variable (D_t) to be negative, indicating that aggressive style of play is lesser valued in the post-lockout period.

The second measure appearing in V_{it} is a player's career major penalties per game. Major penalties are typically called for more violent acts, including fighting and other aggressive behavior that results in serious injury to an opponent.[6] Similar to the case for minor penalties, major penalties may have opposing effects on team's success (and hence for a player's salary). On the one hand, major penalties are costly to teams (more so than minor penalties) as they generally cause a team to play short-handed for 5 minutes thus putting a team at greater risk of giving up a goal (or goals) to an opposing team.[7] Countering this effect are the possible benefits of fighting and other violent acts as these activities may intimidate opposing players and reduce their performance. As with minor penalties, the net effect of major penalties on a team's performance (and the potential effects on player's salaries) is ambiguous, but the rewards to fighting and other major penalties should be reduced in the post-lockout period for the same reasons as noted earlier for minor penalties.[8]

In addition to the measures shown in equation (5.1), two other control variables are included in the model. First, in order to control for the effects of player position a dummy variable is included which takes the value of 1 if the player is a defenseman, 0 otherwise (meaning the player is a forward). The expected value for the coefficient to this dummy variable is positive. The reason for this expectation is that other things equal, including offensive skills, a defenseman is expected to earn a greater salary than a forward since defensemen have the additional role of preventing the opposition from scoring.[9]

Lastly, in order to control for differing team environments team dummies are included in the model. These may be important if, for instance, a particular team has a 'culture' of violent play. For example, the Philadelphia Flyers were known as the 'Broad Street Bullies' in the early 1970s as they frequently engaged in fighting and rough play in an attempt to intimidate their opponents.[10] The Flyers remain one of the more violent teams today. In contrast, the Detroit Red Wings are typically near the bottom of the list in terms of fighting majors.

The data set used to estimate the model shown in equation (5.1) consists

Table 5.1   Summary statistics

Variable	Mean	Std dev.	Min.	Max.
Salary (real 2007 $m)	1.874	1.872	0.170	13.206
Career points per game	0.401	0.259	0	1.992
Career plus-minus per game	−0.013	0.160	−2	2
Career minor penalties per game	0.354	0.231	0	2.046
Career major penalties per game	0.032	0.075	0	2
Career games	389.918	316.826	1	1680

Note: R = 3650.

Source: All data are from NHL.com except for salary data which was collected from USATODAY.com.

of individual player data for the seasons 2001–02 to 2007–08, excluding the 2004–05 lockout season. Thus we have three seasons prior to the lockout and three seasons following, for a total of 3650 player-season observations.[11] Table 5.1 provides summary statistics.

V   ESTIMATION APPROACH AND ANALYSIS OF RESULTS

As described in section II, during the period covered by our data set there were a number of changes in the way NHL players were compensated. The season prior to the lockout there was a minimum player salary of $165 000, but no maximum salary limit. Following the lockout the minimum player salary was boosted to $450 000 (and later raised to $475 000 for the 2007–08 season). In addition, in the post-lockout period the NHL implemented a player maximum salary that was adjusted from season to season.[12] Values for both the player minimum and maximum salaries are reported in Table 5.2.

Given the censoring of the dependent variable, a random effects Tobit estimation is employed.[13, 14] As the natural log of real salaries (in $2007) is used as our dependent variable in equation (5.1), the censoring values used in the Tobit estimation are the natural logs of the minimum and maximum player salaries noted in Table 5.2 (after being converted into $2007 using the consumer price index). A total of four regressions were performed. The first estimates equation (5.1) for the entire six-season period, but leaves out the interaction terms with D_t. The second and third regressions are the same as the first, but for the two sub-periods of

Table 5.2   Player maximum and minimum allowed salaries, by season

Season	Player maximum	Player minimum
2001–02		$165 000
2002–03		$175 000
2003–04		$180 000
2005–06	$7 800 000	$450 000
2006–07	$8 800 000	$450 000
2007–08	$10 060 000	$475 000

2001–02 to 2003–04 (the pre-lockout period) and 2005–06 to 2007–08 (the post-lockout period). Lastly, the fourth regression estimates equation (5.1), including the interaction terms, for the entire period. In all four regressions, team and year dummies are included but the estimated coefficients are not shown.

Estimation results are reported in Table 5.3. As is evident, several coefficient estimates are consistently significant at conventional levels in all four regressions. Specifically, we can see that career points per game has a positive and significant (at the 1 percent level) effect on the log of salaries in each case. Thus, we find the expected result that players are rewarded for their offensive skills, all else equal. Another consistent result is for the coefficients for career games and career games squared. All four regressions produce a positive coefficient for the former and a negative one for the latter with significance being at the 1 percent level in every case. Taken together, these results demonstrate that player salaries increase with experience, but with a diminishing effect.[15] Lastly, the coefficient to the dummy variable defenseman is positive and significant (at the 1 percent level) in all regressions. This result, which is consistent with previous research,[16] implies that all else equal (including offensive production), defensemen tend to be paid more as they have the added ability of preventing the opposition from scoring.[17]

Turning to the plus-minus per game coefficient, it has a negative sign in all four cases but is significant (at the 5 percent level) in the second and fourth regressions. The negative sign suggests that players with a higher per game plus-minus statistic tend to earn lower salaries, a result which is contrary to our expectations. While it is difficult to explain this result, it is interesting to note that the interaction term for the plus-minus per game statistic is positive and significant (at the 5 percent level) indicating that in the post-lockout era two-way play was more valued.[18]

Considering our two measures for penalties, the coefficient to minor penalties per game is positive in all regressions and significant in regressions

Table 5.3   Random-effects Tobit estimation results

Variables	(1) ln(real salary)	(2) ln(real salary) (pre-lockout)	(3) ln(real salary) (post-lockout)	(4) ln(real salary)
Points per game	1.745***	1.630***	1.592***	1.783***
	(0.0596)	(0.0783)	(0.0800)	(0.0648)
Plus-minus per	−0.0817	−0.132**	−0.00303	−0.172**
game	(0.0568)	(0.0674)	(0.0813)	(0.0677)
Minor penalties	0.102*	0.0662	0.0958	0.167***
per game	(0.0536)	(0.0605)	(0.0886)	(0.0561)
Major penalties	−0.0580	−0.0517	−0.599**	0.0517
per game	(0.144)	(0.148)	(0.281)	(0.150)
Post-lockout × points per game				−0.0936 (0.0574)
Post-lockout × plus-minus per game				0.217** (0.0911)
Post-lockout × minor penalties per game				−0.180*** (0.0670)
Post-lockout × major penalties per game				−0.425* (0.235)
Career games	0.00307***	0.00237***	0.00316***	0.00304***
	(9.70e-05)	(0.000129)	(0.000142)	(9.81e-05)
Career games	−2.15e-06***	−1.41e-06***	−2.21e-06***	−2.12e-06***
squared	(8.02e-08)	(1.04e-07)	(1.21e-07)	(8.18e-08)
Defenseman	0.354***	0.356***	0.334***	0.354***
	(0.0286)	(0.0352)	(0.0377)	(0.0287)
Constant	12.55***	12.87***	12.54***	12.51***
	(0.0569)	(0.0733)	(0.0816)	(0.0579)
Team dummies	Yes	Yes	Yes	Yes
Year dummies	Yes	Yes	Yes	Yes
Observations	3650	1845	1805	3650
Number of players	1073	792	800	1073

Notes:
Standard errors in parentheses.
*** $p < 0.01$, ** $p < 0.05$, * $p < 0.1$.

(1) and (4). The positive coefficient is consistent with the view that this measure is capturing aggressive style of play which a team may value above and beyond the negative aspect of having to play short-handed following a minor penalty. Regression (4) provides some interesting results on how the value to aggressive play has changed from the pre- to the post-lockout period. As noted earlier, following the lockout the NHL made a concerted effort to showcase the offensive skills of players and to that end referees were instructed to more closely call minor infractions (hooking, holding, interference, and so on). The coefficient for the interaction between the post-lockout dummy and minor penalties is negative and significant suggesting that aggressive play, while valued by teams in the pre-lockout period, has lost much of its value to teams and players in the post-lockout period. A Wald test did not reject the hypothesis that the sum of the coefficients of career minor penalties per game and its interaction term was equal to zero. Hence, the salary premium for minor penalties apparent in the pre-lockout era was effectively eradicated post-lockout, which is attributable at least partly to increased enforcement of minor penalties.

As for major penalties, regressions (1) through (3) have negative coefficients for career majors per game while regression (4) has a positive one. Only regression (3), however, produces a significant coefficient and its negative sign suggests that players with a career history of committing more major penalties per game were less valued in the post-lockout era. Indeed, the estimated coefficient of -0.6 suggests that a player with a career majors per game value that is one standard deviation above the mean would be expected to earn about 4.5 percent less, all else equal.[19] Regression (4) reinforces this negative post-lockout valuation of violent play as the coefficient to the post-lockout interaction term for career majors per game is negative and significant as well.[20] Hence, salary returns to both major and minor offenses fell post-lockout.

VI CONCLUSION AND SUGGESTIONS FOR FUTURE RESEARCH

We have estimated a salary model for NHL players, both before and after the 2004–05 lockout that brought about an increased enforcement of on-ice infractions. We find that the number of minor penalties spiked markedly upward in the season after the lockout, but then steadily fell after that, ultimately to well below their pre-lockout levels. In contrast, the number of major penalties dropped in the season immediately after the lockout, but then rose towards pre-lockout levels thereafter.

Our salary models show that the returns to both major and minor penalties fell in the post-lockout era. In the case of major offenses, salary returns fell from zero to negative while for minor offenses, returns fell from positive to zero. Thus, not only did the lockout change the absolute number of penalties that were called, it changed the way in which penalties impacted salary. It is worth stressing that the move to greater law enforcement in hockey was accompanied by two other important changes in the game. First, there was a set of rule changes designed to promote more offensive play, including the ability to play longer passes and greater restriction on movement of goalies outside the goal area. These rule changes amount to a change in production technology. Secondly, a tougher salary cap regime post-lockout narrowed the intra-team dispersion of salaries, thus constraining the amounts that 'superstar' players could earn.

These changes potentially affect the returns to particular skills that can be earned by players. On the one hand, if the change in production technology (rule changes) permit more offensive goal scoring opportunities, then salary returns to offensive players should fall. In contrast, defensemen need to be better in ability and performance to counter the greater emphasis on attacking play induced by the rule changes. Their salary returns should rise. In contrast, the tougher salary cap should offset the capability of both offensive and defensive players to increase their salaries. The net effect on salaries of both forwards and defensemen is then indeterminate, a priori. Indeed, our results show no effect of the post-lockout era on returns to offensive play (as shown by the insignificant interaction term between post-lockout era and career points per game, our measure of offensive ability). Further, the salary premium to defensemen is not significantly different comparing post-lockout to pre-lockout periods. But given no change in returns to points per game and to defensemen, we do observe estimated reductions in returns to major and minor offenses.

The attitude of the NHL to player violence remains ambivalent. There is no appetite on the part of the League authorities to eliminate 'thuggery'. In 2009 the NHL commissioner Gary Bettman stated: 'I believe that most of our fans enjoy [the fighting] aspect of the game . . . it is a part of the game [and] I do not think there is any appetite to abolish it'.[21] We have shown that major offenses rose after 2006, while minor offenses fell. The reduction in minor offenses and the accompanying loss of salary premium for these offenses are entirely consistent with an economics of crime model. But the recent rise in major offenses when a salary penalty for such offenses emerged is hard to reconcile with the economics of crime framework and may reflect some underlying team dynamics (for example, fighting is essential for team chemistry and success) that merit further inquiry.

Also for future work, it will be interesting to explore how players' careers have responded behaviorally to the new rules and their enforcement. Did players who were fighters play less or get demoted to lower leagues? Did these players adapt their skills to emphasize their offensive abilities? We suspect that highly aggressive players were able to adapt better, so as to commit fewer penalties, and find a new role on their teams. But we also suspect that specialist fighters would have more difficulty in finding a role in their teams in the post-lockout era.

NOTES

1. See Kahane (2006) for a detailed discussion of the changes implemented by the NHL following the 2004–05 lockout.
2. There are also many other studies examining the salary structure of the NHL where fighting and aggression are not the focus of the analysis, but are included in salary models as control variables. Most of these studies examine discrimination issues, and test for the possible effects of ethnicity (particularly with respect to French Canadians) on salary.
3. Levitt (2002) and Allen (2002) also examine the two-referee experiment from an economics of crime perspective.
4. It should be noted that the vast majority of major penalties are for fighting. Other violent acts may result in a major penalty as well (such as spearing, head-butting and charging that results in serious injury of another player).
5. A player's points are equal to the sum of their goals and assists.
6. Other acts that lead to major penalties include spearing (with the stick), head-butting and kneeing. A complete list can be found on the NHL's official website at: http://www. nhl.com/ice/page.htm?id=26545.
7. If a team is short-handed due to a minor penalty and the opposing team scores before the minor penalty has concluded, the penalty is over and the penalized player is allowed to return to the game. In the case of major penalties, the offending team must play short-handed for the entire 5 minutes of the penalty regardless if the opposing team scores. However, most majors for fighting are, in practice, offsetting (that is, players from both teams receive a major), and thus do not result in a short-handed situation.
8. There is another avenue by which fighting and violent play may affect a player's salary. As noted earlier in section III, Jones et al. (1993) provide empirical support that attendance at hockey games is positively affected (particularly for games played in American cities) by the amount of violence (as proxied by major penalties) that occurs during the game. Thus, to the extent that fighting increases a player's marginal revenue product by increasing attendance this may lead to an increased salary, all else equal.
9. While the plus-minus statistic may partially capture defensive contributions, it is not likely to fully characterize a player's defensive skills.
10. Perhaps the most infamous player was Dave 'The Hammer' Schultz. During the 1974–75 season with the Philadelphia Flyers he amassed a total of 472 penalty minutes over 76 games, or 6.2 minutes per game.
11. Lack of player salary data led to some missing data.
12. As noted in the NHL's 2005 collective bargaining agreement, a player cannot earn more

than 20 percent of a team payroll in a given season. Payroll caps were also put in place, thus fixing a player's possible maximum in any given season. (For more details, see the 2005 CBA at: http://www.nhl.com/ice/page.htm?id=26366).

13. A likelihood-ratio test comparing the random effects Tobit model with the pooled Tobit model rejected the latter (with a p-value of 0.000).
14. It is interesting to note that in the Haisken-DeNew and Vorell (2008) paper there appears to be no control for the censoring of the salary variable in their regressions.
15. Regressions using a player's age and its square produced similar results.
16. For example, Idson and Kahane (2000) and Haisken-DeNew and Vorell (2008).
17. It should be noted that forwards are also expected to play a defensive role during the game. Defensemen, however, have a primary responsibility of preventing the opposition from scoring.
18. Several problems exist with the plus-minus statistic. First, it is correlated with a player's points per game statistic. Secondly, it is affected by the skill level of teammates. Both of these facts may obscure the measure's objective of capturing the offensive and defensive skills of an individual player.
19. Computed using the -0.599 coefficient to career majors per game from regression (3) and the standard deviation for this variable shown in Table 5.1.
20. The p-value for the interaction term is 0.070.
21. Source: CBCSports.ca, http://www.cbc.ca/sports/hockey/story/2009/01/24/fighting-gary bettman.html?ref=rss.

REFERENCES

Allen, W.D. (2002), 'Crime, punishment and recidivism: lessons from the National Hockey League', *Journal of Sports Economics*, **3**, 39–60.

Haisken-DeNew, J. and M. Vorell (2008), 'Blood money: incentives for violence in the NHL', Ruhr Economic Papers, No. 47.

Heckelman, J. and A. Yates (2003), 'And a hockey game broke out: crime and punishment in the NHL', *Economic Inquiry*, **41**, 705–12.

Idson, T. and L.H. Kahane (2000), 'Team effects on compensation: an application to salary determination in the National Hockey League', *Economic Inquiry*, **38**, 345–57.

Jones, J.C.H., D. Ferguson and K. Stewart (1993), 'Blood sports and cherry pie: some economics of violence in the National Hockey League', *American Journal of Economics and Sociology*, **52**, 63–78.

Jones, J.C.H., S. Nadeau and W.D. Walsh (1997), 'The wages of sin: employment and salary effects of violence in the National Hockey League', *Atlantic Economic Journal*, **25**, 191–206.

Jones, J.C.H., S. Nadeau and W.D. Walsh (1999), 'Ethnicity, productivity and salary: player compensation and discrimination in the National Hockey League', *Applied Economics*, **31**, 593–608.

Jones, J.C.H., K. Stewart and R. Sunderman (1996), 'From the arena into the streets: hockey violence, economic incentives and public policy', *American Journal of Economics and Sociology*, **55**, 231–43.

Kahane, L.H. (2006), 'The economics of the National Hockey League: the 2004–05 lockout and the beginning of a new era', in P. Rodríguez, S. Késenne and J. García (eds), *Sports Economics After Fifty Years: Essays in Honour of Simon Rottenberg*, Oviedo: University of Oviedo Press.

Levitt, S.D. (2002), 'Testing the economic model of crime: the NHL's two-referee experiment', *Contributions to Economic Analysis & Policy*, **1**, 1–19.

Paul, R. (2003), 'Variations in National Hockey League attendance', *American Journal of Economics and Sociology*, **62**, 345–64.

Stewart, K., D. Ferguson and J.C.H. Jones (1992), 'On violence in professional team sport as the endogenous result of profit maximization', *Atlantic Economic Journal*, **20**, 55–64.

Vincent, C. and B. Eastman (2009), 'Determinants of pay in the NHL: a quantile regression approach', *Journal of Sports Economics*, **10**, 256–77.

6. Valuing the blind side: pay and performance of offensive linemen in the National Football League

David J. Berri, Brad R. Humphreys and Robert Simmons

INTRODUCTION

Empirical identification of the monetary returns to specialization in economic activities is extremely difficult, particularly where question-naire surveys of managers or workers are used (Green et al., 1998). The limitations of broad questionnaire surveys, containing subjective and possibly unreliable responses, represent one good reason why some econo-mists have recently focused on in-depth analysis of the effects of human resource management policies in particular manufacturing plants. This approach, called 'nano-econometrics' from the pioneering contribution of Ichniowski and Shaw (2003) on US steel plants, allows economists to obtain precise measures of worker performance and rewards.

This chapter is an example of nano-econometrics, using the sports industry as a setting. Kahn's (2000) description of the team sports industry as a labor market laboratory is apposite here. Each of the major North American team sports offers detailed and widely available (that is, not proprietary) data on job tasks (positions within teams), career records, player and team performance and player salaries. In each major sport there is a plethora of online information tracking player performances over many years.

In American professional football, organized in the National Football League (NFL), players have well-defined roles within games. Most plays are designed, at least partly, by the team's coaches and set down in team playbooks. These designs specify assignments for each player on the field of play. In this chapter, we estimate a salary model of offensive line players in the NFL. This group of players has the collective task of protecting the quarterback from being hit ('sacked') by opposition defensive players and providing a player with the ball with room to run without being tackled by

99

opposing players. The offensive line blocks (holds off) defensive players. The longer the amount of time the defense can be held at bay, the greater the opportunity for quarterbacks to execute pass plays, which help the offense gain yards and eventually score points via touchdowns and field goals. Also, the offensive line must block the defense so as to create space for plays by running backs. The blocking schemes that are set down by coaches are scripted in detailed fashion. The individual player must not only carry out their individual assignments, but also work with their fellow linemen to execute the vision of their coaches. All of this must be done without violating the rules of the NFL, which are enforced by the ever-vigilant NFL referees.

Previous work on NFL salary determination has focused on so-called skill positions, which are quarterback, wide receiver, running back and tight end (see Berri and Simmons, 2009, and Berri et al., 2011, for research on the salaries of quarterbacks; Leeds and Kowalewski, 2001, on all skill positions, and Simmons and Berri, 2009, on running backs). There are no published papers on salary determination of offensive line players, probably because their performances are hard to evaluate. In this chapter we offer an analysis of offensive line salaries that estimates the return to performance using two measures of performance: sack yards allowed and penalty yards assessed on specific players. These are of course negative aspects of performance, but they highlight what offensive line players must do.

One key goal for offensive line players is to prevent the quarterback from being sacked. Sacks result in lost yards, making it more difficult for the offense to gain the 10 yards necessary for a first down; which in turn helps the offense progress down the field to score points.[1] The offensive line must avoid giving up penalties, which again result in lost yards. The two most common penalties for offensive line players are holding, essentially an illegal block, and a 'false start' which is an illegal movement of the body prior to the center delivering the ball to the quarterback (called a 'snap'). A holding penalty results in a 10 yard loss, while a false start penalty leads to a 5 yard loss. We should stress that holding penalties are often committed by desperate offensive line players, who did not have the ability to prevent defensive players from penetrating the offensive line.

The offensive line is broken down into further units of specialization. The center plays in the middle of the offensive line, which typically contains five players. His roles are to deliver the ball to the quarterback and having done so to block the defense.[2] The center is accompanied by two guards on either side who assist the center in blocking the defense. Either side of the guards are two 'tackles' who also block, but have a more specific role in preventing the defense from sacking the quarterback. Most sacks emanate from the area outside the offensive line, and the tackles, on the outer part of the line, need to be aware of potential movement from defensive players that could result in sacks.

In his best selling book, *The Blind Side: Evolution of a Game*, Michael Lewis (2006) described the particular case of a then college left tackle, Michael Oher, who now plays for Baltimore Ravens on the left side of the offensive line. Oher's job was to protect a right-handed quarterback from being sacked by a defensive player rushing from the left side of the offensive line (right side of defensive line). Since most quarterbacks are right handed, Lewis termed the outside left area of the offensive line as the 'blind side'. In his book, Lewis suggests that Oher's skill in preventing his quarterback from being sacked was somehow scarce and special. The natural question that follows is whether this specificity of job task generates a salary premium to the worker. We address this question below. We also address three related questions: what is the salary penalty for poor performance, as indicated by penalty yards and sack yards given up? What is the salary return to size? And what is the salary return on draft position?

THE SALARY MODEL

The model of player salaries used here follows the generic Mincer form used in the sports literature, where player salary is assumed to depend on experience, player performance and team characteristics (see Scully, 1974, and Holmes, 2011, for examples from Major League Baseball; Bodvarsson and Partridge, 2001, Hamilton, 1997, Kahn and Shah, 2005, Berri et al., 2007, and Simmons and Berri, 2011, for examples from the National Basketball Association; Kahn, 1992, for an example from the NFL; Idson and Kahane, 2000, and Kahane et al. Chapter 5 in this volume for examples from the National Hockey League; Lucifora and Simmons, 2003, for Italian soccer and Frick, 2011, for German soccer).

Our dependent variable is real player salaries. Basic salary levels are set in the context of a pay scale determined by collective bargaining agreement between the players' union (NFLPA) and team owners.[3] Players receive a base salary, a signing bonus paid in the first year of a contract, performance bonuses and other bonuses not related to performance. Salaries are generally not guaranteed in the NFL, and a player can be released from his contract at any point. The pay scales will reflect player experience in the NFL. Signing bonuses are determined through bilateral bargaining between team owners and the player without union involvement, and paid to the player upon signing a contract. In any season, it follows that the variation in signing bonus will be larger than the variation in basic salary. Over our sample period, it appears that an increasing share of total player salary is accounted for by signing bonuses. For the purposes of salary cap computation, any signing bonuses are pro-rated over the life of the player's contract.

Salary distributions in most occupations are not log-normal and in team sports skewness in the distribution is particularly marked, with a few top players earning substantially more than their colleagues (García del Barrio and Pujol, 2007; Lucifora and Simmons, 2003). Non-normality and excess kurtosis in the dependent variable may result in variations of marginal returns to particular characteristics throughout the salary distribution (Leeds and Kowalewski, 2001). For our sample, a skewness test rejects the joint null of no excess skewness and no excess kurtosis (p value less than 0.001). Hence, we are reluctant to use ordinary least squares to estimate the parameters in our model.

Following earlier contributions on player salaries by Hamilton (1997) and Leeds and Kowalewski (2001), we adopt the quantile regression method for estimation since salaries have a non-normal distribution with substantial skewness and excess kurtosis. At the median, quantile regression differs from ordinary least squares in that it minimizes the sum of absolute residuals rather than the sum of squared residuals (Koenker, 2005). A strong advantage of quantile regression is that it permits estimation of marginal effects of covariates at different points of the distribution of the dependent variable. In our case, we can estimate the impacts of player performance measures on log salary at different salary quantiles.

Our list of explanatory variables begins with *experience*. As with the human capital model, we expect NFL experience to impact player salaries positively, but with diminishing returns to reflect the wear and tear on the body and decline in physical ability (speed and strength) that is clearly apparent in playing careers that average just four years in this highly physical sport. Diminishing returns to experience are captured by a quadratic form with the addition of *experience squared*.

National Football League experience for most players is preceded by the league's player draft. There are seven draft rounds[4] and players drafted in earlier rounds tend to be of higher quality than players drafted in later rounds. Hence, earlier round choices should have greater salaries. Also, players selected in earlier rounds will receive greater technical and coaching support than players selected in later rounds, so the prediction that these players will earn larger salaries is partly self-fulfilling.

The draft is an imperfect predictor of playing talent, especially as performance in the NFL is difficult to predict (see Berri, 2007) and furthermore, teams use the draft partly as a trading exchange for players (Hendricks et al., 2003; Quinn, 2006; Berri and Simmons, 2011).[5] We adopt *first round pick, second round pick* and *third round pick* as dummy variables to reflect draft selection order. The inclusion of these factors allows us to know if the evaluations made on draft day – which have been shown to persist in the National Basketball Association (Camerer and Weber, 1999) and with respect to other positions in the NFL (Berri and Simmons, 2009; Simmons and Berri, 2009) – persist throughout an offensive lineman's career.

For the first three years of a player's career his bargaining power is heavily influenced by what happened on draft day. After three years of experience, a player in the NFL is entitled to 'restricted free agency'. After three years, an NFL player can seek contract offers from rival teams but the current team is entitled to present a matching offer. Such players are denoted by the dummy variable, *Restricted free agent*. NFL players are entitled to unfettered free agency status after four seasons playing experience. Players who have at least four years experience are identified by the dummy variable *experience > 3 years*. Several players remained with their drafting team even though they had acquired free agent status. This is presumably because the drafting team offered the player a contract with valuation at least as high as any alternative offer by another team in the market for free agents. Such players who remain with their original drafting teams despite being free agents are identified by the dummy variable *stayed with same team*. This is set at one until the player switches teams.

Inspection of our data suggests that players often receive lower salary when they change teams. We capture this effect by a dummy variable, *changed teams*, where the value of unity only applies for the first season in which a player represents a different club. This variable was found to have a negative and significant coefficient in the analysis of NFL quarterback salaries of Berri and Simmons (2009). Their rationale was that teams which identified an effective job match with their quarterbacks would offer salaries in excess of outside opportunities, even for free agents. Players who switch teams would then tend to be those deemed surplus to requirements. We anticipate a similar effect for offensive linemen. We predict that both 'veterans' and 'stayers' will earn higher salaries than players who do not have free agent status (see Krautmann et al., 2009 for a full account of conditions for free agency in the NFL). Conversely, we expect players who switch teams will suffer a salary penalty *ceteris paribus*.

Beyond bargaining power, peer esteem also should impact the valuation of a player and therefore impact a player's salary. A useful proxy for peer esteem is selection for the annual Pro Bowl exhibition game (*Pro bowl*). We expect that offensive line players who had at any time previously been selected for the Pro Bowl will receive higher salaries *ceteris paribus*.[6]

Size is an additional attribute that may be rewarded in the player labor market. Given height, a heavier offensive lineman can block more effectively. But extra weight comes at the cost of less speed so we anticipate diminishing returns of salary to size. As defined below, we measure size by body mass index (*BMI*) and assess diminishing returns to size by its square (*BMI squared*).

Our data set identifies four position categories for offensive linemen: center, guard, tackle and offensive lineman. An offensive lineman is a player capable of playing multiple positions on the offensive line and we use this as our base category. We create dummy variables for the other three positions: *center, guard* and *tackle*. Following Lewis's bestselling book, we assess the presence of a salary premium for starting left tackles using a dummy variable for this category (*starting left tackle*). This dummy conflates two attributes, first, that the tackle is operating on the left of the defensive line and, second, that this tackle is categorized as a regular (starting) tackle.

Our two performance measures are penalty yards given up (*penalty yards*) and sack yards given up (*sack yards allowed*). Previous research has argued that yards gained by offensive players is a key determinant of player salaries in the NFL (Berri and Simmons, 2009; Berri et al., 2011; Simmons and Berri, 2011). Our prior view is that yards lost by offensive line players should have a negative, detrimental effect on salaries. Of course, if a player has more game time then it is likely that they will commit more penalties and give up more sacks. We do not have access to detailed playing time data so we control for game time using games started. Salary is assessed at the beginning of each season. To mitigate potential endogeneity concerns, we assess our performance variables (*Games started, Penalty yards, Sack yards*) as measured by previous season totals.

To summarize, our salary model is:

Log real salary = F(Experience, Experience squared, First round pick, Second round pick, Third round pick, Restricted free agent, Experience > 3 years, Stayed on same team, Changed teams, Pro Bowl Selection, BMI, BMI squared, Center, Guard, Tackle, Starting left tackle, Games started, Penalty yards, Sack yards allowed, Team fixed effects, Season fixed effects)

The selected quantiles for estimation are 0.1, 0.25, 0.5 (median), 0.75 and 0.9. Quantiles are estimated with bootstrapped standard errors, to correct for heteroskedasticity.[7]

DATA DESCRIPTION

Our data include detailed information about NFL offensive linemen over the 2000 to 2009 regular seasons. The unit of observation is an individual NFL offensive lineman in a season. In the NFL, offensive line play is

Table 6.1   Summary statistics

Variable	Mean	Std dev.	Min.	Max.
Salary	1 700 066	1 827 212	46 097	14 193 977
Years of experience	5.147	3.322	1	20
First round pick	0.157	0.364	0	1
Second round pick	0.148	0.355	0	1
Third round pick	0.119	0.324	0	1
Experience > 3 years	0.617	0.486	0	1
Tackle	0.237	0.425	0	1
Center	0.176	0.381	0	1
Guard	0.225	0.417	0	1
Starting left tackle	0.118	0.323	0	1
Pro bowl appearance	0.096	0.295	0	1
BMI	37.37	2.31	28.49	47.46
Games started	9.48	6.45	0	16
Penalty yards	23	21	0	169
Sack yards allowed	18	18	0	114

highly inter-related. Unlike many other positions on NFL teams, offensive linemen must cooperate and work as a unit in order to perform well. The data set contains three types of information about offensive linemen: (1) individual performance data for each season, (2) player characteristics and (3) salary data for offensive linemen. The data were assembled from various media sources. The player performance and characteristics data are from the web, including the official NFL website, Stats Incorporated's fee-based STATSPASS web database and www.pro-football-reference. com; the salary data come from the USA Today NFL Salary database. There were 2652 player-year observations consisting of data on 688 unique offensive linemen over the 2000 to 2009 seasons. Table 6.1 contains summary statistics for our data set.

Our salary measure is the amount that each player counts against the salary cap of the team. National Football League players are paid a base salary per year of a contract, a signing bonus paid when the contract is signed, a performance bonus and, occasionally, other bonuses not related to performance. National Football League contracts are not guaranteed, but the signing bonus is paid upon signing of the contract. The NFL salary cap is in fact a cap on total payroll for each team in the league in each season. Each player's compensation must be accounted for against the salary cap according to a relatively complex set of rules that account for all four types of compensation. The salary cap value reflects all four types of compensation in a consistent way. The salary data have been deflated

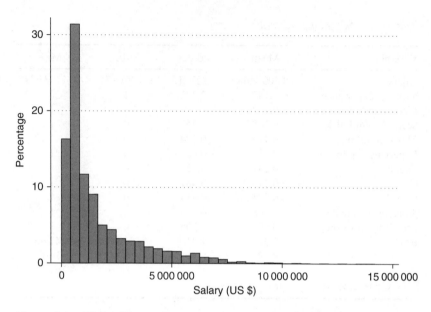

Figure 6.1   NFL offensive linemen salary distribution 2001–09

to real 2009 dollars using the US Consumer Price Index for All Urban
Consumers.

On average, offensive linemen earned $1.7 million dollars. The highest
salary was earned by Minnesota Vikings starting guard, Steve Hutchinson.
As the seventeenth pick in the 2001 NFL draft – in his sixth year of play –
he earned just over $14 million during the 2006 season. The lowest salary
was earned by Baltimore Ravens lineman, Brian Rimpf, a seventh-round
draft choice who played in a single game in 2004 before being cut. Of
special interest is the pay of starting left tackles. Across our sample, these
players were paid on average $3.49 million. In contrast, the average pay of
all other lineman was only $1.47 million. So, as noted, the salary distribu-
tion is not normal. This is illustrated graphically by the long left tail seen
in Figure 6.1.

Any discussion of labor markets in North American sports must address
the reverse order entry draft. The NFL was the first league to establish this
institution (in 1935), and it works by giving the worst team in the previous season the first choice from all incoming amateur players (generally
college players), the second worst team has the second choice, and so on.
The best team in the previous season has the last pick in the round, after
which the worst team again selects, or 'drafts', a player in the next round.

The NFL draft currently has seven rounds. Incoming players generally come from college and university football teams. Since teams have an incentive to select the best players first, the round in which a player is selected is an indicator of the perceived quality of the player before he enters the league. About 16 percent of the observations in our sample are for linemen drafted in the first round, 15 percent for players drafted in the second round and 12 percent for players drafted in the third round.

Under the current collective bargaining agreement between the NFL and the player's union, a player who is drafted by a team remains the property of that team for three seasons. So the NFL draft provides significant monopsony power to each team. But after the third season, a player can become a free agent and sell his services to the highest bidder. In our data set, 61 percent of the observations are for players with more than three years' experience.

Our data set is also segmented by position played. Again, there are three positions, and five players, on the typical offensive line of an NFL team: center, guard and tackle.[8] In the NFL statistics, linemen who play a specific position are identified by that position, while linemen who play multiple positions are identified as 'offensive linemen', a generic description of a lineman who plays multiple positions over the course of a game or season. About 24 percent of the players in our sample are identified as tackles, 22 percent are identified as guards and 18 percent are identified as centers; the rest are jack-of-all-trades 'offensive linemen'.

Of particular interest to this chapter, 12 percent of the observations are for starting left tackles – the tackle playing on the left side of the offensive line – as identified by pro-football-reference.com. About 10 percent of the players in the sample were named to the Pro Bowl game team, an indicator of an exceptional player. On average, a lineman in the sample started 9.5 games in an average season (an NFL teams plays 16 regular season games in the time period we examined).

The size of each lineman is also part of our data set. Relative to an average person in the population, offensive linemen are massive individuals. The primary job of an NFL offensive lineman is to keep the defensive players away from the offensive player with the football, which means moving other massive defensive players in directions they do not want to go. Size, weight and strength are required to perform this job. Body mass index, a common measure of body fat percentage which indicates how large a person is, is the ratio of weight to height squared with the result multiplied by 703. 'Normal' BMI is commonly defined as between 18 and 25. The average BMI for the NFL offensive linemen in our sample is 37, a BMI defined as obese on most scales. Linemen are also tall. The average height of linemen in the sample is 76.4 inches, almost 6 feet 4½ inches.

Our data contain two measures of negative job performance for offensive linemen. We have data on the number of yards of penalties called on each player in each season,[9] and on the number of sack yards allowed by each player. On average, an offensive lineman gave up 18 yards in sacks in a season in this sample. However, the range of this variable is large, with one player giving up 114 sack yards in a season. The average offensive lineman in the sample was penalized 23 yards in false starts and holding over the course of a season. Again, this variable has a large spread, with one player committing more than 160 yards in false starts and holding penalties in a season.

RESULTS AND DISCUSSION

Table 6.2 shows the quantile regression results, parameter estimates and t-statistics, at the 25th, 50th and 75th quantiles. The standard errors were bootstrapped with 200 replications. The quantile regressions were based on 1851 observations; the pseudo-R^2 for the median regression was 0.507. The regression model also included year and team specific effects; the parameter estimates and standard errors for these regression parameters are available on request.

Our results indicate that, consistent with previous research on salaries in the NBA and NFL, draft position has a persistent impact on player compensation. Holding experience and performance constant, players selected in the first round earn a salary premium above those selected in the second round, and players selected in the second round earn a salary premium over players selected in all other rounds. Consequently, just as we observe in the NBA and at other positions in the NFL, we see that initial perceptions of an offensive lineman remain even after decision-makers have observed the player perform in the NFL.

Bargaining power also matters, as we observe statistically significant positive returns to being a restricted free agent and having more than three years of experience. Again, only players with three or more years' NFL playing experience can negotiate with other teams for a contract. As expected, staying on a team beyond three years has a positive impact on salaries while players suffer a penalty when they switch teams. Experience also matters: the turning points for experience are 12, 10 and 9 years at quantiles 0.25, 0.5 and 0.75, respectively. This suggests that offensive linemen at the upper end of the salary distribution reach their peak earning years relatively earlier than offensive linemen at the middle or lower part of the salary distribution.

Size, as indicated by BMI, also matters, although the relationship between size and earnings is nonlinear; turning points are 38.6, 36.7 and

Table 6.2   Parameter estimates and t-statistics, quantile regression model

Variable	25th quantile	50th quantile	75th quantile
Experience	0.218*	0.252*	0.239*
	6.76	8.57	6.40
Experience^2	−0.012*	−0.013*	−0.013*
	−6.77	−8.56	−7.03
First round pick	0.707*	0.634*	0.650*
	11.06	13.13	9.87
Second round pick	0.332*	0.302*	0.283*
	7.05	6.33	5.36
Third round pick	0.064	0.094	0.101*
	1.22	1.88	2.05
Restricted free agent	0.125*	0.236*	0.292*
	2.17	3.99	4.05
Experience > 3 years	0.326*	0.375*	0.607*
	3.84	4.09	5.05
Stayed on same team	0.202*	0.192*	0.148*
	3.72	3.58	2.69
Changed teams	−0.414*	−0.349*	−0.386*
	−6.09	−6.25	−6.80
Pro bowl selection	0.425*	0.361*	0.305*
	6.38	7.43	4.74
BMI	0.270*	0.181	0.230*
	2.68	1.77	2.40
BMI^2	−0.004*	−0.002	−0.003*
	−2.63	−1.82	−2.34
Center	0.099	0.042	0.049
	1.76	0.76	0.87
Guard	0.116*	0.142*	0.089
	2.14	2.85	1.73
Tackle	0.193*	0.207*	0.263*
	3.25	4.01	4.25
Starting left tackle	0.085	0.163*	0.130
	1.33	2.80	1.93
Games started	0.036*	0.046*	0.048*
	8.01	12.84	10.59
Penalty yards	−0.003*	−0.002*	−0.002
	−2.53	−2.15	−1.66
Sack yards allowed	−0.001	−0.002	−0.002
	−0.70	−1.87	−1.17

Note: * Significant at 5 percent level.

37.9 at quantiles 0.25, 0.5 and 0.75 although the point estimate at the median is imprecisely estimated. The implication is that offensive linemen who are not massive enough earn lower salaries, probably because they are less able to perform their assigned task of blocking, and offensive linemen who are too massive are also less effective at performing their job, probably because of reduced mobility.

When it comes to our performance measures, penalty yards consistently matter. At all three quantiles, players who committed more penalty yards in the previous season earn lower salaries than players who committed fewer penalties, other things equal. Allowing sacks, though, was not found to impact compensation. There are two possible reasons for this result. First, it is possible that our other explanatory variables already reflect a player's ability to prevent sacks. For example, we would expect better players to go to Pro Bowls (this positively impacts salaries) and to stay on a team; two factors already captured in our empirical model. In addition, we have noted that linemen must work as a team. It could be that, although sacks are assigned to individuals in our data, the actual blame for allowing sacks should go to the entire line. If that is how decision-makers evaluate performance, we would expect sacks not to matter much in the determination of individual salaries.

What of the motivation for our study, the importance of protecting the quarterback's blind side? Our point estimates suggest a salary hierarchy by offensive line positions with tackles earning more than guards who in turn earn more than centers and other offensive lineman. More precisely, at the 0.25 quantile tackles earn significantly more than centers (p-value $= 0.031$) but do not earn significantly more than guards (p-value $= 0.093$). At the median, tackles again earn significantly more than centers (p-value $= 0.000$) although not significantly more than guards (p-value $= 0.137$). At the 0.75 quantile, tackles earn significantly more than both centers and guards (p-values of 0.002 and 0.001 respectively). Being a starting left tackle, though, doesn't seem to consistently impact pay. At the 0.25 quantile, starting left tackles do not earn significantly more than tackles as a whole. At the median, though, a premium does emerge for starting left tackles over and above regular tackles. This premium amounts to $230 200 (in constant prices) at the point estimate with a 95 percent confidence interval of $65 000 to $415 000. At the 0.75 quantile, the premium for starting left tackles is larger, at $400 000 but less precisely estimated with a 95 percent confidence interval of -$5000 to $874 000. The p-value on this parameter estimate is 0.054, so it is nearly significant at conventional levels. These premia are over and above the returns to performance, draft round, size and peer esteem measures; we note in particular that starting left tackles are more likely than other tackles to have been drafted in the first round (52 percent of round one picks versus 15 percent of other tackles) and more likely to have been selected for the Pro Bowl (28 percent of Pro Bowl selections versus 2 percent). In addition, if starting left tackles are more important than other offensive linemen, then we would not expect to see many starting left tackles in the lower half of the salary distribution; this is consistent with the results shown on Table 6.2.

Our analysis confirms the essential 'Blind Side' story told by Michael Lewis. There is a premium paid to elite starting left tackles in the NFL. But our results have broader implications for economists' understanding of the relationship between pay and performance in the labor market. We have examined the determination of salaries in a setting where individual workers must cooperate with each other and work as a team to produce a valuable output. Our results suggest that individual characteristics (like size, experience, and so on.) all have the usual positive effect on compensation. The predictions of the standard neoclassical model of worker compensation are confirmed in a novel setting. Variations in the earnings of NFL offensive linemen can be explained by the same factors that explain variation in the earnings of factory workers, teachers, and academics.

We also develop evidence that one specific type of non-productive behavior, committing penalties, reduces the earnings of individual members of the team, while another type of non-productive behavior, allowing the quarterback to be sacked, has no negative effect on the earnings of individual team members. This result can help to explain the variation of earnings in other settings where workers must cooperate with each other in a team setting to produce some desired output. For example, the members of a surgical team must work together in an operating theatre, and a nurse who frequently drops instruments might be expected to earn a lower salary than one who does not make such mistakes. Similarly, on a production line in a factory, teams of workers are responsible for performing individual tasks that result in the production of a car or a computer motherboard. Our results suggest that a production worker who sometimes fails to solder a connection on a motherboard would be expected to suffer a salary penalty for this behavior.

NOTES

1. The offense has four plays (downs) in which to gain 10 yards. If the offense uses up four plays and does not gain the necessary 10 yards then possession of the ball is given over to the opposition. Typically, the offense will aim to use up to three downs and will kick (punt) the ball back to the opposition on fourth down if 10 yards have not been gained, unless the head coach considers that the distance needed to gain a first down warrants a regular play on fourth down.

2. The quarterback is typically positioned just behind the center. But he can stand further back in what is known as the shotgun formation. A poor snap could lead to the quarterback dropping the ball, called a fumble. If the fumble is recovered by the offense then typically yards will be lost as well as the down. Sometimes, the fumble will be recovered by the defense so possession of the ball is lost.
3. The NFL operates a salary cap which specifies an upper limit to the ratio of team payroll to gross designated revenues. The salary cap does not specify any limit on individual salaries, hence it is more accurate to refer to this as a cap on payroll. Moreover, the cap can be partly circumvented as some revenues (such as revenues from leasing luxury boxes at stadia) do not count against the cap. Nevertheless, the distribution of team payrolls in NFL is more compressed than in other North American sports and the salary cap can be viewed as binding.
4. Since 1994 the NFL draft has consisted of seven rounds. It was eight rounds in 1993 and 12 rounds in years before 1993.
5. It is common for a player to be traded in the current season in exchange for one or more draft picks of the buying team in future seasons.
6. The data on Pro Bowl selection are from www.pro-football-reference.com. Some selected players do not appear in the Pro Bowl, typically because of injuries.
7. Estimation is via the bsqreg command in Stata 11.0.
8. Again, the center plays in the center of the line and hands the football to the quarterback through his legs (called 'snapping' the ball in the jargon of football); two guards play on either side of the center, and two tackles play outside the two guards. On some occasions, NFL teams will employ additional offensive linemen for one play; for example, if the offense needs to gain only a small number of yards to score or get a first down, the team may use seven or eight linemen on a single play. Some linemen play only one position on the line, while others play multiple positions over the course of a game. One should note, the NFL rules permit unlimited substitution of players throughout the game.
9. The NFL rules are complex; seven officials oversee NFL games and each is assigned specific aspect or area of responsibility on each play. Offensive linemen commonly commit two technical rule violations: false start and holding. A false start occurs when an offensive lineman moves before the ball has been snapped to the quarterback by the center. In general, offensive players cannot move prior to the snap (with the exception of receivers and backs who can move parallel to the line of scrimmage prior to the snap). A false start penalty moves the offense back 5 yards. Holding is an extremely complex rule violation. The NFL rules place specific restrictions on where a player on the offense can place his hands on a defensive player who is being blocked. Violations of these rules are called 'holding'. A holding penalty moves the offense back 10 yards, a more serious violation than a false start.

REFERENCES

Berri, David J. (2007), 'Back to back evaluation on the gridiron', in James H. Albert and Ruud H. Koning (eds), *Statistical Thinking in Sport*, Boca Raton, FL: Chapman & Hall/CRC, pp. 235–56.

Berri, David J. and Rob Simmons (2009), 'Race and the evaluation of signal callers in the National Football League', *Journal of Sports Economics*, **10**(1), 23–43.

Berri, David J. and Rob Simmons (2011), 'Catching a draft: on the process of selecting quarterbacks in the National Football League amateur draft', *Journal of Productivity Analysis*, **35**(1), 37–47.

Berri, David J., Stacey L. Brook and Martin B. Schmidt (2007), 'Does one simply need to score to score?', *International Journal of Sport Finance*, **2**(4), 190–205.

Berri, David J., Jennifer Van Gilder, Lisle O'Neill and Rob Simmons (2011), 'What does it mean to find the face of the franchise? Physical attractiveness and the evaluation of athletic performance', *Economics Letters*, **111**(3), 200–202.

Bodvarsson, Orn B. and Mark D. Partridge (2001), 'A supply and demand model of co-worker, employer and customer discrimination', *Labour Economics*, **8**(2), 389–416.

Camerer, Colin and Roberto A. Weber (1999), 'The econometrics and behavioral economics of escalation of commitment in NBA draft choices', *Journal of Economic Behavior & Organization*, **39**(1), 59–82.

Frick, Bernd (2011), 'Performance, salaries and contract duration: empirical evidence from German soccer', *International Journal of Sport Finance*, **6**(2), 87–118.

García del Barrio, Pedro and Francesco Pujol (2007), 'Hidden monopsony rents in winner-take-all markets: Sport and economic contributions of Spanish soccer players', *Managerial and Decision Economics*, **28**(1), 57–70.

Green, Francis, Stephen Machin and David Wilkinson (1998), 'The meaning and determinants of skill shortages', *Oxford Bulletin of Economics and Statistics*, **60**(2), 167–85.

Hamilton, Barton H. (1997), 'Racial discrimination and professional basketball salaries in the 1990s', *Applied Economics*, **29**(3), 287–296.

Hendricks, Wallace, Lawrence DeBrock and Roger Koenker (2003), 'Uncertainty, hiring and subsequent performance: the NFL draft', *Journal of Labor Economics*, **21**(4), 857–86.

Holmes, Paul (2011), 'New evidence of salary discrimination in Major League Baseball', *Labour Economics*, **18**(3), 320–31.

Ichniowski, Casey and Kathryn Shaw (2003), 'Beyond incentive pay: insiders' estimates of the value of complementary human resource management practices', *Journal of Economic Perspectives*, **17**(1), 155–80.

Idson, Todd L. and Leo H. Kahane (2000), 'Team effects on compensation: an application to salary determination in the National Hockey League', *Economic Inquiry*, **38**(2), 345–57.

Kahn, Lawrence M. (1992), 'The effects of race on professional footballers' compensation', *Industrial and Labor Relations Review*, **45**(2), 295–310.

Kahn, Lawrence M. (2000), 'Sports as a labor market laboratory', *Journal of Economic Perspectives*, **14**(3), 75–94.

Kahn, Lawrence M. and Malav Shah (2005), 'Race, compensation and contract length in the NBA: 2001–2002', *Industrial Relations*, **44**(3), 444–62.

Koenker, Roger (2005), *Quantile Regression*, Cambridge: Cambridge University Press.

Krautmann, Anthony, Peter von Allmen and David J. Berri (2009), 'The underpayment of restricted players in North American sports leagues', *International Journal of Sport Finance*, **4**(3), 161–75.

Leeds, Michael and Sandra Kowalewski (2001), 'Winner take all in the NFL: the effect of the salary cap and free agency on the compensation of skill position players', *Journal of Sports Economics*, **2**(3), 244–56.

Lewis, Michael (2006), *The Blind Side: Evolution of a Game*, New York: W.W. Norton.

Lucifora, Claudio and Rob Simmons (2003), 'Superstar effects in sport: evidence from Italian soccer', *Journal of Sports Economics*, **4**(1), 35–55.

Quinn, Kevin G. (2006), 'Who should be drafted? Predicting future professional productivity of amateur players seeking to enter the National Football League', mimeo, St. Norbert College.

Scully, Gerard W. (1974), 'Pay and performance in Major League Baseball', *American Economic Review*, **64**(6), 915–930.

Simmons, Rob and David J. Berri (2009), 'Gains from specialization and free agency: the story from the gridiron', *Review of Industrial Organization*, **34**(1), 81–98.

Simmons, Rob and David J. Berri (2011), 'Mixing the princes and the paupers: pay and performance in the National Basketball Association', *Labour Economics*, **18**(8), 381–8.

PART III

Attendance

7. Endogeneity in attendance demand models

Roger G. Noll

A hoary econometrics principle is that an ordinary least squares (OLS) estimation of a demand equation in which price is treated as an exogenous independent variable contains a specification error that is likely to produce a biased estimate of the coefficient on price.[1] Price is an endogenous variable that a profit-maximizing supplier chooses on the basis of the cost function and the shape of the demand relationship. In a single-equation OLS model the coefficient on price measures its combined effects on demand (negative) and supply (positive). Only if the exogenous shocks to the equilibrium price and quantity operate to shift the supply curve but not the demand curve will an OLS estimate of the demand equation produce an unbiased estimate of the coefficient on price. If the unexplained shocks affect primarily the demand equation, the coefficient on price will measure primarily the positive response of supply to an increase in price, thereby causing the estimated equation to trace the supply curve rather than the demand curve.

Whether the endogeneity of price creates a problem in using OLS to estimate a demand equation depends on the goal of the regression analysis. If the goal is solely to predict sales as accurately as possible, endogeneity is not an interesting issue. But if the goal is to estimate the marginal attendance effect of a particular variable, then endogeneity is a serious problem. For example, if a goal of a regression is to estimate the price elasticity of demand, a biased estimate of the price coefficient thwarts attaining this goal. Because the price coefficient has opposite signs in supply and demand equations, endogeneity causes an upward bias in the price coefficient and the implied price elasticity of demand is more inelastic than is in fact the case.

If estimating the price elasticity of demand is not a goal of the regression, an OLS model still presents a problem. If some variables in the demand equation also appear in the supply equation, price will be correlated with these independent variables, causing the estimates of these coefficients to be inefficient. Excluding price from the regression is not a solution because then the coefficients on the other variables will measure their combined effects on supply and demand, and so be biased estimates of the true demand coefficients.

The endogeneity problem can be addressed by imposing restrictions on the coefficients in the system of equations. One such identifying restriction is to impose a value on the elasticity of demand, and hence the price coefficient in the demand equation, that is derived from theory or other empirical analysis. Identification also can be achieved if some coefficients on exogenous variables are zero in each equation. A necessary condition for identifying an equation is that each endogenous explanatory variable is explained in part by an exogenous variable that has a zero coefficient in the equation to be estimated (the order condition). The order condition is also sufficient in a two-equation model.[2]

The endogeneity problem can be corrected by using two-stage least squares in which the first stage consists of regressing each endogenous variable on all of the exogenous variables and the second stage uses the fitted values from the first-stage regressions for the endogenous explanatory variables. Thus, to identify the demand equation, in which quantity is the dependent variable, actual prices are replaced by fitted values from a reduced form price regression in which all of the exogenous variables appear on the right-hand side of the equation. Two-stage least squares succeeds because it creates a new exogenous variable – the component of an endogenous variable that is explained by exogenous variables, including the variables that are excluded from the equation of interest – that can be used as an instrument for the endogenous variable.

In supply and demand models the demand equation frequently is identified by assuming that the quantity supplied, but not the quantity demanded, is affected by marginal cost, so that marginal cost (or an instrument for marginal cost, like average cost or input prices) can be used in the first-stage price regression. The supply equation often is identified by assuming that demand, but not supply, is affected by demographic characteristics of buyers, which become the unique exogenous variables in the first-stage quantity equation.[3]

Sports economists who have estimated attendance demand models[4] are aware of the endogeneity problem, but econometric models of attendance in team sports normally do not take endogeneity into account. Notwithstanding possible specification error, sports economists normally include price in the attendance equation. In nearly all of these regressions the price coefficient is either the wrong sign (positive) or, if negative, sufficiently near zero that it implies that suppliers set price on the inelastic portion of the demand curve. Sports economists have generated *ex post* rationalizations for these results, or as Forrest (2012, p. 178) puts it, 'alibis that might explain that, after all, inelastic demand is consistent with profit maximization'.[5] As Kennedy (2007, p. 397) trenchantly observes: 'It is amazing how after the fact economists can conjure up reasons for incorrect signs' when, in fact, the cause is an econometric problem.[6]

A few attendance demand models do address the endogeneity problem. In some cases the analysis simply does not attempt to measaure the effect of price on attendance and instead estimates reduced form equations to serve some other goal (for example, Berri et al., 2004, estimate a reduced form revenue equation). Some studies simply include an assumption about demand elasticity in their list of identifying restrictions (Jones and Ferguson, 1988). A handful of studies use exogenous instruments for price, including lagged price (Villa et al., 2011), stadium capacity (García and Rodríguez, 2002), or both (Coates and Humphries, 2007).

This chapter examines the implications of the endogeneity problem in estimating demand for team sports.[7] The focus is on the economic theory of the supply of tickets to sporting events to explore how supply conditions affect price and hence bias the estimated coefficient on price in a reduced form demand model.

This chapter is organized as follows. The first section addresses the issue of finding appropriate cost variables to identify the demand equation and concludes that this search is futile. The second section examines the problem of estimating demand for a homogeneous product, which in the context of attendance at sporting events requires that seats do not differ in quality. The third section relaxes the homogeneity assumption.

The main conclusions of the analysis to follow are as follows. First, the appropriate specification of attendance demand depends on whether events are sold out. Second, the demand equation cannot be identified if games are not sellouts. Third, if events are sellouts, the elasticity of demand plays no role in determining price and attendance, but the demand equation may be identified because stadium capacity can explain price and may be exogenous to demand. Otherwise, the best approach to estimating attendance demand is the one adopted in several papers in which Colin Jones is a co-author, starting with Jones and Ferguson (1988), which is to impose a value on the price elasticity of demand, which means assuming away the empirical finding that has generated the decades-long debate about its meaning.

USING COST TO IDENTIFY DEMAND

The standard method for identifying the demand equation is to include marginal cost or instruments for marginal cost in the price (supply) regression. This section explains why this standard approach is unlikely to be successful in modeling attendance.

The theory of a profit-maximizing, single-product firm predicts that firms will set price so that marginal revenue equals marginal cost. Assume that the profit function of a team is:

$$\pi = PQ(P) - mQ,$$

in which P is price, Q is attendance and m is the marginal cost of selling a ticket and accommodating a fan. The first-order condition for profit maximization is the following:

$$P = m - Q/Q'. \tag{7.1}$$

Expression (7.1) forms the basis for the standard supply equation in a two-stage least-squares model. Price is regressed on marginal cost (or instruments for marginal cost, such as input prices) and the other exogenous variables, and the estimates of price from this equation are used as an instrument for price in the demand equation. The coefficient on price is then an unbiased estimate of the true coefficient if the model contains no other specification error.

Expression (7.1) yields insights about the elasticity of demand at the equilibrium price that have informed the debate about the findings that the demand for attendance at sports events in price inelastic. Rearranging expression (7.1) yields the following:

$$m = P(1 + e)/e, \tag{7.2}$$

in which $e < 0$ and $|e|$ is the price elasticity of demand. If $m = 0$, expression (7.2) implies that $e = -1$, that is, that price is set at the unit elasticity point on the demand curve. If $m > 0$, the Lerner Index, which is the equilibrium markup of price over marginal cost, is the following:

$$(P - m)/P = -1/e. \tag{7.3}$$

Because profit maximization requires $P - m > 0$, expression (7.3) implies $e < -1$ and so $|e| > 1$, that is, that the firm sets price on the elastic portion of demand. If empirical models find that $|e| < 1$, at least one of the following statements must be true:[8] (7.1) specification error has caused the estimate of the coefficient on price in the demand equation to be biased upwards and the conclusion that demand is inelastic is erroneous; (7.2) the profit equation that sports enterprises maximize is not accurately represented as the revenues and costs associated with attendance; or (7.3) sports enterprises do not maximize profits.

Accounting for Specification Error

The first explanation for a coefficient on price that is too high is that including price in the attendance equation is a serious specification error. As discussed above, the conclusion to be drawn from the theory of the firm is that marginal cost can be used as an instrument for price that can identify the demand equation.

In sports, the short-term marginal cost of attendance is the cost of selling one more ticket and allowing an additional fan to attend the game. As first observed by Demmert (1973), the short-run marginal cost of attendance is very low and does not exhibit much variation among suppliers of events in the same sport. The implication of a marginal cost near zero is that in equilibrium the price elasticity of demand will be near 1. For example, if the marginal cost of selling tickets and accommodating fans is 5 percent of the ticket price, the implied equilibrium price elasticity of demand is approximately 1.05. For dealing with the endogeneity of price in the attendance equation, the more important issue is the lack of variability in short-run marginal cost among sports enterprises. Short-run marginal cost cannot identify the price equation if marginal cost is essentially a constant across teams or, for the same team, over time.

In analyzing the appropriate specification of a supply and demand model in team sports, Fort (2004) argues that team quality affects the marginal cost of attendance because a team can attract more fans by spending more on talented players and coaches. If all teams compete in the same markets for talented inputs, the price of talent will be the same for all teams; however, the marginal quality cost of attendance can differ among teams. In equilibrium, the marginal revenue of team quality equals its marginal cost. A variant of Fort's team profit function is:

$$\pi = PQ(P,x) - mQ(P,x) - wx,$$

where x is quality, w is the unit wage of skills, and P, Q and m are defined as in expression (7.1), the first-order condition for quality is as follows:

$$w/(\delta Q/\delta x) = (P - m). \tag{7.4}$$

The left side of equation (7.4) is the cost of attracting one more fan by improving quality. Because teams do not all set the same price, the left side of expression (7.4) must vary among teams. If talent markets are competitive, teams face the same price of talent, w, so the source of variation in expression (7.4) must be $\delta Q/\delta x$, which implies that the relationship between team quality and attendance is not linear. If attendance exhibits diminishing returns to talent, which is consistent with the proposition that fans value competitive balance, the marginal attendance effect of team quality is decreasing in talent. From expression (7.4), diminishing returns to talent implies that high values of $\delta Q/\delta x$ are associated with low values of attendance, price and team quality.

For purposes of identifying the demand equation, the relevant question is whether marginal attendance productivity of talent, $\delta Q/\delta x$, or perhaps an instrument for it, is a valid exogenous variable in the price equation but not the attendance equation. The arguments of $\delta Q/\delta x$ are price, team quality and the exogenous variables in the attendance equation. Hence, the marginal quality cost of attendance is endogenous in the price equation and so cannot be used as an exogenous instrument for price. Moreover, any exogenous variable that affects the marginal productivity of talent appears in both the demand and supply equations and so does not satisfy the order condition for identification.

The sad news from the preceding analysis is that one cannot adopt a normal identification strategy of using cost as an instrument for price. Neither marginal cost nor any instrument for marginal cost can be regarded as a unique exogenous variable in the first-stage price regression.

The Opportunity Cost of Lower Attendance

The second explanation for a coefficient on price that is not sufficiently negative is that the firm's profit maximization problem is not accurately characterized in the preceding analysis (Heilmann and Wendling, 1976; Coates and Humphreys, 2007; Krautman and Berri, 2007). Net revenue from attendance exceeds ticket sales because teams also profit from non-ticket game-day revenue sources, such as concessions, in-stadium advertising, and, in many cases, parking, all of which are related to the number of fans who attend the event. These other revenues create an opportunity cost for a decision to exclude more fans by raising ticket prices, in which case this opportunity cost is a candidate for explaining price and identifying demand.

A variant of the profit function from Heilmann and Wendling (1976) is the following:

$$\pi = PQ(P) + R(Q(P)) - mQ,$$

where $R(Q(P))$ is the net revenue accruing to the team from sources other than ticket sales that depend on attendance. The first-order condition for this profit function then is the following:

$$P = m - Q/Q' - R',$$ (7.5)

which can be rearranged to become:

$$(P - m)/P = 1/|e| - R'/P.$$ (7.6)

Thus, the profit-maximizing Lerner Index is less than the inverse of the elasticity of demand, with the difference being the ratio of the marginal revenue from other sources to the price of a ticket. If the marginal cost of attendance (m) is zero, expression (7.6) implies the following:

$$|e| = P/(P + R').$$ (7.7)

The relative importance of non-ticket revenues and ticket sales in the profit equation differs among sports, so expression (7.7) implies that the equilibrium price elasticity of demand also should vary among sports. For example, if non-ticket game-day revenues are a small fraction of ticket prices (for example, the National Basketball Association in the US), $|e|$ should be close to unity. If non-ticket revenues are at least as important as ticket sales (for example, the lowest classifications of American minor league baseball), the value of $|e|$ should not exceed 0.5. Thus, the plausibility of this explanation for finding that demand is inelastic depends on the sport, but could explain an elasticity of demand substantially less than unity for a sport in which non-ticket game-day profits are comparable in importance to revenues from ticket sales.

Expression (7.5) also has implications for identification. If teams exhibit little or no variation in m, they still might exhibit variation in marginal non-ticket revenues, R'. If so, expression (7.5) suggests that a measure of the marginal profitability of non-ticket game-day revenues might be used as an instrument for price. A possible measure of the marginal profitability of non-ticket revenue sources is average non-ticket revenue, which works as an instrument if the profitability of these products exhibits constant returns to scale in attendance.

Unfortunately, non-ticket game-day revenue is not likely to be a valid identifier. Revenue from these sources is endogenous because teams decide the variety and prices of these products. Nevertheless, teams often sign long-term contracts with other firms to provide these products, in which case these revenues are exogenous in the short run. But even if this variable is exogenous, attendance plausibly could be affected by the variety and prices of these products (Coates and Humphreys, 2007). If so, non-ticket average revenue cannot be used as an instrument for price to identify demand because it appears in both equations.

The Dubious Test for Profit Maximization

As the orginal perpetrator of using estimates of the price elasticity of demand as a 'test' for profit maximization, I confess that this test is not valid. The reason that this test is erroneous sheds interesting light on specification of attendance demand.

Consider a simple alternative to profit maximization, which is that teams maximize on-field victories subject to a budget constraint. If so a firm has the following objective function:

$$W = F(x)$$

where W is wins and F is a function that maps team quality, x, into victories. The maximization of wins is subject to the budget constraint:

$$K + PQ(P,x) > mQ(P,x) + wx,$$

where K is the owner's cash contribution to operations and all other terms have the same definitions as in the preceding analysis. The owner's optimization problem is to maximize:

$$W = F(x) - \lambda(K + PQ(P,x) - mQ(P,x) - wx), \qquad (7.8)$$

where λ is the Lagrange multiplier. Except for K, the term inside the Lagrange multiplier in expression (7.8) is the profit function when team quality is a choice variable for the firm. Because K is a constant and x does not depend on price, the first-order condition for maximizing expression (7.8) is identical to the first-order condition for price in the simple profit-maximization model, which is expression (7.1). Hence, the equilibrium price elasticity of demand in the win-maximization model is that same as in the profit-maximization model. Thus, the finding that demand is inelastic rejects the win-maximization model.

The price-elasticity test also is doubtful as a test of the validity of a model of a sports enterprise as maximizing the utility of the owners. As originally proposed by Sloane (1971, p. 136) owner utility is a function of attendance, team quality, profits and league viability. The last depends on the quality of the team and the subsidy a team gives to other members, which in turn is depends on team quality. Hence league viability is taken into account in the functional relationship between team quality and utility. The implied objective function is then:

$$U(\pi, x, Q) = U(PQ(P \cdot x) - mQ(P,x) - wx, x, Q(P,x)). \qquad (7.9)$$

If profits and wins were the only arguments in the utility function, the equilibrium price elasticity would not differ among utility maximization, win maximization and profit maximization models. In finding the maximum of expression 7.9, the first-order condition for price is that the marginal utility of profit multiplied by the marginal profit of a price change equals zero. Because the marginal utility of profit always is positive, the marginal profit of a price change must be zero, which is the same first-order condition for price as in the other models. But if attendance is a separate argument of the utility function, the first-order condition for price contains another additive term: the product of the marginal utility of attendance and the marginal effect of price on attendance. The new equation that is the counterpart to expression (7.1) is then as follows:

$$P = m - Q/Q' - U_Q/U_\pi, \qquad (7.10)$$

where U_Q/U_π is the marginal utility of attendance divided by the marginal utility of profit. Because the marginal utilities of attendance and profit are both positive, expression (7.10) implies that the equilibrium price elasticity of demand is lower than in the other models. If $m = 0$, the price elasticity of demand is given by:

$$|e| = 1/(1 + U_Q/U_\pi) < 1.$$

The equilibrium price elasticity that is derived from Sloane's model is similar to the result from the model that includes attendance-related revenues other than ticket sales. Thus, whether the demand for tickets is inelastic is actually a test of whether attendance contributes value beyond revenues from ticket sales, regardless of whether this added value comes from profit or owner utility. Because attendance can add value to either utility or profit from other sources, the presence of inelastic demand for tickets is a test of whether attendance creates value beyond ticket sales and not of the motivation of owners.

SUPPLY OF HOMOGENEOUS SEATS

An important complication in estimating the demand for sports is that the product being supplied – a seat at a sporting event – is not a homogeneous product. That is, a fan's enjoyment of the event depends on seat location, which causes suppliers to price tickets on the basis of seat quality. The analysis in this section ignores heterogeneity in seats for the purpose of developing a baseline model of supply and demand that transparently

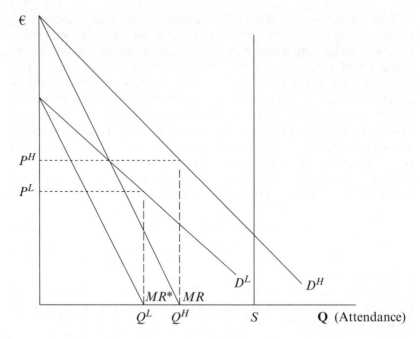

Figure 7.1   Price and attendance with high stadium capacity

illustrates the endogeneity problem and the implications of sellouts. The next section relaxes this assumption.

The point of this section is illustrated in Figures 7.1 and 7.2. In these figures the vertical axis is a value measure (here euros) and the horizontal axis is a quantity measure (here attendance).

Figure 7.1 depicts supply and demand conditions for two teams, one of which faces high demand, D^H, and the other faces low demand, D^L. These demand relationships can be interpreted as pertaining to teams in large and small markets, respectively. Figure 7.1 also shows the stadium capacity for both teams, S, which exceeds the equilibrium demand for both teams. Price and quantity are written as P^i and Q^i, respectively, with i indexing demand ($i = L,H$). The equilibrium price and quantity is determined by the point at which marginal revenue equals marginal cost. As is standard in the literature on attendance demand, marginal cost is assumed to be zero. Equilibrium prices are P^L and P^H and equilibrium values for attendance Q^L and Q^H.

Figure 7.1 shows that when stadium capacity exceeds equilibrium attendance for all teams and all teams have the same marginal cost, price and quantity both will be increasing as the demand curve shifts outward.

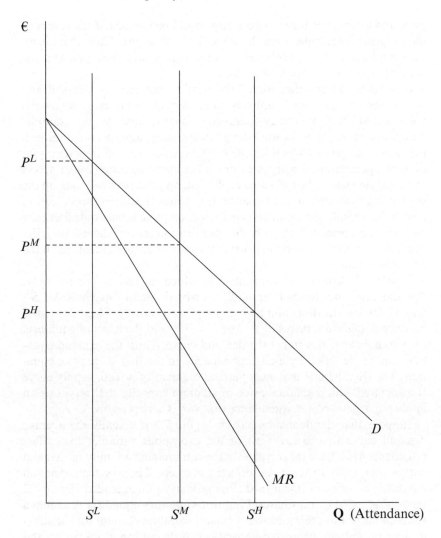

Figure 7.2 Price and attendance with varying stadium capacity

In Figure 7.1, $P^L < P^H$ and $Q^L < Q^H$. Thus, if attendance is regressed on price, the coefficient will be positive. In principle the exogenous independent variables that affect attendance can account perfectly for the difference between D^L and D^H. That is, if the differences between the two teams in all non-price variables were fully taken into account, the underlying demand relationships for both teams would be identical. Because both teams have the same marginal cost of attendance (here zero), the equilibrium price and attendance for the two teams would be identical if the values of the exogenous variables were the same for both teams. Thus, there is no variance in price to be explained by other exogenous variables, and the demand equation cannot be identified.

In practice the specification of the relationship between demand and the exogenous variables is unlikely to be perfect. Some exogenous variables that affect demand may be missing from the equation (for example, a measure of variation in the interest in the sport among communities). For some exogenous variables their instruments may be imperfect (for example, population density is an imperfect instrument for ease of access to the playing site). The estimated coefficient on price then will soak up the unexplained variance in the equation that arises from these specification errors. As a result, the estimated coefficient on price is biased. Indeed, the coefficient on price reflects only the specification error if there is no independent source of variation in price that can be used as an identifier in the price regression.

Figure 7.2 depicts a circumstance in which all teams face the same demand curve, but teams have stadiums with different capacities, S^L, S^M and S^H for low, medium and high capacity, respectively. These capacities produce equilibrium prices of $P^L > P^M > P^H$, and the locus of equilibria for varying capacities traces the demand curve. Thus, the demand equation can be identified by including capacity in the first-stage price equation. The trick here is that each vertical segment of a team supply curve is associated with a shadow price of stadium capacity that serves as an implicit marginal cost of attendance that varies across teams.

Suppose that the demand curve in Figure 7.2 is actually the average demand curve that arises if all of the exogenous variables that affect attendance take their mean values. One can imagine a family of demand curves that apply to teams in different markets. The true team demand curves are a series of downward sloping lines in an amended Figure 7.2 (as in Figure 7.1), and the resulting price/quantity equilibria resemble a shotgun blast. But the exogenous demand variables account for the shifts in demand among teams and capacity then determines price, so a valid two-stage least squares estimate is possible.

A potential problem with using capacity to identify the demand equation is that capacity may be an endogenous variable that is selected on the basis of demand. Surely when sports facilities are constructed, the underlying popularity of the sports that will use the facility enters into the decision about capacity. The potential salvation for capacity as an exogenous identifier is that sports facilities have a long useful life, implying that capacity is exogenous for nearly all teams in nearly all years. But stadium capacity still is likely to bear some relationship to attendance because the variables that determine the popularity of a sport are likely to be correlated through time.

The crucial issue for identification is whether shocks to demand after a facility is built are correlated with capacity. Capacity can be used to trace changes in price along the demand curve, and hence in the first-stage price equation, only if capacity is uncorrelated with shifts in demand through time.

A test for whether capacity can identify the demand is to regress capacity on the current values of the exogenous variables that appear in the demand equation. If the fit is good, then capacity is a weak identifier and cannot be expected to allow an unbiased estimate of the coefficient on price in the attendance equation (Wooldridge, 2001). A poor fit implies that capacity is mainly exogenous to demand, but it still can be a weak identifier. For example, in leagues such as the NFL in which capacity does not exhibit much variation among teams, the fact that capacity passes a test for endogeneity is likely to be small comfort because its variance is too small to provide much explanatory power for price.[9]

A similar set of observations applies to the common use of lagged price as an exogenous instrument for current price. The relevant statistical concept for identification is not whether the current values of the other exogenous values possibly could cause historical prices, but whether mathematically historical prices can be approximated by a linear combination of the current values of these variables. If the fit of a regression of lagged prices on current values of exogenous variables is good, lagged prices are a weak identifier. If the fit is poor but a substantial amount of the variation in current prices is explained by lagged prices, the latter may be a valid instrument for the former, but such a result raises the question about why this correlation exists. Because in any period price is not really exogenous, the cause of an intertemporal correlation of price is almost certainly due to an omitted exogenous variable that enters either the cost function or the demand function. In this case, lagged price actually is an instrument for this variable. Without further information about the identity of the omitted variable and the mechanism through which it affects price, one cannot tell whether incorporating it into the price equation identifies the demand equation.

SUPPLY FROM A MULTI-PRODUCT FIRM

The previous analysis departs from reality because sports facilities have seats of varying quality. A ticket to a sports events is not a homogeneous product, but tickets for seats of differing quality are separate products that are imperfect substitutes. This section explores the decision by a profit-maximizing sports team about how to price seats of varying quality, given that lower prices for lower quality seats can 'cannabilize' sales of better seats at higher prices.

To simplify for clarity, assume that a team has a fixed supply of good seats, S_G, and bad seats, S_B. This section ignores the issues of the endogeneity of team quality and the presence of attendance-related revenue other than ticket sales. The results that arise from generalizing the model to follow parallel the results for the case of homogeneous seats. Hence, here we assume that the team maximizes profits subject to the constraints that sales of both types of tickets cannot exceed the respective capacities:

$$\pi = P_G Q_G(P_G, P_B) + P_B Q_B(P_B, P_G) - m(Q_G - Q_B) - \lambda_G(Q_G - S_G) - \lambda_B(Q_B - S_B), \tag{7.11}$$

where the variables are as defined above except that the subscripts, G and B, refer to good and bad seats. The assumption that the marginal cost of attendance is equal for good and bad seats simplifies the results and is no great sacrifice of reality if the marginal costs of both types of attendance are near zero.

The first-order conditions for expression (7.11), rearranged to form the Lerner Index, are:

$$(P_G - m)/P_G = (1/|e_G|) - (P_B/P_G)(\delta Q_B/\delta P_G) + \lambda_G \tag{7.12}$$

$$(P_B - m)/P_B = (1/|e_B|) - (P_G/P_B)(\delta Q_G/\delta P_B) + \lambda_B. \tag{7.13}$$

If the two types of seats are substitutes, then the terms involving the cross-elasticity of demand are positive. Suppose first that the capacities constraints are not binding, in which case λ_B and λ_G are zero. The prices that would satisfy expressions (7.12) and (7.13) if the cross-elasticity terms were zero exceed the equilibrium prices because of the effects of the second terms on the right-hand side of the equations. The intuition here is that if a team is given the opportunity to sell bad seats it will do so, even if offering those seats cannibalizes some sales of good seats.

If the capacity constraints are binding, the shadow price of a seat is positive. The prices that would satisfy (7.12) and (7.13) if capacities were not binding would be too low, which means that the prices under binding capacity constraints are higher than the equilibrium prices without constraints. The shadow price of each type of capacity is the implicit marginal capacity cost that would make existing prices profit maximizing. If these capacities also are exogenous, then when used as an instrument for prices they identify the demand equations. Thus, if a team sells out most of the time, the capacities associated with each distinct ticket price are plausible candidates for exogenous variables to identify the demand equation.

Unfortunately, at least some of these capacities are almost certain to be weak identifiers, even if the total capacity of facilities varies among teams in a league. The reason is that, for the most part, variation in capacity is likely to be concentrated in the lowest quality seats. That is, the quality of seats is determined by the position and distance of the seat in relation to the playing area. Obviously, physics, not economics, determines the number of front-row seats, so teams are not likely to exhibit much variability in the number of top quality seats that they offer. As a result, regressing price on capacity is not likely to produce a useful instrument that identifies the demand equation for better seats.

Attendance demand studies frequently deal with the heterogeneity of seats by constructing an average price over all types of seats. In the above model, an illustration would be to construct the average price, $P_A = (P_G S_G + P_B S_B)/(S_G + S_B)$. In some cases, total capacity is then used as an exogenous variable to explain average price in a first-stage regression, the fitted values from which are then used as the instrument for price in the second-stage regression. This procedure cannot possibly identify demand if capacity is not binding because capacity is not an instrument for any price variable.

If capacity is binding, the effects of using capacity as an instrument for price require taking into account the true structure of the supply and demand relationship for the team as a multi-product firm (two types of seats). That is, the true structural model has two separate demand and supply equations. The estimated supply and demand equations are then sums of the two true equations. The actual sum of the true demand equations is:

$$Q_G + Q_B = a + b_G P_G + b_B P_B + \mathbf{c}\mathbf{Z}, \qquad (7.14)$$

where scalers a, b_G and b_B and vector $\mathbf{c}$ are parameters to be estimated and $\mathbf{Z}$ is a vector of exogenous variables. One can imagine two approaches to using capacity to identify the prices in this regression.

One approach is to undertake separate first-stage regressions on the two prices, with the capacities for the two types of seats exogenous variables that do not appear in the demand equation. Two problems arise from using this approach. The first is that the estimated coefficients on prices in expression (7.14) combine two effects: the effect of a price for a given seat quality on demand for that quality of seat (a measure of own elasticity) and the effect of the price for one quality of seat on demand for the other quality (a measure of cross-elasticity). The second is that for good seats the identifier is weak because of lack of variation across teams, in which case the equation is not really identified.

The other approach is to use average price as a single price variable and to estimate a first-stage regression of price on total capacity and the other exogenous variables. The actual estimating equation is then:

$$Q_G + Q_B = a + b(P_G S_G + P_B S_B)/(S_G + S_B) + \mathbf{c}\mathbf{Z} \qquad (7.15)$$

This procedure amounts to imposing another restriction on the price coefficients, b_G and b_B, that they each are equal to b multiplied by the share of seats at the associated quality. The resulting estimated value of b is even less meaningful than the estimates of separate coefficients in expression (7.14). The restrictions have no basis in economics, and hence yield poor estimates of the underlying coefficients in (7.14). Moreover, by imposing this restriction, the presence of a weak instrument for P_C is allowed to infect the estimated hybrid coefficient on P_B.

The take-home message of this analysis is that the use of average ticket prices, even when the averages are based on capacities instead of sales, is not a valid procedure. The best that one can do is to match each ticket price to the number of seats at that capacity and then, for the subset of prices for which its seat capacity is not a weak instrument, include only fitted values of those prices in the demand equation.

CONCLUSIONS

The preceding analysis supports fairly gloomy conclusions. The first conclusion is that identifying an attendance demand equation by finding a good instrument for price is not likely to succeed. Second, the only plausible instrument is capacity, and this is likely to work only for bad seats when teams have mostly sellouts and when capacity exhibits substantial variation among teams in a league. Third, demand models ought to include separate equations for each quality of seat, and every equation should contain instruments for each price, derived from first-stage regressions of price on all exogenous variables, including all the capacities for each seat quality. Most likely, such an estimation is impossible, in which case the best strategy is to assume that the theory is accurate and to restrict the value of the price coefficient that cannot be reliably estimated. These coefficients should be based on the assumption that the own price elasticity of demand is one adjusted downward for the proportion of revenues from attendance-related sources other than ticket sales.

NOTES

1. For a parsimonious explanation of the endogeneity problem in the public domain, see Daniel McFadden, *Lecture Notes*, ch. 6, at http://elsa.berkeley.edu/users/mcfadden/e240b_f01/e240b.html (accessed 14 October 2011).
2. If an equation has $N > 1$ endogenous right-hand side variables, a sufficient (rank) condition for identifying the equation is that N (or more) exogenous variables have zero coefficients in the equation to be estimated and that set of coefficients on these variables in the other equations are linearly independent.
3. Another common independent variable in demand equations is income, but income plausibly has a non-zero coefficient in the supply equation because it may be related to the salaries of employees and hence marginal cost. If so, income does not identify either equation.
4. For surveys of the demand for team sports, see Borland and MacDonald (2003), Cairns et al. (1985), Fort (2006) and García Villar and Rodríguez Guerrero (2009).
5. As discussed more fully elsewhere in this chapter, the competing explanations for the finding that demand is price inelastic are: (1) teams do not maximize profits; (2) other revenues, such as concessions and parking, are increased by attendance so that the profitability of the marginal ticket exceeds the ticket price; (3) travel costs to attend games reduce the elasticity of demand for tickets; and (4) larger stadiums have lower average ticket prices, all else equal, because they have more bad seats, which leads to a downward bias in the estimated effect of lower prices on attendance in a model that does not account for seat quality.
6. I am as guilty as anyone of ignoring this problem and offering alibis – see Noll (1974).
7. Other econometric issues that must be taken into account in estimating attendance demand are not discussed here unless they factor in to dealing with the endogeneity problem. One is proper measurement of key variables, such as price (given that teams offer different seat locations at different prices) and competitive balance (for which the relevant variable is the measure of relative team quality that enters the utility functions of fans). Another is the functional form of the demand and supply relationships. Still another is heteroskedasticity, which is likely to arise from population differences and differences in the sample variance of exogenous variables among localities. A common tool for dealing with this problem is to use the generalized method of moments (GMM) to produce more efficient estimates of the coefficients (Wooldridge, 2001).
8. A fourth explanation for inelastic demand is that ticket prices do not equal the full cost of attendance, which also includes travel costs (Noll, 1974; see Forrest, 2012, for a survey of studies of the effect of travel cost on sports demand). If attendance demand is a function of total costs of attendance, then a change of z percent in ticket price will lead to less than a z percent change in total costs, which means that at any given ticket price the demand for tickets is less elastic than it would be if travel costs were zero. Thus, teams face a demand curve that is less elastic at each price. Assuming a marginal cost of attendance, the profit-maximizing ticket price still occurs at the unit elasticity point of the residual demand for tickets, but the equilibrium price will be higher (and attendance lower) than would be the case if travel costs were zero. Hence, travel costs do not explain inelastic demand at the equilibrium price.
9. Coates and Humphreys (2007) find that in analyzing NFL attendance, using capacity in the first-stage price regression yields coefficients on both price and the total cost of attending a game that have the wrong sign. Two possible explanations for this result are that capacity is a weak identifier or that variation in capacity among teams actually is an instrument for an omitted variable or other specification error in the demand equation.

REFERENCES

Berri, David J., Martin B. Schmidt and Stacey L. Brook (2004), 'Stars at the gate: the impact of star power on NBA gate revenues', *Journal of Sports Economics*, **5** (1), 33–50.

Borland, Jeffrey and Robert MacDonald (2003), 'Demand for sport', *Oxford Journal of Economic Policy*, **19** (4), 478–502.

Cairns, John A., Nicholas Jennett and Peter J. Sloane (1985), 'The economics of professional team sports: a survey of theory and evidence', *Journal of Economic Studies*, **13** (1), 3–80.

Coates, Dennis and Brad R. Humphreys (2007), 'Ticket prices, concessions and attendance at professional sporting events', *International Journal of Sport Finance*, **2** (3), 161–70.

Demmert, Henry (1973), *The Economics of Professional Sports*, Lexington, MA: Lexington Books.

Forrest, David (2012), 'Travel and population issues in modelling attendance demand', in Stephen Schmanske and Leo H. Kahane (eds), *The Oxford Handbook of Sports Economics*, vol. 2, New York: Oxford University Press, pp. 175–89.

Fort, Rodney (2004), 'Inelastic sports pricing', *Managerial and Decision Economics*, **25** (2), 87–94.

Fort, Rodney (2006), 'Inelastic sports pricing at the gate? A survey', in Wladimir Andreff and Stefan Szymanski (eds), *Handbook on the Economics of Sport*, Cheltenham, UK and Northampton, MA, USA: Edward Elgar Publishing, pp. 700–708.

García, Jaume and Plácido Rodríguez (2002), 'The determinants of football match attendance', *Journal of Sports Economics*, **3** (1), 18–38.

García Villar, Jaume and Plácido Rodríguez Guerrero (2009), 'Sports attendance: a survey of the literature 1973–2007', *Revista di Diritto Ed Economia dello Sport*, **5** (2), 111–51.

Heilmann, Ronald L. and Wayne R. Wendling (1976), 'A note on optimum pricing strategies for sports events', in Robert Engel Machol and Shaul P. Ladany (eds), *Management Science in Sports*, New York: North Holland, pp. 91–100.

Jones, J.C.H. and D.G. Ferguson (1988), 'Location and survival in the National Hockey League', *Journal of Industrial Economics*, **36** (4), 443–57.

Kennedy, Peter (2007), *A Guide to Econometrics*, Malden, MA: Blackwell.

Krautman, Anthony C. and David J. Berri (2007), 'Can we find it in the concessions? Understanding price elasticity in professional sports', *Journal of Sports Economics* **8** (2), 183–91.

Noll, Roger G. (1974), 'Attendance and price setting', in Roger G. Noll (ed.), *Government and the Sports Business*, Washington, DC: Brookings Institution, pp. 115–58.

Sloane, Peter J. (1971), 'The economics of professional football: the football club as a utility maximizer', *Scottish Journal of Political Economy*, **18** (2), 121–146.

Wooldridge, Jeffrey M. (2001), 'Applications of generalized method of moments estimation', *Journal of Economic Perspectives*, **15** (4), 87–100.

Villa, G., I. Molina and R. Fried (2011), 'Modeling attendance at Spanish professional football leagues', *Journal of Applied Statistics*, **38** (6), 1189–206.

8. Estimation of temporal variations in fan loyalty: application of multi-factor models*

Young Hoon Lee

INTRODUCTION

Sports attendance has been the subject of extensive study in the sports economics literature (Noll, 1974; Siefried and Eisenberg, 1980; Humphreys, 2002; Schmidt and Berri, 2004; Krautmann and Hadley, 2006; Poitras and Hadley, 2006; Ahn and Lee, 2007; Krautmann and Berri, 2007; Lee and Fort, 2008). Many studies have centered on the testing of the uncertainty outcome hypothesis. For example, Lee and Fort (2008) categorized uncertainty of outcomes into game uncertainty, playoff uncertainty and consecutive season uncertainty, and presented empirical evidence that the attendance of fans of Major League Baseball (MLB) is sensitive to changes in playoff uncertainty, but not to other types of uncertainty. Inelastic pricing has also been studied fairly extensively (Fort, 2004; Ahn and Lee, 2007; Krautmann and Berri, 2007). It is expected that sports teams will set their ticket prices in elastic regions, as most sports teams are local monopolistic firms. This is something of a puzzle, as inelastic pricing has been found recursively in a variety of empirical analyses of attendance. Krautmann and Berri (2007) have taken into account the fact that ticket price does not capture the full cost of attending a game. In this view, the ticket-price elasticity of attendance should be low, as teams that set prices higher would suffer revenue losses attributable to parking, concessions and merchandise sales. Ahn and Lee (2007) presented a dynamic profit-maximization model in which inelastic pricing is found to be the optimal strategy for lifetime profit maximization if habit-formation is inherent to game attendance. Additionally, Poitras and Hadley (2006) developed a model that explains the stadium effect on team revenue over the life of the stadium, and determine that newly constructed stadiums can generate additional revenues sufficient to pay the construction cost.

Consumer preference appears to play a substantial role in attendance decisions. Fan loyalty appears to be an obvious characteristic of consumer preference and fan demand. Even some teams that never make it to the post-season appear to have steady attendance. Sellouts often occur even when a good team hits hard times, and seem especially relevant in the context of international competition, despite the quality of the 'home' team. Finally, sellouts seem quite common even for weaker teams in some leagues, such as the National Football League and National Hockey League in the United States. The case of Korean sports offers an especially interesting puzzle from the loyalty perspective. Korean national teams (particularly soccer) have many strongly loyal fans, but individual professional teams do not. This difference clearly contributes to the financial picture of Korean pro teams.

In the marketing literature, brand loyalty has been studied extensively (Tucker, 1964; Dick and Basu, 1994; Chaudhuri and Holbrook, 2001). Brand loyalty is defined as repeated consumption under stress changes by rival goods. Previous studies into this subject have focused on analyses of individual consumers. Tucker has suggested that some consumers become brand loyal, even when there is no substantial difference between brands other than the brand itself, according to the results of his experiment. This topic has also been the subject of extensive study in the field of sports management (Wakefield and Sloan, 1995; Bristow and Sebastian, 2001; Gladden and Funk, 2002; Bauer et al., 2008). Bristow and Sebastian (2001) analyzed individual fans' behavior by surveying fans of the Chicago Cubs. They determined that fans who attended Cubs games frequently in childhood were more likely to become loyal fans. Bauer et al. (2008) developed a model to measure brand image in the sport industry, and evaluated the relationship between brand image and fan loyalty. They presented empirical evidence to suggest that a team's brand image plays a significant role in fostering loyal fan behavior and that the non-product-related brand attributes (team history, logo and stadium) have stronger effects than the product-related attributes (coach, star player and team play).

However, fan loyalty remains a relatively untouched topic in the literature of sports economics. Only a handful of studies have assessed fan loyalty in the context of attendance demand (Depken, 2000, 2001; Ahn and Lee, 2007; Lee and Smith, 2008). Depken (2000, 2001) estimated fan loyalty for sports teams and evaluated its effects on public-funding decisions by citizens or relocation decisions by team owners. Depken (2000) estimated the attendance demand equation of the MLB teams via the application of the stochastic production frontier model of Aigner et al. (1977). He identified fan loyalty as a significant factor in explaining the outcome of stadium referenda. Depken (2001) also estimated fan loyalty for National Football League teams, and determined that a low level of fan loyalty is a motivating factor in the owner's decision to relocate his franchise to a new host city. Unlike extant studies in the sports management literature, which generally collect survey data to measure individual levels of fan loyalty, Depken attempted to estimate team levels of fan loyalty by controlling all variables that affect attendance. His empirical studies were limited in that they assumed that fan loyalty has a specific truncated distribution and in that only cross-sectional comparison of loyalty was conducted; additionally, Depken's study did not assess loyalty over time.

The measurement of fan loyalty is crucial to the study of loyalty comparisons across teams and/or determinants of loyalty. The principal objective of this study was to improve the coarse measurement of loyalty by applying advanced econometric models to the loyalty estimation. First, we make no distributional assumptions of fan loyalty, such as in Depken's study (2000, 2001). Second, we retrieve the restriction of time-invariant fan loyalty. It is unlikely that the level of fan loyalty for a team remains constant over time. For example, the Chicago Cubs have frequently been recognized as a team with fiercely loyal fans, but it is not clear that this was the case in the 1960s. This chapter intends to estimate not only the fan loyalty differences between different teams, but also temporal variations in fan loyalty. Econometric models that can be applied for this purpose include the multi-factorial models that have been well established in the field of finance (Bai, 2003, 2009; Bai and Ng, 2002; Ahn et al., 2007). The multi-factor model that has been frequently applied in the finance literature is adopted for the sake of this objective. We assume that fan loyalty consists of several common factors with interactions between individually different loadings.

ECONOMETRIC MODEL

Depken (2000) used a panel dataset consisting of the MLB teams (26 teams over 1990–96) and set the attendance regression equation as

$$y_i = X_i\beta + \varepsilon_i \tag{8.1}$$

in which y is attendance and X represents various factors influencing attendance. As Depken applied a stochastic frontier model, ε_i is a composite error term of statistical noise and a term representing fan loyalty. The fan loyalty term is assumed to have a specific distribution truncated at zero and normal distribution is also assumed for the statistical noise term. Therefore, the estimates of attendance equation are obtained via the maximum likelihood method. Even though a panel data sample is utilized, only the estimated average fan loyalty is reported. For this purpose, the traditional panel data model with individual effects might also prove useful:

$$y_{it} = X_{it}\beta + \alpha_i + \varepsilon_{it} \tag{8.2}$$

in which the individual effects term, α_i represents the average fan loyalty for team i and ε_{it} is an idiosyncratic error.

Stochastic frontier models are designed for the estimation of technical efficiency. Thus, the regression equation is either a production function or cost function, and the inefficiency term is positive since it represents the gap between the production (cost) frontier and the actual output (cost). Attendance equation is neither a production function nor a cost function. Therefore, the assumption that fan loyalty has a specific truncated distribution is not necessary. This chapter intends to assess the temporal fluctuations in fan loyalty for individual teams without any distributional assumption. Then, the attendance regression specification becomes:

$$y_{it} = X_{it}\beta + \alpha_{it} + \varepsilon_{it} \tag{8.3}$$

Now, α_{it} changes across different teams as well as over seasons. One way to estimate the attendance equation and α_{it} is to apply multiple factor models. More specifically, the models are panel data models with multiple time-varying individual effects, as follows:

$$y_{it} = x'_{it}\beta + \lambda'_i\theta_t + \varepsilon_{it} = x'_{it}\beta + \sum_{j=1}^{p}\theta_{tj}\lambda_{ij} + \varepsilon_{it} \tag{8.4}$$

Here $i = 1,\ldots, N$, $t = 1,\ldots,T$, and N and T are the numbers of cross-sectional and time-series observations, respectively. α_{it} has a factor structure. λ_i is a $p \times 1$ vector of factor loadings and θ_t is a $p \times 1$ vector of common factors such that $\lambda'_i\theta_t = \theta_{t1}\lambda_{i1} + \ldots + \theta_{tp}\lambda_{ip}$. The unobservable common factors affect everyone, but because the factor loadings λ_{ij} vary over cross-sectional units, they do not affect everyone equally. The p is the number of factors that will be estimated.

Extensive studies have been conducted into this type of econometric model (Lee, 1991; Lee and Schmidt, 1993; Ahn et al., 2001, 2007; Bai 2003, 2009). Lee and Schmidt (1993) considered a single-factor model ($p = 1$) and suggested a consistent estimator of the concentrated least square. Ahn et al. (2001) also considered a single-factor model, but suggested more efficient estimation by the generalized method of moments. Ahn et al. (2007) presented a stochastic frontier model, the efficiency term of which has a multiple factor structure; they proposed a sequential test to estimate a true number of factors. Their estimation is restricted to cases in which N is large and T is small (so asymptotic analyses are as $N \to \infty$ with T fixed). Lee (1991) considered the multiple factor model with a large N and a small T, and suggested the concentrated least squared estimator under some restrictions: specifically, that a number of factors are known and a error term is identically independently distributed. On the other hand, Bai (2003, 2009) considered the case in which both N and T are large. The proposed estimation method is conceptually the same as the concentrated least squares elucidated by Lee (1991) and Lee and Schmidt (1993). The estimator of β is obtained by the least squared method on the weighted mean difference equation, and the estimation of θ_p can be obtained by the eigenvalue problem. He also suggested information criteria to determine the number of factors, along with the simulation results.

In this empirical study, the MLB sample includes 30 teams, but we use only 23 teams in order to keep the panel dataset balanced. The time span of our study begins in the 1975 season and ends in 2009. This may introduce a small sample issue. As our sample has more time-series observations than cross-sectional observations, it is not legitimate to apply the method of Ahn et al. (2007) which considers the case in which N is large and T is small. Rather, we apply Bai's (2009) method to this MLB panel dataset, although the small sample problem persists.

Bai (2009) proposed the least square objective function and the least square estimators of β and θ are as follows:

$$SSE(\beta, \theta, \lambda) = \sum_{i=1}^{N} (y_i - x_i \beta + \lambda_i' \theta)' (y_i - x_i \beta + \lambda_i' \theta). \qquad (8.5)$$

$$\hat{\beta} = \sum_{i=1}^{N} (x_i' M x_i)^{-1} \sum_{i=1}^{N} (x_i' M y_i), \quad M = I_T - \theta \theta' / T \qquad (8.6)$$

$$\hat{\theta} = \text{the eigenvectors of } \sum_{i=1}^{N} (y_i - x_i \hat{\beta})(y_i - x_i \hat{\beta})'$$

corresponding to the p largest eigenvalues. $\qquad (8.7)$

Since the solutions of (8.6) and (8.7) are not closed form, $(\hat{\beta}, \hat{\theta})$ are obtained via iteration. For the selection of the number of factors, Bai proposed two different information criteria which lead to a consistent estimator:

$$CP(p) = \hat{\sigma}^2(p) + \hat{\sigma}^2(\bar{p})\,[p\,(N+T) - p^2]\frac{\ln NT}{NT} \qquad (8.8)$$

$$IC(p) = \ln\hat{\sigma}^2(p) + [p(N+T) - p^2]\frac{\ln NT}{NT} \qquad (8.9)$$

in which p is the number of factors and $\bar{p}$ is the maximum number of factors.

The assumptions made by Bai (2009) rule out time-invariant regressors and constant terms, but allow for serial and cross-section weak dependence of the idiosyncratic error term, as well as its heteroskedasticity. The inclusion of factors in excess of the true number of factors does not hurt the consistency of $\hat{\beta}$, but does degrade its efficiency. On the other hand, underestimation of p will cause $\hat{\beta}$ to become inconsistent if omitted factors are correlated to regressors.

The regression analysis of attendance is based on equation (8.4). The dependent variable is the logged attendance per game ($\ln APG$). The regressors represent ticket price, winning performance, playoff uncertainty, stadium factor, income, population and macro shocks attributable to labor strikes. First, we include winning performance both in the current season and in the previous season. The inclusion of past performance takes into consideration the fact that a large portion of purchased tickets are season tickets. The purchasing decision of season tickets is based on the expectation of winning performance in the upcoming season. This expectation is dependent upon the winning performance in the previous season that just ended. Therefore, we add a win percentage of the previous season ($WPCT_{t-1}$) and a dummy variable (PO_{t-1}), indicating whether a home team advanced to the playoffs in season $t-1$. Lee (2009) presented empirical evidence suggesting that the playoff uncertainty among three different types of uncertainty (game uncertainty, playoff uncertainty and consecutive season uncertainty) is the most significant in terms of its influence on attendance in the MLB. Here, games back behind the division leader (GB) represent playoff uncertainty. Extensive and consistent empirical results of the new stadium effect on attendance have been noted (Poirtras and Hadley, 2006). In this study, we employed $NEWST$ in accordance with the methods of Ahn and Lee (2007) and Poitras and Hadley (2006). $NEWST$ equals 4 in the first year of a new or renovated stadium, 3 in the second year, 2 in the third year and 1 in the fourth year. This four-year reverse trend captures the aging effect.

We consider the market size effect by including population (POP) and a dummy variable for New York, Los Angeles, and Chicago ($BigCity$).

Since the three largest cities all have multiple teams, it is possible that a city population variable does not reflect the actual effect of market size for the cities. In this case, the coefficient of *BigCity* is negative. On the other hand, it may be also possible that the log-linear regression equation does not explain variation in attendance properly in the range of an extremely large population. Per capita personal income is included as a control variable for the income effects. The final variable of the strike dummy (*Strike*) takes into account previous empirical findings showing that strikes have temporary impacts on attendance (Schmidt and Berri, 2004). A strike has a value of one for $t = 1981, 1994, 1995$ and a value of zero for all other years. Therefore, the regression equation (8.4) becomes as follows:

$$\ln APG_{it} = \beta_0 + \beta_1 \ln p_{it} + \beta_2 WPCT_{it} + \beta_3 WPCT_{it-1} + \beta_4 GB_{it} + \beta_5 \ln INC_{it} +$$
$$\beta_6 NEWST_{it} + \beta_7 \ln POP_{it} + \beta_8 BigCity_{it} + \beta_9 PO_{it-1} + \beta_{10} Strike_{it} + \sum_{j=1}^{p} \theta_{tj} \lambda_{ij} + \varepsilon_{it}$$

$$(8.10)$$

DATA AND EMPIRICAL RESULTS

We analyze a panel dataset from Major League Baseball. The MLB dataset consists of 23 teams and a time period from 1975 through 2009. The data for the 1989–90 period was omitted, because ticket price data for the period was not readily available. There are 30 MLB teams, but among them seven teams (Arizona Diamondbacks, Colorado Rockies, Florida Marlins, Seattle Mariners, Tampa Bay Devil Rays, Toronto Blue Jays and Washington Nationals) were excluded from our analysis. As the Bai model is developed for a balanced data panel, teams entering the MLB after 1975 could not be effectively used in the sample dataset. We also dropped Toronto from our study dataset, because fluctuations in the exchange rate between US and Canadian dollars could influence our empirical results if they were included.

Table 8.1 contains the sample means and standard deviations of the primary variables in the dataset. The winning percentage (*WPCT*), attendance per game (*APG*), number of games back behind the leader of a division (*GB*) and ticket prices (*P*) were taken directly from Professor Fort's Sports Business Data Pages. We also obtained from the US Census Bureau the per capita personal income (*INC*) and population (*POP*) of the metropolitan statistical area in which each team is located. The ticket prices and income measures are real terms in 2009 dollar values.

Table 8.2 shows the estimation results of various estimation methods. The first column includes the ordinary least squares (OLS) estimates.

Table 8.1   Descriptive statistics

	Mean	Standard deviation	Maximum	Minimum
Attendance per game: *APG*	25955	9460	53070	3787
Ticket price (in 2009 $): *P*	16.840	7.061	72.970	9.249
Win %: *WPCT*	0.505	0.069	0.704	0.265
Games back: *GB*	13.3	11.4	47.0	0.0
Real income ($1000): *INC*	37.450	78.525	65.054	22.586
Population (1000): *POP*	5576	4660	19070	1385

The signs of the coefficient estimates are as expected except for ticket price; 53.6 percent of variations in attendance can be explained by this regression. The second column shows the within-estimation results when the attendance equation includes individual effects. This is similar to Depken's specification. The within estimation presents a negative estimate of price, but it is statistically insignificant. The strike dummy has negative estimates in both OLS and within estimation while it is insignificant.

Columns 3–5 display the estimation results of the multiple factor models. In this application, we set $\bar{p} = 5$. The first step is to estimate the number of factors. The two different information criteria in equations (8.8) and (8.9) suggest contradictory results. *CP* has a minimum value when $p = 3$, whereas *IC* is minimized when $p = 1$. Bai and Ng (2002) provide extensive simulation results relevant to the determination of factor number. According to their simulation, *CP* and *IC* generally perform better than *AIC* and *BIC*; however, in cases of small sample, *CP* tends to overestimate, whereas *IC* tends to underestimate. In an in-depth analysis of their simulation, we note that *CP* frequently estimates $\hat{p} = \bar{p}$ ($\bar{p} = 8$ in Bai and Ng, 2002) when overestimation occurs. Our results are consistent with those simulation results in that *CP* suggests a larger number of factors than does *IC*. Therefore, it is possible for $\hat{p} = 3$ to be over-parameterization and for $\hat{p} = 1$ to be under-parameterization. However, we choose to estimate the number of factors based on the CP criterion for the following reasons. First, the CP estimate does not hit the maximum number of factors. In these cases in Bai and Ng (2002), the estimates of p are fairly close to the true value of p. Second, the estimation results with $p = 3$ resemble those with $p = 2$ with regard to the sign and magnitude of estimates, as well as their t-values, whereas those with $p = 1$ differ significantly. Considering that the over-parameterization of p does not ruin the consistency of $\hat{\beta}$, whereas under-parameterization may, we can assert that $p = 3$ is more likely close to the true p.

Table 8.2 Attendance equation estimation

Variable	OLS Coeff	OLS t-stat.	Within Coeff	Within t-stat.	Factor model ($p = 1$) Coeff	Factor model ($p = 1$) t-stat.	Factor model ($p = 2$) Coeff	Factor model ($p = 2$) t-stat.	Factor model ($p = 3$) Coeff	Factor model ($p = 3$) t-stat.
$\ln P$	0.262	8.90	-0.043	-1.02	0.048	1.92	-0.067	-2.76	-0.120	-4.06
$WPCT_t$	1.032	5.21	1.157	4.99	1.418	6.79	1.453	8.63	1.602	10.62
$WPCT_{t-i}$	1.144	9.97	1.309	9.75	1.236	10.69	1.202	12.26	1.280	15.94
GB	-0.006	-5.42	-0.006	-4.34	-0.004	-3.01	-0.004	-3.58	-0.003	-3.43
$\ln INC$	0.475	9.19	1.230	13.53	0.881	14.46	0.830	12.31	0.778	12.78
$NEWST$	0.046	5.30	0.061	6.07	0.058	7.53	0.059	9.21	0.043	6.90
$\ln POP$	0.083	8.74	0.141	1.68	0.046	1.07	0.053	1.14	0.073	1.76
$BigCity$					0.037	0.44	0.188	2.35	0.191	2.69
PO_{t-i}	0.055	1.51	0.089	2.10	0.098	2.83	0.143	4.50	0.136	4.83
$Strike$	-0.026	-1.12	-0.013	-0.49	-0.068	-2.57	-0.081	-3.71	-0.076	-4.15
Constant	3.847	6.47								
Sig^2					0.032		0.020		0.014	
R^2	0.536		0.751		0.806		0.875		0.911	

143

The estimated coefficient of ticket price statistically significantly differs from zero; it is negative and has an absolute value of less than one. This finding is consistent with the recurrent inelastic pricing outcome in sports (Fort, 2004; Ahn and Lee, 2007). The next estimate concerns the effect of playing performance on attendance measured by winning percentage. The estimate implies that an increase in one percentage point (for example, an increase from 0.51 to 0.52) draws a 1.6 percent increase in attendance. Since a large portion of total gate tickets are sold before a season begins in the form of season tickets, the expectation of home team performance in the forthcoming season t, given information about season $t - 1$, should necessarily influence attendance. We assume that an adaptive expectation, coupled with winning performance in season $t - 1$, forms the expectation. $WPCT_{t-1}$ has a positive and statistically significant estimate of 1.28. This is slightly less than the estimate of $WPCT_t$. It implies that winning performance in the current season has a slightly more profound impact on attendance than winning performance in the previous season. The postseason dummy (PO_{t-1}) also has positive effects on attendance, as anticipated. The estimate implies that post-season participation boosts attendance in the next season by 19 percent.

The playoff uncertainty measured by games back also turns out to be statistically significant. The estimate implies that a number of 10 games back behind its division winner causes attendance to fall by 3 percent. The significant effect of playoff uncertainty on attendance is also consistent with previous empirical findings (Lee and Fort, 2008; Lee, 2009; Krautmann et al., 2011). In particular, Krautmann et al. (2011) empirically analyze the effect of playoff uncertainty with monthly data, and determine that the real impact occurs at the end of the season.

The next four estimates concern the effects of income, stadium and market size. The income elasticity is estimated to be 0.78 and the newly constructed or renovated stadium significantly boosts attendance. The coefficient estimate implies that the attendance in the first season increases by 17.2 percent and the effect afterward, in the fourth season, becomes 4.3 percent. Population turns out to be significant in determining attendance, and a dummy of *BigCity* also has a positive and significant estimate. The final variable controls for the negative effect of labor strikes. It is statistically insignificant in both OLS and within estimation, but is significant in the multi-factor models. According to the estimate generated thusly, strikes in 1981, 1994 and 1995 decreased attendance per game by an average of 7.6 percent.

Figure 8.1 shows temporal variations in three common factors, representing league-wide common movements of fan loyalty, and thus attendance. These are somewhat akin to macro-shocks in consumption

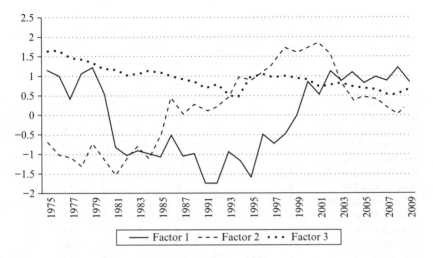

Figure 8.1   Temporal trends in common factors

or investment. The first common factor decreased dramatically in the early 1980s when the labor strike induced a work stoppage and stayed low until the mid-1990s. It bounced back shortly after the labor strike ended in 1996, and has evidenced a minor downhill trend in the 2000s. The second common factor has remained more or less constant in the early period, and increased steadily from the late 1980s to 2000, but declined in the 2000s. The third common factor evidenced the least temporal variation. It declined slightly over the entirety of the sample period. Taking into account temporal variations in all three factors together, MLB had increasing attendance in the 1990s, whereas the trend turned, albeit in a less dramatic manner, in the 2000s. A study of the causes of the temporal changes in common factors would be intriguing, but we will leave this topic for future studies.

Table 8.3 ranks the average fan loyalty estimates over different periods. For the whole sample period (1975–2009), the St Louis Cardinals and Baltimore Orioles are the top two teams in terms of fan loyalty, whereas the Chicago White Sox and Oakland Athletics have the least loyal fans. However, significant variations in fan loyalty have been determined to exist. For example, the Baltimore Orioles are among the teams that have evidenced dynamic changes in fan loyalty. They suffered from a lack of fan support until the early 1980s, but suddenly began to enjoy top levels of fan support beginning in the late 1980s. On the other hand, the New York Mets, San Francisco Giants and Oakland Athletics are teams that have stayed at the bottom of the fan loyalty

Table 8.3   Fan loyalty estimates

Team	1975–79	1980–84	1985–89	1990–94	1995–99	2000–04	2005–09	Total
St Louis Cardinals	6	5	1	2	2	2	3	1
Baltimore Orioles	16	14	2	1	1	1	6	2
LA Dodgers	3	3	3	3	5	10	7	3
Philadelphia Phillies	1	1	4	5	8	14	8	4
Cincinnati Reds	2	4	6	9	11	11	5	5
San Diego Padres	5	9	8	13	6	4	1	6
Kansas City Royals	7	2	5	4	12	16	15	7
Boston Red Sox	9	6	7	8	10	12	12	8
Milwaukee Brewers	8	8	11	15	13	7	4	9
Detroit Tigers	4	10	13	18	15	8	2	10
Texas Rangers	12	13	9	6	3	5	11	11
Atlanta Braves	13	11	10	7	9	15	16	12
Chicago Cubs	15	18	14	11	7	6	13	13
Cleveland Indians	19	22	15	12	4	3	9	14
Houston Astros	10	12	16	19	16	13	10	15
LA Angels	11	7	12	10	17	19	20	16
Pittsburgh Pirates	18	21	18	17	14	9	14	17
New York Mets	17	19	21	22	20	18	17	18
New York Yankees	14	15	19	21	21	20	19	19
Minnesota Twins	22	17	17	14	18	21	22	20
San Francisco Giants	21	23	23	23	19	17	18	21
Chicago White Sox	20	16	22	20	23	22	21	22
Oakland Athletics	23	20	20	16	22	23	23	23

rankings throughout the sample period, even though the Giants accumulated loyal fans from the late 1990s and then, continued to improve their ranking to seventeenth and eighteenth in the 2000s. This may be interpreted as the effect of a superstar. Barry Bonds left the Pittsburgh Pirates and signed a free-agent contract with the Giants in 1993 and enjoyed a brilliant career until he retired in 2007. One of the highlight moments in this regard is the 2001 season, when he hit 73 homeruns by breaking the previous single season homerun record of Mark McGwire. His long tenure as a player on the Giants and consistently excellent performance may have helped to attract and retain loyal fans (Kahane and Shmanske, 1997).

Compared with the estimation results of Depken's study (2000), which estimated fan loyalty during 1990–96 via the maximum likelihood estimation method, our average estimates in 1990–94 were more or less similar to his estimates. The top three teams in terms of fan loyalty in Depken's

(2000) study are the Colorado Rockies, St Louis Cardinals, and Baltimore Orioles. In this empirical study, the Rockies were excluded from the sample, but the Cardinals and Orioles were ranked during 1990–94 as the second and the first, respectively. Conversely, the bottom three teams in Depken's study (2000) were the Pittsburgh Pirates, Chicago White Sox and Detroit Tigers; in this study, they are estimated as ranks 17, 20 and 18, respectively, among 23 teams. A noticeable discrepancy between the two studies is the case of the Cleveland Indians. The Indians are the team with the fourth-highest fan loyalty in Depken's study, while this study ranks them twelfth during the 1990–94 period; however, their rank rises to fourth in 1995–99.

Figure 8.2 displays temporal changes in fan loyalty and attendance per game of the top and bottom three teams. Notably, ranges of fan loyalty were smaller for the top three teams than for the bottom three. In particular, the Dodgers and Cardinals evidenced little variation in this regard over the 1975–2009 period. The bottom three teams have experienced more ups and downs. As discussed above, the Giants were one of the lowest-ranked teams earlier, but increased their loyalty level in the 2000s, even though the Giants continue to rank among the bottom of the fan loyalty rankings. The White Sox evidenced the most dramatic temporal changes in fan loyalty. Their loyalty level increased rapidly until the 1993 season, but suddenly fell down quickly during 1995–96. This implies that a team with lesser fan support is sensitive to macro-shocks, such as the 1994–95 labor strike. Attendance appears to be more stable over time in the top teams than in the bottom teams. These empirical findings are reasonable, since once a team has established great fan loyalty, it tends to remain constant and insensitive to environmental changes. On the other hand, the attendance enjoyed by a team with few loyal fans should be sensitive to environmental changes.

Figure 8.3 addressed the fan loyalty estimates of two teams located in Chicago. The Chicago Cubs are well known for their legendary fan loyalty. Therefore, many studies have addressed its famed fan loyalty and its determinants (Bristow and Sebastian, 2001). However, over the periods being discussed here, there have been no studies conducted addressing temporal patterns of fan loyalty. The sample average ranking of the Cubs is not impressive; it resides in the middle of the ranking list. Its loyalty level was low in 1975, but increased continuously until the 1994 labor strike. Afterward, it stayed constant throughout the 2000s. The contribution to attendance can be measured. The fan loyalty estimates were -0.78 and -0.11 in 1975 and 1994, respectively; attendance per game was 67 percent higher in 1994 because of the increase in fan loyalty. On the other hand, the intra-city rival, the White Sox, experienced ups

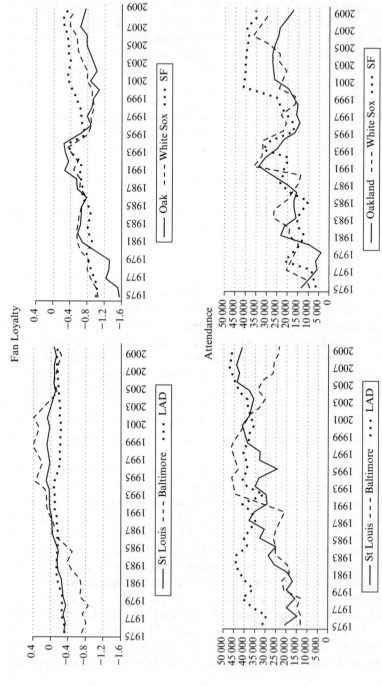

Fan Loyalty

Attendance

Figure 8.2   Temporal trends in fan loyalty and attendance of the top and bottom teams

148

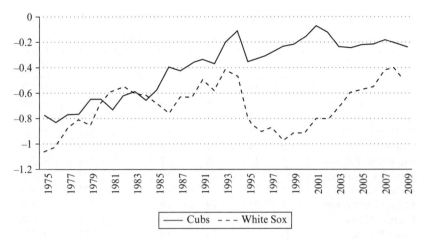

Figure 8.3   Chicago Cubs and White Sox: fan loyalty

and downs in loyalty, but its loyalty ranking remained consistently at the bottom.

The determinants of fan loyalty are quite intriguing, and the study thereof would easily warrant another paper. However, we have conducted a descriptive analysis of the properties of teams with more loyal fans in Table 8.4. The 23 teams are listed by their fan loyalty ranking and their corresponding rankings of population, attendance and win percentage are shown in the next three columns. The final two columns show the correlation coefficient of *APG* and *WPCT* and the coefficient of variation of *APG*. At the bottom, average numbers of various variables are compared for teams with strong loyalty and weak loyalty. The average population ranking of the top three teams with regard to fan loyalty is 10.33, whereas the bottom three teams have an average ranking of 7.67. That is, a smaller market size may help to attract and retain loyal fans. We did not attempt to determine whether or not the difference was statistically significant via a hypothesis test. Since attending a baseball game is time-consuming, other entertainment activities such as watching movies and going to the opera constitute rival goods. Certainly, larger metropolitan cities offer a variety of entertainment, which makes the switching costs low. From this perspective, it can be reasonably conjectured that a team in a larger city find it difficult to enjoy stronger fan support. The attendance ranking between the top and the bottom teams is extremely wide. It implies that fan loyalty is a core determinant of attendance. The fourth column compares the rankings of *WPCT* and shows that the top teams have slightly better winning performance, on

Table 8.4   Descriptive analyses of fan loyalty and the relevant variables

Team	Loyalty	POP	APG	WPCT	Corr of APG and WPCT[1]	CV of APG[2]
St Louis Cardinals	1	13	3	5	0.407	0.278
Baltimore Orioles	2	16	4	13	−0.121	0.363
LA Dodgers	3	2	1	3	0.227	0.114
Philadelphia Phillies	4	5	7	7	0.625	0.242
Cincinnati Reds	5	19	11	8	0.427	0.184
San Diego Padres	6	17	15	23	0.501	0.296
Kansas City Royals	7	20	20	18	0.525	0.276
Boston Red Sox	8	8	4	13	−0.121	0.363
Milwaukee Brewers	9	21	19	19	0.243	0.291
Detroit Tigers	10	6	16	20	0.536	0.276
Texas Rangers	11	7	13	16	0.217	0.325
Atlanta Braves	12	12	10	4	0.855	0.456
Chicago Cubs	13	3	8	21	0.409	0.325
Cleveland Indians	14	18	17	14	0.711	0.528
Houston Astros	15	9	12	6	0.377	0.346
LA Angels	16	2	5	11	0.600	0.269
Pittsburgh Pirates	17	15	23	22	−0.048	0.27
New York Mets	18	1	9	15	0.647	0.395
New York Yankees	19	1	2	1	0.437	0.295
Minnesota Twins	20	14	21	17	0.670	0.400
San Francisco Giants	21	10	14	12	0.493	0.468
Chicago White Sox	22	3	18	9	0.598	0.312
Oakland Athletics	23	10	22	10	0.596	0.374
Average	12	10.087	11.913	12.478	0.427	0.324
Top 3	2	10.333	2.667	7.000	0.171	0.252
Bottom 3	22	7.667	18.000	10.333	0.562	0.385

Notes:
1.   Corr: correlation coefficient.
2.   CV: coefficient of variation.

average, than the bottom teams. This is consistent with the implication of the habitual attending model, in that chronic winning success attracted more attendance in the past and then the current attendance increases via the mechanism of habit-formation. The average correlation coefficient of the top three teams between *APG* and *WPCT* is only 0.17 – fairly close to zero – but it is 0.56 for the bottom three teams. Therefore, attendance is not sensitive to the current winning performance after a team has established loyal fan support. The variation of attendance again is smaller in the top teams than in the bottom teams.

CONCLUDING REMARKS

This study empirically analyzed the attendance of MLB baseball teams with the assessment of temporal variations in fan loyalty. For this purpose, the balanced panel dataset of 23 teams over the period 1975–2009 is assessed using multi-factor models. That is, this study assumes that fan loyalty has a factor structure with common factors and corresponding loadings. This specification allows for the estimation of temporal variations in the fan loyalty of each individual team and does not impose a specific distributional assumption of the fan loyalty variable.

The estimation results show a substantially large disparity of fan loyalty across different teams. Fan loyalty, by its nature, is not supposed to change dramatically over time. The estimates are consistent with this proposition, but there appear to be moderate temporal variations in fan loyalty. It was also found here that fan loyalty is a core factor in determining attendance. There are broad differences between teams with and without strong fan support. Therefore, a team should take into account its management practices in the relation with fan loyalty to enhance its revenues. The study of fan loyalty determinants has emerged as an intriguing and practically useful one. In this study, we only attempted a rough descriptive study to determine whether there are any particular properties in teams with strong fan support. It has been determined that (1) teams with loyal fans enjoy consistently large attendance insensitive to environmental changes, (2) winning performance helps to improve the degree of a team's fan loyalty, and (3) the switching cost argument that switching cost is a determinant of brand loyalty, is confirmed in the sense that teams in larger cities have less loyal fan support, as there are more varieties of rival entertainment options and thus lower switching costs in larger cities.

From the author's perspective, consumer preference plays a more important role in consumption decisions in sports industries than in manufacturing industries, as emotional factors such as nostalgia and reminiscences are involved in the utility function of attending a sports game. However, the literature is still in its infancy and there is a great deal of conceptual space to be filled in the future.

NOTE

*   This work was supported by the National Research Foundation Grant funded by the Korean Government (MEST) (KRF-2009-220-B00008).

REFERENCES

Ahn, S.C. and Y.H. Lee (2007), 'Life-cycle demand for Major League Baseball', *International Journal of Sport Finance*, **2** (2), 79–93.

Ahn, S.C., Y.H. Lee and P. Schmidt (2001), 'GMM estimation of linear panel data models with time-varying individual effects', *Journal of Econometrics*, **101**, 219–55.

Ahn, S.C., Y.H. Lee and P. Schmidt (2007), 'Stochastic frontier models with multiple time-varying individual effects', *Journal of Productivity Analysis*, **27** (1), 1–12.

Aigner, D.J., C.A. Knox Lovell and P. Schmidt (1977), 'Formulation and estimation of stochastic production function models', *Journal of Econometrics*, **6** (1), 21–37.

Bai, J. (2003), 'Inferential theory for factor models of large dimension', *Econometrica*, **71**, 135–71.

Bai, J. (2009), 'Panel data models with interactive fixed effects', *Econometrica*, **77** (4), 1229–79.

Bai, J. and S. Ng (2002), 'Determining the number of factors in approximate factor models', *Econometrica*, **70**, 191–221.

Bauer, H.H., N.E. Stokburger-Sauer and S. Exler (2008), 'Brand image and fan loyalty in professional team sport: a refined model and empirical assessment', *Journal of Sport Management*, **22**, 205–26.

Bristow, D.N. and R.J. Sebastian (2001), 'Holy cow! Wait 'til next year! A closer look at the brand loyalty of Chicago Cubs baseball fans', *Journal of Consumer Marketing*, **18** (3), 256–75.

Chaudhuri, A. and M.B. Holbrook (2001), 'The chain of effects from brand trust and brand affect to brand performance: the role of brand loyalty', *Journal of Marketing*, **65** (2), 81–93.

Depken, C.A. (2000), 'Fan loyalty and stadium funding in professional Baseball', *Journal of Sports Economics*, **1**, 124–38.

Depken, C. (2001), 'Fan loyalty in professional sports'. *Journal of Sports Economics*, **2** (3), 275–84.

Dick, A.S. and K. Basu (1994), 'Customer loyalty: toward an integrated conceptual framework', *Journal of the Academy of Marketing Science*, **22** (2), 99–113.

Fort, R. (2004), 'Inelastic sports pricing', *Managerial and Decision Economics*, **25**, 87–94.

Gladden, J.M. and D.C. Funk (2002), 'Developing an understanding of brand associations in team sport: empirical evidence from consumers of professional sport', *Journal of Sport Management*, **16** (1), 54–81.

Humphreys, B.R. (2002), 'Alternative measures of competitive balance in sports leagues', *Journal of Sports Economics*, **3**, 133–48.

Kahane, L. and S. Shmanske (1997), 'Team roster turnover and attendance in Major League Baseball', *Applied Economics*, **29**, 425–31.

Krautmann, A., and D. Berri (2007), 'Can we find it at the concessions? Understanding price elasticity in professional sports', *Journal of Sports Economics*, **8** (2), 183–91.

Krautmann A. and L. Hadley (2006), 'Demand issues: the product market for professional sports', in J. Fizel (ed.), *Handbook of Sports Economics Research*, New York: M.E. Sharpe, pp. 175–89.

Krautmann, A., Y.H. Lee and K. Quinn (2010), 'Playoff uncertainty and pennant races', *Journal of Sports Economics*, **12** (5), 495–514.

Lee, Y.H. (1991), 'Panel data models with multiplicative individual and time effects: application to compensation and frontier production functions', unpublished PhD dissertation, Michigan State University.

Lee, Y.H. (2009), 'The impact of post-season restructuring on the competitive balance and fan demand in Major League Baseball', *Journal of Sports Economics*, **11**, 136–56.

Lee, Y.H. and R. Fort (2008), 'Attendance and the uncertainty of outcome hypothesis in baseball', *Review of Industrial Organization*, **33** (4), 281–95.

Lee, Y.H. and P. Schmidt (1993), 'A production frontier model with flexible temporal variation in technical inefficiency', in H. Fried, C.A.K. Lovell and S. Schmidt (eds), *The Measurement of Productive Efficiency: Techniques and Applications*, Oxford: Oxford University Press, pp. 237–55.

Lee, Y.H. and T. Smith (2008), 'Why are Americans addicted to baseball? An empirical analysis of fandom in Korea and the U.S.', *Contemporary Economic Policy*, **26** (1), 32–48.

Noll, R.G. (1974), 'Attendance and price setting', in R.G. Noll (ed.), *Government and the Sports Business*, Washington, DC: Brookings Institution Press, pp. 115–57.

Poitras, M. and L. Hadley (2006), 'Do new major league ballparks pay for themselves?', *Journal of Business*, **79**, 2275–99.

Schmidt, M.B. and Berri. D.J. (2004), 'The impact of labor strikes on consumer demand: an application to professional sports', *American Economic Review*, **94**, 334–47.

Siefried, J.J. and J.D. Eisenberg (1980), 'The demand for Minor League Baseball', *Atlantic Economic Journal*, **8**, 59–69.

Tucker, W.T. (1964), 'The development of brand loyalty', *Journal of Marketing Research*, **1** (3), 32–5.

Wakefield, K.L. and H.J. Sloan (1995), 'The effects of team loyalty and selected stadium factors on spectator attendance', *Journal of Sport Management*, **9**, 153–72.

9. The determinants of football match attendance in Spanish football: an empirical analysis

Jaume García and Plácido Rodríguez

1 INTRODUCTION

Attendance at football stadiums in Spanish First Division could be considered almost constant for the past two decades. As can be observed in Table 9.1, overall attendance in the First Division is about 8 to 9 million spectators each season. The increment in the 1995–96 season is the consequence of 22 teams instead of 20 in Spanish First Division football. In the Second Division, from the 1997/98 season there are 22 teams.

The main categories of spectators are both season ticket holders who buy their seat at the beginning of the season, and occasional spectators who get their ticket for a single match. The other spectators are people invited by the club for institutional reasons; the latter do not pay to go into the stadium. Season ticket holders are about 75 percent of total spectators. The participation of three categories of spectators and their evolution in the last data set of this study (1995–96 season) and the last season (2011–12) for the First Division is shown in Table 9.2.

The analysis of the factors that affect live attendance is one of the most important topics in the sport economics literature.[1] There is a large number of empirical articles on this issue referred to different professional sports, and European football in particular.[2] We can distinguish different groups depending on: the type of data used (time series and/or cross section at club level, data on individual matches for one or several seasons); the explanatory factors included, in particular, the consideration of price effects; the definition of the sector variables; the definition of the endogenous variables; and whether they estimate a single equation model or a set of equations.[3]

In this chapter we analyse to what extent the sectored variables which influence attendance have different effects depending on whether we consider attendance of season ticket holders or occasional spectators. In order

Table 9.1   Attendance in the Spanish First and Second Division football leagues

Seasons	First Division (million)	Second Division (million)	Total (million)
92/93	8.4	1.7	10.1
93/94	8.6	2.0	10.6
94/95	9.8	1.8	11.6
95/96	11.1	1.8	12.9
. . .	. . .	. . .	. . .
08/09	9.3	3.7	13
09/10	9.6	3.5	13.1
10/11	9.8	3.6	13.4
11/12	9.8	3.0	12.9

Source: Memorias de la Liga de Fútbol Profesional.

Table 9.2   Structure of attendance in Spanish professional football First Division

	1995–96	2011–12
Season ticket holders	76%	76%
Occasional spectators	18%	16.3%
Invitations	6%	7.6%

Source: Memorias de la Liga de Fútbol Profesional (1995/1996 and 2011/2012)

to do this we estimate demand equations for types of attendance, using data on individual matches played in the First Division of the Spanish football league in the seasons from 1992–93 until 1995–96, a total of 1580 observations.

The chapter is organized as follows. In section 2 we describe the data and the definition of the variables used in the empirical analysis. In section 3 we present the estimation results for both types of attendance equations, evaluating the importance of each group of variables in explaining live attendance. We end with a summary of the main conclusions.

2   DATA AND VARIABLES

Most of the data used in this chapter comes from the information supplied by the Liga de Fútbol Profesional corresponding to the seasons from

1992–93 until 1995–96. Some additional information has been obtained from other sources as indicated in Table 9A.1 in the appendix.

As mentioned above, we estimate two attendance equations: occasional spectators' attendance and season ticket holders' attendance. The dependent variable in the occasional attendance equation is the number of tickets sold for each match, whereas in the other equation is the number of season ticket holders attending the match. The explanatory factors are grouped into six categories: economic factors, market size, *ex ante* quality, current quality, outcome uncertainty and opportunity cost of a match.

In the occasional attendance equation, the explanatory economic variables included are the ticket price and income. The price is the minimum adult ticket price. The use of this price is relevant in order to have a homogeneous measure for different clubs. For instance, several clubs establish special prices for children or make price discrimination between men and women. The income variable is the real income per capita in the province of the home team. In the case of the season ticket holders' equation we do not include these variables because they affect the fact of being a season ticket holder but not whether or not this individual is attending a particular match. Instead, we control for the fact of the fixture being a 'Club's Day match', that is, a match which season ticket holders have to pay to attend.

For the size of the market factors, we use the number of people who are resident in the province as a measure of the size of the potential market in the case of the occasional spectators' attendance. When there is more than one club in the province, the population is divided between the number of clubs using the same percentage as the number of season ticket holders that each club has. Additionally, although evidence for Spanish football does not seem to support the view of some capacity constraint, we have included a variable measuring the maximum number of tickets which can be sold (capacity). This allows us to also control particular situations, as in the case of Barcelona where the 'real' capacity is small because of the large number of season ticket holders. We use the total number of season ticket holders as the size of the market variable in the second attendance equation.

Quality variables can be divided into two categories: *ex ante* quality variables which are constant during the season or fixed in advance, and current quality variables which capture the recent performance of both teams. In the first group we include the budget (in real terms) of the local and the visiting teams in the occasional spectators' equation, but only that of the visiting team in the season ticket holders' equation because that of the local team (as a proxy of quality) affects the decision of purchasing a season ticket but not the attendance to a particular match. As far as we know, Falter and Perignon (2000) is the first article to use the budget variables as proxies of quality, since the budget includes the salaries of the players which are good proxies of their productivity.[4] We also include two dummies for those matches where the visiting team is either Barcelona or Real Madrid, historically the two most important teams in Spain; a dummy for those games of special interest because of historical or regional rivalry; and, finally, a dummy indicating whether season ticket holders have to pay to attend the match (Club's Day match), a usual practice of most Spanish clubs. This is an indicator of the club's expectation about the quality (or interest) of the game.[5] Among the current quality variables we include two variables: the number of home and visiting team wins in the last three games.

With respect to the outcome uncertainty variables, we distinguish between season uncertainty and match uncertainty. In the first group we include two dummies for those matches where the home team has either no chance of winning the championship or is definitely in a promotion or relegation position. Match uncertainty is proxied by the difference between the standings of the teams.

The last group of variables is that which captures the opportunity cost of attending a football match: weather conditions; if the match is televised or not; and if the match is played on a week day. These variables are modelled by dummies. We define two dummies for the weather conditions where the omitted dummy corresponds to rainy days. We expect the worse the weather conditions are, the smaller the attendance will be. If the game is televised we distinguish if the match is televised on public or private channels for subscribers. In both cases we hope that televising games will reduce attendance, especially if the match is televised by a public channel. If a match is played on a week day, rather than at the weekend, attendance should decrease.

Finally, as fully discussed in García and Rodríguez (2002), we take into account that we have a panel data set. So, we have the possibility of controlling different types of unobserved factors. In that sense, we control the potential season effects. We do not control for home team effects because the effect of some relevant variables is affected because these variables, like market size, income or *ex ante* quality, do not have match variability.

Descriptive statistics of the variables used in the econometric exercise are reported in Table 9.A.1 of the appendix.

3   RESULTS

The specification we use is based on that in García and Rodríguez (2002) but using a log-log linear specification for the endogenous variable and the continuous explanatory variables (price, income, market size and budget). We have also simplified the specification to avoid collinearity problems and to make easier the interpretation of the effects of the variables of the different groups considered. The results for the attendance equations are presented in Table 9.3. Both equations have been estimated by ordinary least squares (OLS) (controlling for unobserved heteroskedasticity) and also treating them as seemingly unrelated equations, without observing significant differences between both sets of estimates. It is also worth mentioning that the explanatory power of both estimated equations is significantly different, as measured in terms of the adjusted R^2 (0.59 for occasional attendance and 0.90 for season ticket holders' attendance).

Given the 'log' specification we have chosen, the coefficient of the (log) price estimates the price elasticity. As happens in most empirical papers in this literature, price elasticity is less than 1 in absolute value. There are some contributions trying to explain this finding. For example, ticket price is only a part of the real cost of seeing live matches. In addition, clubs can have a utility function in which profits are only one of the arguments in the club objective function. The estimated elasticity is in line with that reported in García and Rodríguez (2002) for the log linear model (−0.630).

The income elasticity is positive and less than 1, meaning that attendance at a football stadium is a normal good. A similar estimate of this elasticity was found in García and Rodríguez (2002) for the log linear specification without home team fixed effects. As mentioned above, including these variables has a substantial effect on the point estimates and the precision of the coefficients of those variables without variability between fixtures.

In the season ticket holders' equation we have included, as an economic variable, a dummy capturing a kind of price effect related to whether season ticket holders have to pay to attend particular matches (Club's Day match variable). The results imply an approximate expected decrease in the attendance of season ticket holders of 12.6 percent for those special fixtures.

With respect to the size of the market, results are substantially different in magnitude when considering both types of attendance. The effect is much more important in the season ticket holders' equation given that, on the one hand, the size of the market is better proxied in this case and, on the other hand, payment is previous and compulsory to attending the match. In fact, the 'elasticity' of this type of attendance to the size of the market is almost 1, meaning that a 1 percent increase in the number of season ticket holders almost translates into a 1 percent increase in this attendance.

The *ex ante* quality variables all have a significant and positive effect on the corresponding type of attendance. The effect of the budget variable

Table 9.3 *Estimates of the attendance equations (endogenous variable: log(attendance)) (N = 1580)*

	Occasional spectators				Season ticket holders			
	OLS		SURE		OLS		SURE	
	Coef.	p-value	Coef.	p-value	Coef.	p-value	Coef.	p-value
Economic variables								
Price (log)	−0.613	(0.000)	−0.631	(0.000)				
Income (log)	0.486	(0.000)	0.576	(0.000)				
'Club's Day' match					−0.126	(0.000)	−0.126	(0.000)
Market size variables								
Population (log)	0.131	(0.011)	0.215	(0.000)				
Stadium capacity (log)	0.194	(0.000)	0.142	(0.000)				
Number of season ticket holders (log)					0.939	(0.000)	0.945	(0.000)
Ex ante quality								
Budget (h) (log)	0.553	(0.000)	0.457	(0.000)	0.029	(0.003)	0.029	(0.005)
Budget (v) (log)	0.285	(0.000)	0.294	(0.000)				
Away team Barcelona	0.813	(0.000)	0.791	(0.000)				
Away team Real Madrid	0.771	(0.000)	0.744	(0.000)				
Rivalry	0.741	(0.000)	0.745	(0.000)	0.028	(0.365)	0.029	(0.302)
'Club's Day' match	0.302	(0.000)	0.303	(0.000)				
Current quality								
No. of wins in the last 3 games (h)	0.143	(0.000)	0.142	(0.000)	0.037	(0.000)	0.037	(0.000)
No. of wins in the last 3 games (v)	0.043	(0.041)	0.042	(0.052)	−0.004	(0.546)	−0.005	(0.520)

Table 9.3   (continued)

| | Occasional spectators | | | | Season ticket holders | | | |
| | OLS | | SURE | | OLS | | SURE | |
	Coef.	p-value	Coef.	p-value	Coef.	p-value	Coef.	p-value
Uncertainty								
No chance to win the championship (h)	−0.177	(0.001)	−0.180	(0.000)	−0.038	(0.023)	−0.037	(0.021)
No chance of leaving relegation zone (h)	−0.967	(0.001)	−0.982	(0.000)	−0.322	(0.000)	−0.321	(0.000)
Difference in league positions (h-v)	0.012	(0.000)	0.012	(0.000)	0.001	(0.332)	0.001	(0.213)
Opportunity cost								
No rain, hot	0.409	(0.000)	0.427	(0.000)	0.076	(0.000)	0.075	(0.000)
No rain, cold	0.270	(0.000)	0.282	(0.000)	0.063	(0.002)	0.062	(0.003)
Televised by public channels	−0.359	(0.000)	−0.358	(0.000)	−0.072	(0.002)	−0.075	(0.001)
Televised by a private channel	−0.253	(0.000)	−0.253	(0.000)	−0.039	(0.049)	−0.041	(0.048)
Not played on the weekend	−0.246	(0.000)	−0.248	(0.000)	−0.047	(0.014)	−0.047	(0.036)
Season dummies								
1993–94	0.179	(0.000)	0.181	(0.000)	0.081	(0.000)	0.082	(0.000)
1994–95	0.128	(0.014)	0.127	(0.010)	0.129	(0.000)	0.128	(0.000)
1995–96	−0.071	(0.161)	−0.071	(0.140)	0.068	(0.000)	0.067	(0.000)
Constant	−7.248	(0.000)	−7.876	(0.000)	−0.069	(0.575)	−0.128	(0.328)
R^2 (adjusted)	0.590		0.589		0.904		0.904	

Note: (h) and (v) refer to the home team and the away team respectively.

is more important in the case of the home team.[6] Also, the dummies capturing whether Barcelona or Real Madrid are the visiting teams have an important and significant effect on the occasional spectators' attendance, not being included in the season ticket holders' equation because its effect was mainly captured by the budget of the visiting team. Notice that the effect of the *ex ante* variables (budget of the visiting team and dummy for rivalry) is more important for the occasional spectators. Finally, the Club's Day match, which is a proxy for quality in the payment equation, has a significant and positive effect, in contrast to the (negative) effect of this variable in the second type of attendance as proxy of a price effect.

Home team recent performance (current quality) matters and has a positive effect on both types of attendance but, as in previous cases, is more relevant for occasional spectators. The recent performance of the visiting team has an almost negligible effect. The effect of the uncertainty variables follows a similar pattern, in that payment attendance is more sensitive to changes in these variables.

The coefficients of opportunity cost variables have the expected sign but are significantly different for both equations. Weather conditions matter, in that worse conditions (rain and/or cold) reduce both types of attendance. On the other hand, the fact that the match is broadcast also reduces attendance, although more so in the case of public broadcasts than private broadcasts by subscription. Finally, the day of the match is also important in terms of attendance. Those matches not played during the weekend have a smaller expected attendance.

Although the previous comments on the estimated coefficients pointed out the higher sensitiveness of the occasional spectators' attendance to changes in the explanatory variables, we also provide some additional statistical evidence of this finding, in Table 9.4. We evaluate the relevance of each group of variables in explaining both types of attendance by looking at the increase in the residual sum of squares when omitting a group of variables from the basic model (as reported in Table 9.3) and by performing the corresponding F test for the null hypothesis of a zero effect for the variables in a particular group.[7]

Both statistics in Table 9.4 show that the worsening of the explanatory power by omitting a group of variables is more important for the occasional spectators' attendance, with the exception of the size of the market variables. As mentioned above and as expected, the total number of season ticket holders is the strongest determinant of their attendance. The adjusted R^2 of a model which only includes this market size variable is 0.894, which compares with that of the basic model, 0.904. By contrast, the adjusted R^2 in the occasional spectators' equation when including only the market size variables is 0.299 compared to 0.590 in the basic model.

Table 9.4 Significance of each set of explanatory variables

	Occasional spectators					Season ticket holders				
	RSS	%	K	r	F-test	RSS	%	K	r	F-test
Basic model	705.32		24			80.69		18		
Set of excluded variables										
Economic variables	766.13	8.62	22	2	66.46	81.84	1.43	17	1	21.08
Size of the market	738.03	4.64	22	2	39.73	573.52	610.77	17	1	>1000
Ex ante quality	984.19	39.54	18	6	108.36	81.13	0.55	16	2	4.43
Current quality	732.53	3.86	22	2	27.56	81.91	1.51	16	2	12.98
Uncertainty	728.13	3.23	21	3	11.98	82.61	2.38	15	3	7.81
Opportunity cost	753.94	6.89	19	5	18.71	82.38	2.09	12	6	6.36
Season effects	721.19	2.25	21	3	12.18	83.88	3.95	15	3	15.61

Notes:
The basic models are those in the first and third columns of Table 9.1.
RSS: residual sum of squares.
%: percentage increase in the RSS by omitting the corresponding group of variables in the basic model.
K: number of parameters.
r: number of restrictions.
F-test: value of the F statistic for testing the null hypothesis of the coefficients of the variable in a particular group being equal to 0.

When looking at the statistics reported in Table 9.4 for each attendance equation separately, we can conclude that *ex ante* quality variables have the most important effect on the occasional attendance equation followed by the group of economic variables. On the other hand, for the second attendance equation, the economic variable (Club's Day match), followed by the season dummies, is the most relevant explanatory factor, apart from the huge effect of the total number of season ticket holders, mentioned above.

4   CONCLUSIONS

In this chapter we have analysed the determinants of attendance in Spanish football for occasional spectators and for season ticket holders by estimating the corresponding attendance equations using six groups of explanatory variables which refer to economic factors, size of the market, *ex ante* quality, current quality, outcome uncertainty and opportunity costs.

By looking at the estimation results and at the evidence from statistics to capture the relevance of the different groups of explanatory variables, we conclude that, although the season ticket holders' equation shows a higher adjusted R^2, because of the extremely high explanatory power of the market size variable (the total number of season ticket holders), the occasional spectators' attendance is more sensitive to changes in the variables of the other groups.

Some other findings worth to point out are the following:

- As is usual in this type of demand equations, the elasticity for occasional attendance is less than 1 in absolute value.
- The attendance behaviour of occasional spectators with respect to income is according to attendance being a normal good.
- The Club's Day variable has a different sign in both attendance equations, which is consistent with the different role this variable plays in each equation, that is, a proxy for *ex ante* quality for occasional spectators and a proxy for a price effect in the season ticket holders' attendance.
- The weather conditions, broadcasting of the match and the day of the match also play an important role as determinants of both types of attendance.

NOTES

1. See Schofield (1983), Cairns (1990), Downward and Dawson (2000), Dobson and Goddard (2001), Szymanski (2003), Borland and Macdonald (2003), Krautman and Hadley (2006), Brook (2006), Fort and Lee (2006) and García and Rodríguez (2003, 2009).
2. See Hart et al. (1975), Bird (1982), Jennet (1984), Cairns (1987), Kuypers (1995), Szymansky and Smith (1997) and García and Rodríguez (2002).
3. See Demmert (1973), Stewart et al. (1992), Boyd and Boyd (1998) and Ferguson et al. (2000), among others.
4. García and Rodríguez (2002, 2006) use budget variables when estimating pay attendance and television audiences in the Spanish football, respectively.
5. Notice that this variable plays a different role in the two attendance equations.
6. We have not included two variables referring to the number of players in each team who have participated in their national team because these variables are highly correlated with the budget variables.
7. Notice that there is no exact relationship between these two statistics because the F test is calculated from the OLS estimates controlling for heteroskedasticity and in this case the F test has no exact direct relationship to the residual sum of squares of the basic model and that of the restricted model.

REFERENCES

Bird, P.J. (1982), 'The demand for league football', *Applied Economics*, **14**, 637–49.
Borland, J. and R. Macdonald (2003), 'Demand for sport', *Oxford Review of Economic Policy*, **19** (4), 478–502.
Boyd, D.W. and L.A. Boyd (1998), 'The home field advantage: implications for the pricing of tickets to professional team sporting events', *Journal of Economics and Finance*, **22**, 169–79.
Brook, S.L. (2006), 'Evaluating inelastic ticket pricing models', *International. Journal of Sport Finance*, **3** (1), 140–50.
Cairns, J.A. (1987), 'Evaluating changes in league structure: the reorganization of the Scottish Football League', *Applied Economics*, **19**, 259–75.
Cairns, J.A. (1990), 'The demand for professional team sports', *British Review of Economic Issues*, **12**, 1–20.
Demmert, H.G. (1973), *The Economics of Professional Team Sports*, Lexington, MA: Lexington Books.
Dobson, S.M. and J.A. Goddard, (2001), *The Economics of Football*, Cambridge. Cambridge University Press.
Downward, P. and A. Dawson, (2000), *The Economics of Professional Team Sports*, London: Routledge.
Falter, J.M. and C. Perignon, (2000), 'Demand for football and intramatch winning probability: an essay on the glorious uncertainty of sports', *Applied Economics*, **32**, 1757–65.
Ferguson, D.G., J.C.H. Jones and K.G. Stewart (2000), 'Competition within a cartel league conduct and team conduct in the market for baseball players services', *The Review of Economics and Statistics*, **82**, 422–30.
Fort, R. and Y.H. Lee, (2006), 'Stationarity and Major League Baseball attendance analysis', *Journal of Sport Eonomics*, **7**(4), 408–15.

García J. and P. Rodríguez, (2002), 'The determinants of football match attendance revisited: empirical evidence from the Spanish football league', *Journal of Sports Economics*, **3** (February), 18–38.

García, J. and P. Rodríguez, (2003), 'Análisis empírico de la demanda en los deportes profesionales: un panorama', *Revista Asturiana de Economía*, **26** (January–April), 23–60.

García, J. and P. Rodríguez, (2006), 'The determinants of the TV audience for Spanish football: a first approach', in P. Rodríguez, S. Késenne and J. García (eds), *Sports Economics after Fifty Years. Essays in Honour of Simon Rottenberg*, Oviedo: Ediciones de la Universidad de Oviedo, pp.147–67

García, J. and P. Rodríguez, (2009), 'Sports attendance: a survey of the literature 1973–2007', *Rivista di Diritto ed Economia dello Sport*, **5** (2), 111–51.

Hart, R.A., J. Hutton and T. Sharot (1975), 'A statistical analysis of association football attendances', *Applied Statistics*, **24**, 17–27.

Jennett, N. (1984), 'Attendances, uncertainty of outcome and policy in Scottish league football', *Scottish Journal of Political Economy*, **31**, 176–98.

Krautman, A. and Hadley, L. (2006), 'The product market for professional sports', in J. Fizel (ed.), *Handbook of Sports Economics Research*, Armond: M.E. Sharpe, pp.175–89.

Kuypers, T. (1995), 'The beautiful game? An econometric study of why people watch English football', working paper, Department of Economics, University College London.

Schofield, J.A. (1983), 'Performance and attendance at professional team sports', *Journal of Sports Behaviour*, **6**, 196–206.

Stewart, K.G., Ferguson, D.G. and Jones, J.C.H. (1992), 'On violence in professional team sport as the endogenous result of profit maximization', *Atlantic Economic Journal*, **20**, 55–64.

Szymanski, S. (2003), 'Economic design of sporting contests', *The Journal of Economic Literature*, **41** (4), 1137–87.

Szymanski, S. and R. Smith, (1997), 'The English football industry: profit, performance and industrial structure', *International Review of Applied Economics*, **11**, 135–53.

APPENDIX

Table 9A.1   Descriptive statistics and sources

Variable	Mean	St. dev.	Source[3]
Attendance			
Occasional spectators	3772.59	5101.24	LNFP
Season ticket holders	17809.72	15554.03	LNFP
Economic variables			
Price[1]	2047.53	662.16	LNFP
Income[1]	1292.86	277.44	BBVA
Size of the market			
Population[2]	1089.36	1058.43	BBVA
Stadium's capacity	17889.61	12018.90	LNFP
Number of season ticket holders	23365.98	22407.57	LNFP
Ex ante quality			
Budget (h)[1]	1790.54	1736.59	LNFP
Budget (v)[1]	1776.39	1727.63	LNFP
Away team Barcelona	0.0487		
Away team Real Madrid	0.0487		
Rivalry	0.0468		
'Club's Day' match	0.0563		LNFP
Current quality			
No. of wins in the last 3 games (h)	0.9127	0.8255	
No. of wins in the last 3 games (v)	1.0551	0.8805	
Uncertainty			
No chance of winning the championship (h)	0.1791		
No chance of leaving relegation zone (h)	0.0089		
Difference in league positions (h-v)	0.3329	8.2663	
Opportunity cost			
No rain, hot	0.5361		*Dinámico*
No rain, cold	0.3627		*Dinámico*
Televised by public channels	0.1006		LNFP
Televised by a private channel	0.0987		LNFP
Not played on the weekend	0.0715		LNFP

Notes:
1. These variables are expressed in real terms (1991 pesetas). Income in thousands of pesetas and budgets in millions of pesetas.
2. Population is in thousands.
3. LNFP: Liga Nacional de Fútbol Profesional.
BBVA: Fundación BBVA, *Renta nacional de España y su distribución provincial.*
Dinámico: Football yearbook.

PART IV

Economic Impact

10. Estimating economic impact using *ex post* econometric analysis: cautionary tales

Robert Baumann and Victor A. Matheson

INTRODUCTION

Since the seminal work of Baade and Dye (1988) over twenty years ago, the analysis of the economic impact of sports teams, stadiums and major athletic events on host economies has elicited significant attention from sports economists. There are two main reasons. First, the topic has considerable public finance implications. Over the past two decades over 100 stadium and arena construction projects have taken place at a cost totaling in excess of $30 billion in the US and Canada alone (Baade and Matheson, 2011). Since over half of this cost has been borne by state and local governments, it is reasonable to ask whether taxpayers are getting a good return on their investment.

The second reason for the consideration is the clear difference between the *ex ante* economic benefit estimates provided by economists working in a consulting capacity at the behest of sports organizers and the *ex post* estimates provided by economists working in a scholarly setting. *Ex ante* economic impact numbers are typically generated by predicting the number of visitors to an event and the average spending per visitor. Multiplying these two figures together provides an estimate of the direct economic impact. A multiplier is then applied to the direct economic impact to arrive at an estimate of total economic impact. Invariably the total economic impact of sports teams and events estimated in this manner is extremely impressive.

Critics of this process point out several flaws in this methodology. First, *ex ante* economic impact reports tend to report the gross rather than the net economic impact of spectator sports. Local residents who spend their money on sports have less disposable income to spend on other goods and services in the local economy. Sports may simply shift spending around but not cause an increase in local incomes. Similarly, sports fans may displace other consumers. Finally, the multipliers used are often implausibly large and, even when reasonable looking multipliers are used, rarely do they account for the unique circumstances that surround professional sports (Matheson, 2009; Siegfried and Zimbalist, 2002).

In order to test the effects of these theoretical deficiencies, numerous researchers have followed Baade and Dye (1988), including Coates and Humphreys (1999; 2002), Baade and Matheson (2002, 2004), Baade et al. (2008), Hagn and Maennig (2008), Jasmand and Maennig (2008) and Feddersen and Maennig (2010), to name just a few. These economists have performed *ex post* analyses of the performance of economic variables in local economies in the wake of new stadium construction, mega-events, and franchise relocation. An *ex post* evaluation of economic impact examines some aspect of a local economy, such as personal income, employment, income per capita, taxable sales or visitor arrivals, and compares the data before, during and after an event, new stadium construction or franchise move. If the *ex ante* estimates are correct, then shifts of a similar magnitude should be observable in the data. In fact, these types of studies have typically found that sporting events, teams and stadiums create a fraction of the economic benefits predicted in *ex ante* studies.

While the flaws of *ex ante* studies are clear, it is also easy for errors to be made in *ex post* economic impact analyses. The purpose of this chapter is to highlight what types of errors can be made in *ex post* analyses and to explain the intuition behind why such errors occur.

DATA

In order to motivate the discussion of potential econometric errors and to provide concrete examples, this chapter utilizes a time-series cross-section (also called a dynamic panel) data set on college athletics in the US. The National Collegiate Athletic Association (NCAA) is the largest governing body for intercollegiate sports in the US. With nearly 1100 member schools, the organization serves as both a rule-making body as well as the primary sponsor for championships in intercollegiate sports among its members. While several other collegiate athletic associations exist, including the 290-member National Association of Intercollegiate Athletics and the roughly 500-member National Junior College Athletic Association, the NCAA is both the largest and most prominent organization, and its members also include the biggest and most highly funded athletic programs in the country. The NCAA categorizes its member schools into one of three divisions based on school size, recruiting rules, athlete eligibility and the availability of scholarship money for athletes. Division I is the highest level of competition and comprises 338 schools ranging from

Table 10.1   Championship variables

Men's sports	Women's sports	Coed sports
Cross country	Cross country	Rifle
Soccer	Soccer	Skiing
Volleyball	Volleyball	Fencing
Water polo	Water polo	
Baseball	Softball	
Basketball	Basketball	
Gymnastics	Gymnastics	
Hockey	Hockey	
Swimming	Swimming	
Golf	Golf	
Lacrosse	Lacrosse	
Tennis	Tennis	
Track and field indoor	Track and field indoor	
Track and field outdoor	Track and field outdoor	
Fencing	Fencing	
Wrestling	Bowling	
	Field hockey	
	Rowing	

large state universities to smaller private colleges. The NCAA sponsors championships in 37 different sports, including the different championships held for men and women athletes in most sports. Table 10.1 lists the sports with a championship. Football was excluded from the sample of national championships since the national championship in football for the top schools is not administered by the NCAA, and the 'true' national champion is the source of some dispute.

This chapter uses data from 1969 through to 2005 for 60 metropolitan areas that are home to a university with a football team belonging to one of the six major Division 1 athletic conferences in the country. In addition, Provo, Utah, Colorado Springs, Colorado, and South Bend, Indiana, homes to Brigham Young, Air Force and Notre Dame, respectively, are added to the sample, bringing the total number of cities examined up to 63. While the list of cities in the sample is somewhat ad hoc, the sample covers the home city for the majority of universities that one would normally consider to have a major athletic program. Indeed, schools in these cities account for just under 800 of the 995 national championships awarded in various sports by the NCAA during this time period. Restricting the sample to these major athletic programs provides for a manageable data set and ensures that the host city is large enough be included within one

Table 10.2   Summary statistics

Variable	Mean	Standard deviation	Observations
Personal income ($000s)	$31 056 541	$55 985 830	2268
Percent change in personal income	3.17%	3.22%	2205
Per capita income	$25 472	$6528	2268
Percent change in per capita income	1.70%	2.90%	2205
Employment	500 602	835 812	2330
Percent change in employment	2.25%	2.69%	2330

of the Census Bureau defined metropolitan statistical areas (MSAs). In most cases, only a single major university resides in each MSA; however, in some cases, notably Los Angeles, two or more Division 1 schools may have won national championships and no differentiation is made for which school within an MSA was named champion. For each MSA, we have data on total personal income, per capita income and employment. Table 10.2 presents the summary statistics for the levels and percentage changes of all three variables. The only caveat is that our sample frame ends at 2005 for employment and 2004 for personal income and per capita income. We merge these economic data with the championship information to create dummy variables for each champion in a given year.

Up to this point, the data are similar to that used in many other *ex post* analyses of the economic impact of sports. What is of crucial importance here, however, is that *there is no conceivable mechanism by which national championships in the vast majority of NCAA Division 1 sports can have any meaningful impact on MSA-wide economic variables.* Outside of football, which is not examined in this study, and men's basketball, most intercollegiate sports have relatively few followers. National championships are low budget, sparsely attended events that generate little media coverage. In addition, most national championships are held at neutral venues, so the winner of a national championship will typically not benefit from any tourism inflows, small though they may be, nor do winning teams receive any monetary rewards from the NCAA. Therefore, any economic impact would have to rely on psychological effects on local workers, capital or labor inflows as a result of an advertising effect, or other indirect factors. While Coates and Humphries (2002) and Davis and End (2010) suggest that psychological factors may be at work in explaining an identified increase in economic activity among cities that win the Super Bowl in the National Football League, such an explanation for championships in minor college sports borders on the absurd. In fact, should winning a championship in any of the sports examined in this chapter turn out to have a significant effect on any of the MSA economic variables, the only logical conclusion to draw is one of spurious correlation or model misspecification. The results of this chapter show how easy it is to end up with statistically significant results for minor sporting events given incorrect econometric modeling.

MODELS I AND II: LEVELS WITHOUT FIXED EFFECTS FOR YEARS OR MSAS

Given we have data for 63 MSAs over 36 (1969–2004 for personal income and per capita income) or 37 (1969–2005 for employment) years, we begin by using panel data techniques to account for time-invariant effects of each MSA. While we have the alternative of estimating separate models for each MSA, as is done in Baade and Matheson (2004), we lose the control group of the remaining MSAs. However, pooling data into a panel also makes heteroskedasticity far more likely. We include panel-corrected standard errors to allow the error variance to be different across MSAs. Whether the data are pooled or not, it is likely autocorrelation exists within each MSA. We will return to this issue later in the chapter.

Ignoring for now the potential problem of unit roots, which are almost certain to exist when dealing with time series involving economic data in levels, Table 10.3 presents only the statistically significant estimates in a least squares model with the championship variables as the only covariates. The insignificant controls are available upon request. At this point, MSA-level fixed effects and yearly dummies are not included. Table 10.3 shows that nearly half (47 out of 99 total) of the championship dummy variables are statistically significant across the three dependent variables. As stated previously, the only explanations for statistically significant championship variables are spurious correlations and/or model misspecification.

In most sports, team quality is likely to persist over a long period of time due to coaching quality, program reputation and/or institutional support, and therefore championships are commonly dominated by a small number of schools. If these universities happen to be located in MSAs with an above (below) average level of income, employment, or per capita income, then the championships in those sports will show up as being correlated to high (low) incomes, and so on. For example, West Virginia University (WVU) has won half of the NCAA rifle championships in our sample. WVU is located in Morgantown, West Virginia, a town that is both significantly smaller and poorer that the typical 'college town' in the data set.

Table 10.3 Levels result – no city or year dummy variables included (model I)

Personal income		Per capita income		Employment	
Men's cross country	−1.87e+07 ($p = 0.084$)	Men's cross country	2682.9 ($p = 0.050$)	Men's cross country	−285 781 ($p = 0.065$)
Women's cross country	−2.59e+07 ($p = 0.041$)	Women's cross country	2730.2 ($p = 0.089$)	Women's cross country	−371 869 ($p = 0.040$)
Women's volleyball	4.35e+07 ($p < 0.001$)	Women's field hockey	7321.4 ($p < 0.001$)	Women's field hockey	498 236 ($p = 0.015$)
Men's volleyball	1.43e+08 ($p < 0.001$)	Women's soccer	3003.0 ($p = 0.030$)	Women's volleyball	640 211 ($p < 0.001$)
Men's water polo	4.27e+07 ($p < 0.001$)	Women's volleyball	4604.7 ($p = 0.003$)	Men's volleyball	2 287 268 ($p < 0.001$)
Women's water polo	1.65e+08 ($p < 0.001$)	Men's water polo	5092.0 ($p < 0.001$)	Men's water polo	551 036 ($p < 0.001$)
Softball	4.43e+07 ($p < 0.001$)	Men's gymnastics	1886.6 ($p = 0.077$)	Women's water polo	1 755 717 ($p < 0.001$)
Men's hockey	4.43e+07 ($p < 0.001$)	Men's hockey	6507.6 ($p < 0.001$)	Baseball	228 629 ($p = 0.094$)
Women's hockey	1.05e+08 ($p = 0.031$)	Women's hockey	17 446.4 ($p = 0.005$)	Softball	623 453 ($p < 0.001$)
Rifle	−2.44e+07 ($p = 0.072$)	Rifle	−3265.3 ($p = 0.057$)	Men's hockey	693 716 ($p < 0.001$)
Wrestling	−1.72e+07 ($p = 0.036$)	Men's track & field indoor	−2695.6 ($p = 0.069$)	Women's hockey	1 407 786 ($p = 0.006$)
Women's lacrosse	9.84e+07 ($p < 0.001$)	Women's lacrosse	11 973.8 ($p < 0.001$)	Rifle	−387 342 ($p = 0.054$)
Men's tennis	1.86e+07 ($p = 0.049$)	Men's tennis	3543.4 ($p = 0.003$)	Wrestling	−281 901 ($p = 0.019$)
Women's rowing	1.13e+08 ($p < 0.001$)	Women's tennis	7184.1 ($p < 0.001$)	Women's lacrosse	1 498 449 ($p < 0.001$)
		Women's rowing	16 288.1 ($p < 0.001$)	Men's tennis	252 915 ($p = 0.066$)
		Ski	3901.7 ($p = 0.023$)	Women's rowing	1 287 247 ($p < 0.001$)
				Ski	−333 334 ($p = 0.097$)
No. of sports	37				

Note: All results are estimated by a least squares model with standard errors that are robust to heteroskedasticity across MSAs.

The negative coefficients on income personal income and employment for the rifle championships in Table 10.3 clearly reflect the size and wealth of Morgantown rather than the influence of perhaps the smallest of all NCAA championship sports. Similarly, teams from the Los Angeles MSA have dominated men's and women's water polo and men's volleyball, leading to highly statistically significant results on employment and personal income for these championships.

Indeed, the necessity of including city effects places a major constraint on the types of events that can be examined using *ex post* econometric analysis. Standard *ex post* techniques can only examine variables in which there is some type of movement between cities since the inclusion of city-level fixed effects causes perfectly collinearity between the fixed effect and the event dummy variable. For example, the Super Bowl can be examined because it changes location every year, but major college football bowl games such as the Rose Bowl cannot be easily studied since the game takes place in the same city on the same day every year. Even if one observes a large surge in spending in Pasadena every New Year's Day, it would be nearly impossible to disentangle whether the boost in economic activity was due to the Rose Bowl or other unique features of the Pasadena economy on that day. Similarly, studies of stadiums and arenas must concentrate on changes in sports infrastructure, such as new stadiums or renovations to existing facilities, rather than on the potential impact of existing stadiums.

It is also not sufficient to account only for differences between cities. Table 10.4 shows statistically significant estimates in least squares estimations on all three dependent variables but includes MSA-level fixed effects. Again, many championship dummy variables are statistically significant particularly in women's sports, which constitute 28 of the 35 significant championship variables across the three estimations. Given the NCAA did not begin to sponsor championships in women's sports until 1981, this finding is likely the byproduct of the upward trend in each dependent variable. Similar spurious correlations are likely if time trends are not properly accounted for when examining the economic impact of any sport in which team or playoff expansion has occurred or the number of games played per season has changed.

MODEL III: LEVELS

Even when MSA-level fixed effects and yearly dummies are included, many economic variables are almost certain to have a unit root given a reasonable time period. Using Dickey-Fuller and Phillips–Perron tests,

Table 10.4 Levels result – city but no year dummy variables included (model II)

Personal income		Per capita income		Employment	
Women's field hockey	8.66e+06 ($p = 0.077$)	Women's field hockey	4301.9 ($p = 0.002$)	Women's field hockey	175 284 ($p = 0.001$)
Women's volleyball	2.09e+07 ($p < 0.001$)	Women's soccer	4745.5 ($p < 0.001$)	Women's volleyball	230 816 ($p < 0.001$)
Women's water polo	4.50e+07 ($p < 0.001$)	Women's volleyball	3202.9 ($p = 0.006$)	Women's water polo	294 387 ($p = 0.002$)
Softball	1.51e+07 ($p < 0.001$)	Women's gymnastics	2887.0 ($p = 0.043$)	Baseball	−85 295 ($p = 0.012$)
Men's basketball	−6.23e+06 ($p = 0.047$)	Women's hockey	10 500.5 ($p = 0.021$)	Softball	162 271 ($p < 0.001$)
Women's gymnastics	1.42e+07 ($p = 0.006$)	Women's lacrosse	6105.0 ($p < 0.001$)	Men's basketball	−86 115 ($p = 0.010$)
Women's hockey	5.21e+07 ($p = 0.001$)	Women's tennis	4308.7 ($p < 0.001$)	Women's hockey	499 836 ($p < 0.001$)
Men's swimming	−5.52e+07 ($p = 0.069$)	Women's rowing	9526.1 ($p < 0.001$)	Women's golf	123 589 ($p = 0.003$)
Women's track & field indoor	7.77e+06 ($p = 0.080$)	Coed fencing	5624.4 ($p < 0.001$)	Women's lacrosse	340 260 ($p < 0.001$)
Women's golf	9.29e+06 ($p = 0.019$)	Ski	−4490.9 ($p = 0.004$)	Women's tennis	81 629 ($p = 0.055$)
Women's lacrosse	3.27e+07 ($p < 0.001$)	Women's bowling	8025.1 ($p = 0.077$)	Women's rowing	407 732 ($p < 0.001$)
Men's tennis	−7.44e+06 ($p = 0.039$)				
Women's rowing	4.88e+07 ($p < 0.001$)				
No. of sports	37				

Note: All results are estimated by a least squares model with standard errors that are robust to heteroskedasticity across MSAs.

our three dependent variables – per capita income, personal income and employment – fail all MSA-specific unit root tests except in one case: Pullman, WA, which is the home of Washington State University. This MSA rejects the existence of a unit root for personal income in both Dickey–Fuller and Phillips–Perron tests. The unit roots in all MSAs but one are almost certainly a result of the upward trend in all three dependent variables over our time frame.

Table 10.5   Levels result – city and year dummy variables included (model III)

Personal income		Per capita income		Employment	
Women's volleyball	1.64e+07 ($p = 0.004$)	Men's cross country	1401.8 ($p = 0.059$)	Women's volleyball	177180 ($p = 0.004$)
Women's basketball	−5.52e+07 ($p = 0.038$)	Men's water polo	−600.7 ($p = 0.052$)	Women's basketball	−49631 ($p = 0.021$)
Women's water polo	3.694e+07 ($p = 0.002$)	Women's soccer	1633.8 ($p = 0.010$)	Women's water polo	205019 ($p = 0.001$)
Men's track and field outdoor	−5.03e+06 ($p = 0.075$)	Softball	−772.2 ($p = 0.086$)	Men's water polo	−23633 ($p = 0.089$)
Women's rowing	3.65e+07 ($p < 0.001$)	Women's rowing	3699.5 ($p < 0.001$)	Women's rowing	275948 ($p < 0.001$)
Coed fencing	−8.45e+06 ($p = 0.007$)	Women's lacrosse	2036.8 ($p < 0.001$)	Women's soccer	−32434 ($p = 0.095$)
Women's lacrosse	2.47e+07 ($p = 0.085$)			Women's lacrosse	244984 ($p = 0.045$)
Men's gymnastics	2.87e+06 ($p = 0.036$)			Men's track and field outdoor	−53724 ($p = 0.019$)
				Men's gymnastics	42068 ($p = 0.021$)
				Coed fencing	−84500 ($p 0.012$)
No. of sports	33				

Note: All results are estimated by a least squares model that includes MSA-level fixed effects, yearly dummies, and standard errors that are robust to heteroskedasticity across MSAs.

We also execute three time series panel unit root tests: Hadri (2000), Levin et al. (2002) and Im et al. (2003). These tests differ by their flexibility when faced with other econometric problems. For example, Hadri (2000) allows for heteroskedasticity, which is common in time-series panels. Im et al. (2003) and Levin et al. (2002) allows for an overall time trend and also MSA-specific fixed effects and time trends. All three tests suggest a unit root is present in each of our three independent variables.

Table 10.5 presents only the statistically significant estimates in estimations on all three dependent variables. Although not presented, MSA-level fixed effects and yearly dummies are included. Those results are available upon request. Including MSA-level fixed effects and yearly dummies forces us to omit four championships – women's bowling (Nebraska), men's fencing (Notre Dame), rifle (West Virginia) and women's hockey (Minnesota) – which we observe in only one year or only one champion. As stated above, the only explanations for statistically significant championship variables are spurious correlations and/or model misspecification. Table 10.5 shows statistically significant championship controls at $\alpha = 0.1$: six in the per capita income estimation, eight in the personal income estimation, and 10 in the employment estimation. Given there are 33 championship variables, such a high percentage of significant variables is almost certainly the fault of the unit root caused by the upward trend of each dependent variable. Of these 24 significant estimates, 14 are positive. Though not presented in Table 10.5, it is also worth noting that nearly all of the year dummies are statistically significant with an upward trend except for recessions during the time frame.

Some of the sports appear multiple times in the significance lists. The most notable examples are women's lacrosse and women's rowing, which have a positive and significant effect on each economic variable. The University of Maryland (Washington, DC MSA) has won the majority of women's lacrosse championships, including five during the 1990s. Given there are MSA-specific fixed effects and yearly dummy variables, this suggests DC grew faster than the national average during the economic expansion that started in 1992. The same is true for Seattle, which is the home for the University of Washington which won three women's rowing national championships during the same expansion. While the time dummies absorb the national macroeconomic trends, these spurious correlations are caused by the above average volatility in Seattle and Washington, DC.

MODEL IV: PERCENTAGE CHANGES

A common solution to unit root problems is to transform the variables into first differences or percent changes. The MSA-specific Dickey–Fuller and Phillips–Perron tests and the three time-series panel unit root tests all suggest these two transformations substantially lessen the unit root problem found in the levels. For our three dependent variables, the percentage change performs slightly better than the first difference in these tests, so we use that transformation in the following results. This puts all MSAs on the same playing field, but somewhat obscures the total dollar impact of an event. For example, an event that produces $100 million of benefit would appear significant in a small MSA and insignificant in a large MSA.

Table 10.6   Percentage change results (model IV)

Personal income		Per capita income		Employment	
Women's fencing	1.64e+07 (p = 0.004)	Men's water polo	−0.0127 (p = 0.059)	Women's fencing	0.0136 (p = 0.072)
Men's baseball	−0.0059 (p = 0.027)	Women's basketball	−0.0094 (p = 0.077)	Coed fencing	0.0079 (p < 0.001)
Men's water polo	−0.0145 (p = 0.057)	Men's hockey	−0.0079 (p = 0.097)	Women's basketball	−49 631 (p = 0.021)
Men's golf	−0.0040 (p = 0.077)	Women's tennis	−0.0099 (p = 0.002)	Men's water polo	−0.0054 (p = 0.046)
Women's tennis	−0.0112 (p = 0.001)			Women's track and field indoor	−0.0092 (p = 0.005)
				Women's golf	−0.0056 (p = 0.067)
				Women's tennis	−0.0100 (p = 0.095)
				Men's track and field outdoor	0.0045 (p = 0.027)
No. of sports	33				

Note: All results are estimated by a least squares model that includes MSA-level fixed effects, yearly dummies, and standard errors that are robust to heteroskedasticity across MSAs.

Table 10.6 presents the results. As before, MSA-level fixed effects and time dummies are included but not presented for brevity. Per capita income has four significant championship variables, personal income has five, and employment has eight. In addition, five of these 18 significant variables are positive. These percentages of significance and positive significance are more in line with the random spurious correlations though not a perfect fit. Assuming no model misspecification, the expected number of randomly significant variables is 10 (compared to our 18) given a 10 percentage threshold for significance and 33 championship variables in three estimations.

Similar to the levels estimations, some of the sports appear multiple times in the significance lists. Women's tennis is negative and significant for all three economic variables, while men's tennis is negative and but near significance (*p*-values of 0.188 and 0.302) in two of three economic variables. Stanford University (San Jose–Sunnyvale–Santa Clara MSA) is a dominant program in both men's and women's tennis. However, most of its women's tennis championships occur during recessions including championships during the early 1980s, early 1990s and early 2000s. Meanwhile, their men's team tended to win during expansions, most notably six during the 1990s. In addition, the economy of the San Jose–Sunnyvale–Santa Clara MSA is more volatile than the rest of the nation. For that MSA, each economic variable has a standard deviation at least 50 percent higher than the national average. We conclude these significant championship variables are a result of this volatility.

MODEL V: INSTRUMENTAL VARIABLES-GENERAL METHOD OF MOMENTS MODELS

Models I through to IV treat the data as if it were a panel, but it could be argued our data more resemble a time-series cross-section (TSCS), which is also called a dynamic panel. Much has been written about the difference, but the main issues are whether 'T is large enough to do serious averaging over time, and also whether it is large enough to make some econometric problems disappear' (Beck and Katz, 2004, p. 3). Given $T = 35$ in our data set, this likely passes the threshold mentioned by Beck and Katz, which means we are probably better off using techniques designed for TSCS data. In addition, we use no explanatory variables to control for the macroeconomy other than MSA-level fixed effects and yearly dummies. Part of this rationale is avoiding the likely endogeneity that is caused by including another macro control. But this means the error term includes a greater amount of information, and this information is almost certain to be correlated over time within an MSA. In other words, it is highly likely Models I and II suffer from autocorrelation.

An autocorrelation test appears in Wooldridge (2002), where the null hypothesis is no autocorrelation. We perform this test for each of our 63 MSAs since it is not appropriate for TSCS data. For our three dependent variables, 55 (personal income), 52 (per capita income) and 61 (employment) of 63 reject the null hypothesis of no autocorrelation at $\alpha = 0.1$. Since autocorrelation produces incorrect standard errors, our significance tests in models I and II are suspect.

One solution to removing the inertia in the error is to include the lagged dependent variable as a regressor. Unfortunately, this addition biases the fixed effect estimators because that model is equivalent to a least squares estimation that transforms the data to deviations of MSA-specific means.

It is these means that create a correlation between the independent variables and the error term. As N approaches infinity, Nickell (1981) shows the amount of inconsistency is of order T^{-1}. This may seem small given $T = 35$ in our sample, but $N = 63$ is not nearly close enough to infinity to assume this result.

There are two solutions to produce consistent estimates in this framework. One option is to choose a technique from the Instrumental Variable-General Method of Moments (IV-GMM) family of estimators, which include Anderson and Hsiao (1982), Arellano and Bond (1991) and Blundell and Bond (1998). All three methods first difference the equation and use past information about the lagged dependent variable as instruments for the lagged dependent variable, that is, the endogenous regressor. The main difference between Anderson and Hsiao (1982) and Arellano and Bond (1991) is the level of identification. Anderson and Hsiao (1982) propose an exactly identified IV strategy that uses the second lag to instrument for the endogenous first lag. In comparison, the Arellano and Bond (1991) technique is over-identified because the researcher can use as many higher-order lags as the data will allow. Blundell and Bond (1998) propose a different estimator for small-sample cases which are more likely to produce weak instruments. One advantage of all of these methods is that any potentially endogenous independent variable can be instrumented in the same way.

For this exercise, we choose the Arellano and Bond (1991) estimator for two reasons. First, it is accepted that this estimator is more efficient than Anderson–Hsiao. Second, the Blundell and Bond (1998) estimator provides very similar results suggesting we have very little small-sample bias. We also add that Arellano and Bond (1991) has corrections for MSA-specific heteroskedasticity and downward-biased standard errors caused by the IV approach (Windmeijer, 2005).

Table 10.7 presents results for the Arellano and Bond (1991) technique. Per capita income has four significant championship controls, personal income has three, and employment has six. Of these 12 significant estimates, five are positive. The lagged dependent variable is significant in two of the three dependent variables. The estimates of the coefficient on the lagged dependent variable are 0.971 (personal income, $p = 0.032$), 0.612 (per capita income, $p = 0.436$) and 0.951 (employment, $p = 0.013$). We conclude that this model finds a large amount of autocorrelation, but a great number of significant championship variables remain. We also note that men's basketball, which has a positive and significant effect on employment, cannot be ruled out as spurious because of its high profile.

Table 10.7 Lagged dependent variables – Arellano–Bond (model V)

Personal income		Per capita income		Employment	
Women's field hockey	0.0143 ($p = 0.055$)	Men's water polo	−0.0239 ($p = 0.072$)	Women's field hockey	0.0049 ($p = 0.075$)
Women's water polo	0.0788 ($p = 0.033$)	Women's gymnastics	−0.0089 ($p = 0.083$)	Football	0.0064 ($p = 0.025$)
Women's gymnastics	−0.0111 ($p = 0.076$)	Wrestling	0.0123 ($p = 0.019$)	Men's water polo	−0.0090 ($p = 0.038$)
Wrestling	0.0143 ($p = 0.068$)	Women's tennis	−0.0099 ($p = 0.002$)	Men's basketball	0.0084 ($p = 0.012$)
				Women's swimming	0.0192 ($p = 0.015$)
				Women's track and field indoor	−0.0110 ($p = 0.002$)
				Men's golf	−0.0035 ($p = 0.074$)
				Women's lacrosse	0.0082 ($p = 0.018$)
Lags used as instruments	2,3	Lags used as instruments	3,4,5,6,7	Lags used as instruments	2,3
Hansen over-ident. test	$\chi^2 = 0.30$ ($p = 0.584$)	Hansen over-ident. test	$\chi^2 = 1.57$ ($p = 0.815$)	Hansen over-ident. test	$\chi^2 = 0.14$ ($p = 0.708$)
Lagged dep. var.	0.9708 ($p = 0.032$)	Lagged dep. var.	0.6125 ($p = 0.436$)	Lagged dep. var.	0.9511 ($p = 0.013$)
No. of sports	33				

Note: All estimations are done using the percent change of the dependent variable. The optimal number of lags is determined using the Hansen (1982) over-identification test, which has a null hypothesis of no over-identification.

MODELS VI AND VII: LAGGED DEPENDENT VARIABLE MODELS

While introducing a lagged dependent variable allows us to model autocorrelation, the IV correction can produce several unintended consequences especially if the instruments are weak or the sample is small. Kiviet (1995) and later Bruno (2005) take a different path by first estimating the amount of bias in a lagged dependent variable model that does not correct its endogeneity. Once the bias is estimated, it adjusts the estimates. This result is inspired by Nickell (1981), who first derived the amount of inconsistency in these models.

The Monte Carlo evidence tends to favor the Kiviet correction to IV-GMM models (see Judson and Owen, 1999; Bun and Kiviet, 2003; Bruno, 2005), but there are two other issues with the Kiviet correction. First, its bias correction formula includes the parameter values of the autoregressive coefficient and the error variance. Since these are unobservable, Kiviet (1995) recommends using consistent estimates from either the Anderson–Hsiao, Arellano–Bond, or Blundell–Bond techniques. Although all of these produce consistent estimates, sample sizes in macroeconomic data tend to be small and this introduces extra noise in the estimation. Second, there is only an asymptotic formula for the standard errors (see Bun and Kiviet, 2001). Bruno (2005) outlines a bootstrap technique based on the normal distribution that we use here.

Beck and Katz (2004) argue a Kiviet correction to a lagged dependent variable model may not even be necessary. Their Monte Carlo evidence that suggests omitting a Kiviet correction given $T > 20$ since there is little difference in bias and mean squared error above this threshold. However, they also find the Kiviet correction produces a lower mean squared error in cases with high autocorrelation, which is what the results from the Model III suggest. For this reason, we include estimates with and without the Kiviet correction. Since least squares is well known to produce inconsistent estimates in models with lagged dependent variables, we estimate the 'without Kiviet' models with maximum likelihood. Finally, we use robust standard errors to guard against heteroskedasticity across MSAs.

Table 10.8 lists the significant championship variables using the Kiviet-corrected technique, and Table 10.9 presents the same for the maximum likelihood estimation, that is, no Kiviet correction. Both estimations produce 11 significant championship variables, and some of the sports overlap. The significant controls are also more likely to be negative than positive. Of the 22 significant estimates, eight are positive. There are also similarities in the autoregressive term estimates. For the personal income and employment estimations, the Kiviet and lagged dependent variable models produce very similar and highly significant estimates of the AR process. In the per capita income model, this term is insignificant. We also note the autoregressive component is closer to zero in these models compared to the Arellano–Bond approach.

The results of models VI and VII are both reassuring and highlight an inherent problem in statistical inference. With only 11 significant championship variables, each model produces roughly the number of significant

Table 10.8   Lagged dependent variables – Kiviet correction (model VI)

Personal income		Per capita income		Employment	
Men's water polo	−0.0146 ($p = 0.006$)	Men's water polo	−0.0130 ($p = 0.010$)	Men's basketball	0.0055 ($p = 0.085$)
Men's track and field indoor	−0.0181 ($p = 0.003$)	Men's track and field indoor	−0.0193 ($p = 0.001$)		
Men's hockey	−0.0090 ($p = 0.093$)	Men's track and field outdoor	0.0092 ($p = 0.092$)		
Men's tennis	0.0109 ($p = 0.037$)	Men's tennis	0.0112 ($p = 0.025$)		
Women's tennis	−0.0103 ($p = 0.069$)	Women's tennis	−0.0101 ($p = 0.062$)		
Lagged dep. var.	0.2143 ($p < 0.001$)	Lagged dep. var.	0.0267 ($p = 0.202$)	Lagged dep. var.	0.3823 ($p < 0.001$)
No. of sports	33				

Note: All estimations are done using the percent change of the dependent variable. We use the Anderson–Hsiao method to obtain the consistent estimates necessary for the Kiviet correction to be calculated. The other IV-GMM techniques that produce consistent estimates (Arellano–Bond and Blundell–Bond) do not substantially change the results. The variance-covariance matrix is calculated using a bootstrap method over 500 iterations.

results that one would normally expect from a regression with 99 independent sports variables, suggesting that the modeling technique has been largely successful at eliminating spurious correlation. On the other hand, an unsophisticated reading of the results may lead one to believe that the 11 remaining sports with statistically significant championship coefficients really are driving economic growth rather than being the result of pure chance. Of course, an economic policy using the promotion of women's collegiate fencing as a tool to spur economic growth is likely to be a spectacular failure. It is important to remember that researchers should resist placing too much emphasis a single econometric result in any estimation that utilizes a large vector of sports-related variables.

CONCLUSIONS

Economic impact studies are vital to the literature and public policy debates. While the academic literature agrees that *ex post* studies produce better estimates than *ex ante* approaches, there is no consensus on the

Table 10.9   Lagged dependent variables – MLE: no Kiviet correction (model VII)

Personal income		Per capita income		Employment	
Men's water polo	−0.0156 ($p = 0.013$)	Men's water polo	−0.0139 ($p = 0.002$)	Men's basketball	0.0059 ($p = 0.092$)
Men's hockey	−0.0115 ($p = 0.005$)	Men's hockey	−0.0089 ($p = 0.080$)	Men's track and field indoor	−0.0097 ($p = 0.073$)
Women's fencing	0.0092 ($p = 0.003$)	Men's track and field indoor	−0.0152 ($p = 0.017$)		
		Men's track and field outdoor	0.0085 ($p = 0.085$)		
		Men's tennis	0.0107 ($p = 0.018$)		
		Women's tennis	−0.0122 ($p = 0.028$)		
Lagged dep. var.	0.2325 ($p < 0.001$)	Lagged dep. var.	0.0037 ($p = 0.861$)	Lagged dep. var.	0.3914 ($p < 0.001$)
No. of sports	33				

Note: All estimations are done using the percent change of the dependent variable. We use maximum likelihood to calculate the estimates.

right empirical techniques. Part of this problem is data specific. In this chapter, we consider methods for data with multiple time observations for multiple geographic areas, which are known as dynamic panels or time-series cross-sections. We build an econometric model where NCAA championships can impact one of three economic indicators based on the assumption that a championship outside of the two highest profile sports (football and men's basketball) should have no economic impact. We reach the following conclusions:

First, both city and time effects must be considered which limits the number and type of events that can be examined using *ex post* analysis. Second, unit roots are a major problem. At a minimum, economic impact studies require a long enough time period to map out the 'typical' path of the economic indicator. Any length that accomplishes this is almost certain to have an upward trend and ignoring this problem produces many spurious correlations. In addition, since there has been an increase in the number of NCAA sports over our sample, we find a high number of significant and positive championship effects in our estimations that are almost certainly false. Such problems will also occur in any league that has experienced expansion or an increase in the number of contests played per season.

The common solutions to unit root problems, namely first differencing and percentage changes, are the right antidote but there are important implications to both especially when the variance of the dependent variables across groups is high. A percentage change approach will put different groups on a level playing field. In our data, a percentage change means that any impact on, say, Ames, Iowa (home of Iowa State University) is comparable to a much larger MSA like Los Angeles (home of both University of Southern California and University of California Los Angeles). However, if the event is speculated to have a constant impact across MSAs, say $400 million for hosting a Super Bowl, then first differences are more direct.

Third, fixed effects (and to a lesser extent time dummies) cure some econometric problems but also create others. Since geographic areas follow different growth paths, a fixed effect purges time-invariant growth factors. This also lessens – but usually does not eliminate – heteroskedaticity. Time dummies absorb macroeconomic effects that impact all of the geographic areas, which will purge some generic business cycle problems from the data. Unfortunately, fixed effects create biased estimates in a model with autocorrelation via the demeaning process of the data.

Fourth, the solution for autocorrelation is complicated, and in some cases the researcher may be better off ignoring this problem than correcting it. Since the autocorrelation creates the endogeneity that biases the estimates, one answer is an instrumental variable approach (that is, IV-GMM). The advantage of these techniques is they do not require the researcher to search for instruments as they are embedded in the data. However, it is not assured that higher-order lags will be good instruments. The Kiviet correction offers an alternative approach that is usually preferred to IV-GMM estimators in Monte Carlo settings, but relies on the initial values set by an IV-GMM model which may be improperly specified. Because of this ambiguity, Beck and Katz (2004) argue that simply including a lagged dependent variable as a regressor or in some cases ignoring autocorrelation altogether with a simple fixed effects estimator may be preferable. After all, it is usually better to have inefficient estimates (that is, ignoring autocorrelation) than biased ones (that is, using an improper fix). This is especially true for TSCS data with 'larger' T, say $T > 30$. We feel that corrections for autocorrelation should consider all of the above approaches. In our models, these techniques decrease the percentage of significant championship variables which is an indicator that models that recognize autocorrelation are closer to the true result for our data.

Fifth, the effect of an event or championship need not be in only one period. In our examples, we consider a one-year bump to winning a championship since our a priori assumption in these models is that championship variables should be insignificant. However, there are other contexts where the effect of the event is felt for several periods following the event. For example, Baade et al. (2008) find the effect of Hurricane Andrew on Miami MSA was initially negative right after the storm and then positive as rebuilding efforts began.

Finally, the only cure for spurious correlations is a well-specified model since economic impact studies have serious potential for omitted variable bias. Most often an event is measured as a simple dummy variable in the period it occurred, but clearly some other large event may be the true driver of the effect. In fact, the ability to isolate the economic impact of some event is another reason why fixed effects and time dummies are so important to these studies. This problem increases with the length of the time period, that is, monthly versus yearly data. Since none of our techniques eliminate all of the significant championship variables, we echo the advice that is in Austin et al. (2006) who warn against 'the hazards of testing multiple, non-prespecified hypotheses' (p. 968).

REFERENCES

Anderson, T.W. and C. Hsiao (1982), 'Formulation and estimation of dynamic models using panel data', *Journal of Econometrics*, **18** (1), 47–82.

Arellano, M. and S.R. Bond. (1991), 'Some tests of specification for panel data: Monte Carlo evidence and an application to employment equations', *Review of Economic Studies*, **58**, 277–97.

Austin, P.C., M.M. Mamdani, D.N. Juurlink and J.E. Hux (2006), 'Testing multiple statistical hypotheses results in spurious associations: a study of astrological signs and health', *Journal of Clinical Epidemiology*, **59**, 964–9.

Baade, R. and R. Dye (1988), 'Sports stadiums and area development: a critical view', *Economic Development Quarterly*, **2** (3), 265–75.

Baade, R. and V. Matheson, with R. Baade, (2002), 'Bidding for the Olympics: Fool's Gold?', in *Transatlantic Sport: The Comparative Economics of North American and European Sports*, C.P. Barros, M. Ibrahimo and S. Szymanski (eds), London: Edward Elgar Publishing, pp. 127–51.

Baade, R. and V. Matheson (2004), 'The quest for the cup: assessing the economic impact of the World Cup', *Regional Studies*, **38** (4), 343–54.

Baade, R. and V. Matheson, with R. Baade (2011), 'Financing professional sports facilities', in Z. Kotval and S. White (eds), *Financing for Local Economic Development*, 2nd edn, NewYork: M.E. Sharpe pp. 323–42.

Baade, R., R. Baumann, and V. Matheson (2008), 'Selling the game: estimating the economic impact of professional sports through taxable sales', *Southern Economic Journal*, **74** (3), 794–810.

Beck, N. and J.N. Katz (2004), 'Time-series-cross-section issues: dynamics, 2004', working paper, The Society for Political Methodology, Washington University in St. Louis.

Blundell, R. and S. Bond (1998), 'Initial conditions and moment restrictions in dynamic panel data models', *Journal of Econometrics*, **87**, 115–43.

Bruno, G. (2005), 'Estimation, inference and Monte Carlo analysis in dynamic panel data models with a small number of individuals', *Stata Journal*, **5** (4), 473–500.

Bun, Maurice J.G. and Jan F. Kiviet (2001), 'The accuracy of inference in small samples of dynamic panel data models', Tinbergen Institute Descussion Paper No. 01-006/4.

Bun, Maurice J.G. and Jan F. Kiviet (2003), 'On the diminishing returns of higher-order terms in asymptotic expansions of bias', *Economics Letters*, **79** (2), 145–52.

Coates, D. and Humphreys, B. (1999), 'The growth effects of sports franchises, stadia, and arenas', *Journal of Policy Analysis and Management*, **14** (4), 601–24.

Coates, D. and Humphreys, B. (2002), 'The economic impact of post-season play in professional sports', *Journal of Sports Economics*, **3** (3), 291–9.

Davis, M. and C. End (2010), 'A winning proposition: the economic impact of successful National Football League franchises', *Economic Inquiry*, **48** (1), 39–50.

Feddersen, A. and W. Maennig (2010), 'Sectoral labour market effects of the 2006 FIFA World Cup', *Hamburg Contemporary Economic Discussions*, no. 33.

Hadri, K. (2000), 'Testing for stationarity in heterogeneous panel data', *The Econometrics Journal*, **3** (2), 148–61.

Hagn, F. and W. Maennig (2008), 'Employment effects of the Football World Cup 1974 in Germany', *Labour Economics*, **15** (5), 1062–75.

Hansen, Lars Peter (1982), 'Large sample properties of generalized method of moments estimators', *Econometrica*, **50** (4), 1029–54.

Im, K.S., M.H. Pesaran and Y. Shin (2003), 'Testing for unit roots in heterogeneous panels', *Journal of Econometrics*, **115**, 53–74.

Jasmand, S. and W. Maennig (2008), 'Regional income and employment effects of the 1972 Munich Olympic Summer Games', *Regional Studies*, **42** (7), 991–1002.

Judson, K.A. and A.L. Owen (1999), 'Estimating dynamic panel data models: a guide for macroeconomists', *Economics Letters*, **65**, 9–15.

Kiviet, J.F. (1995), 'On bias, inconsistency, and efficiency of various estimators in dynamic panel models', *Journal of Econometrics*, **68**, 53–78.

Levin, A., C.F. Lin and C.S.J. Chu (2002), 'Unit root tests in panel data: asymptotic and finite-sample properties', *Journal of Econometrics*, **108**, 1–24.

Matheson, V. (2009), 'Economic multipliers and mega-event analysis', *International Journal of Sport Finance*, **4** (1), 63–70.

Nickell, S. (1981), 'Biases in dynamic models with fixed effects', *Econometrica*, **49**, 1417–26.

Siegfried, J. and A. Zimbalist (2002), 'A note on the local economic impact of sports expenditures', *Journal of Sports Economics*, **3** (4), 361–6.

Windmeijer, F. (2005), 'A finite sample correction for the variance of linear two-step GMM estimators', *Journal of Econometrics*, **126** (1), 25–51.

Wooldridge, J. (2002), *Introductory Econometrics: A Modern Approach*, 2nd edn, New York: South-Western College.

11. Should I wish on a stadium? Measuring the average effect on the treated[1]

Gabriel M. Ahlfeldt and Georgios Kavetsos

---

1 INTRODUCTION

Sports facility franchises and hosting of major sports events have often been claimed to be associated with a positive impact on growth, tourism, employment and wages. The empirical literature has, however, clearly rejected the presence of direct benefits to the host community and has seriously questioned these arguments (Siegfried and Zimbalist, 2000).

A relatively new strand of the related literature has focused on the impact professional sports facilities have on prices of proximate properties. The main result is that stadia have a positive impact on the desirability of the location, thus inflating sales and rent prices in their vicinity. The existing evidence is based on stadium-specific case studies, where it is unclear whether the positive impact on prices is attributed to the fandom, area regeneration/accessibility, the stadium's architectural design, or neighbourhood trends that might be correlated with the effect of the stadium thus biasing its impact.

In this chapter we perform a pooled analysis of 27 professional sports stadia in Greater London. Using 2000–2007 property data from the Nationwide Building Society, we are able to estimate the average effect on the treated area based on all major sports facilities in the Greater London Authorities. Our findings support those of the existing literature suggesting that stadia have a positive impact on prices of proximate properties.

2 SPORTS STADIA AND PROPERTY PRICES

The urban economics literature has long been investigating the links between property prices and neighbourhood characteristics, such as the impact on schools (Gibbons and Machin, 2003, 2006), airports (Tomkins et al., 1998), transport links (Gibbons and Machin, 2005) and crime (Gibbons, 2004). As a neighbourhood amenity, sports stadia are also likely to have a significant impact of some sort on the value of proximate properties. In fact, a number of studies, most of them based on the US experience, have aimed at identifying stadium effects on property prices over the past decade. In what follows, we offer a brief overview of the most significant of these.

Carlino and Coulson (2004) study the impact of a National Football League (NFL) franchise on property rents. They estimate that the presence of the NFL franchise increases annual rents by 8 percent in the city and by 4 percent in the wider metropolitan area, an effect they attribute to fandom and civic pride of individuals, wishing to relocate to the area thus pushing rents upwards.[2]

Given the existence of the NFL franchise in Carlino and Coulson (2004), it is hard to distinguish the effect of the stadium itself. Focusing on the construction of the FedEx Field in Maryland, Tu (2005) attempts to estimate the effect of the stadium prior to it being linked to a franchised team. The hedonic analysis provided in his study offers substantial evidence suggesting that prices of proximate properties significantly increase by about 5 percent following each completion phase of the construction. Furthermore, Feng and Humphreys (2008) focus on the case of the Nationwide Arena and Crew Stadium in Columbus, Ohio. Their results indicate a positive effect of both stadiums on proximate property prices.

Results of European-based studies are along the same lines. Ahlfeldt and Maennig (2009, 2010) estimate the impact of the Velodrom and Max-Schmelling Arena on land values in Berlin. For both cases, they find that the stadiums impose a positive effect on land values up to 3 kilometres away. Notably though, these stadia are considered as architectural landmarks, which further induce the effect on prices probably because of the increased identification felt by citizens and fans.

Ahlfeldt and Kavetsos (2013) study the case of the New Wembley and the Emirates Stadium in London. The choice of the two stadia offers an interesting contrast. The New Wembley was constructed on the same site as the historic Wembley stadium, has an impressive architectural design and is the home of the English national football team. The Emirates Stadium is the home of Arsenal FC, one of the most successful English football teams, who relocated to this modern, though not especially impressive, stadium. The authors find significant positive effects on proximate properties in both cases, as well as significant anticipation effects.

Moreover, relevant research has provided evidence regarding the announcement of stadium construction. Dehring et al. (2007) for example, study a series of stadium construction announcements in Dallas City in order to host an NFL franchise, to find that those promoting construction have a significant positive impact on property values. Similar arguments though regarding the distinction between the effect of the stadium and the team also come into play here.

Kavetsos (2012) on the other hand investigates the impact of the announcement of London's successful bid to host the 2012 Olympic Games in July 2005. Arguing that London had unexpectedly won the bid, thus ruling out anticipation effects, he finds a positive and significant impact on property prices in host boroughs and up to 9 miles around the main stadium.[3] Despite the fact that the legacy plans of the main stadium at the time did not involve the relocation of a professional sports team, the study is unable to separate the effect of the regeneration of the Olympic site in a modern park.

Finally, looking at the impact of stadiums from another perspective, Coates and Humphreys (2006) study voting preferences regarding the decision to subsidise the construction or renovation of facilities in Green Bay and Houston, US. The evidence here also points towards an appreciation of property wealth, business trade or fandom, as referenda indicate that precincts proximate to the facilities tend to agree on average with the subsidization plan. Interestingly, Ahlfeldt et al. (2010) find the opposite effect when investigating the referendum on the Munich Allianz-Arena in Germany, indicating that (perceived) proximity cost may vary across sports and countries.

3 DATA, METHODOLOGY AND RESULTS

This chapter presents evidence based on a pooled analysis of 27 professional sports stadia in Greater London. These are presented in Figure 11.1 below. We further use property transactions data from the Nationwide Building Society spanning the period 2000–2007, which we merge with location control variables generated from EDINA Digimaps, the national pupil database and the UK 2001 census. Hence, we are able to estimate the average effect on the treated based on all major sports facilities in the Greater London Authorities.

Assuming a maximum walking distance of 2 kilometres, we draw 2-kilometre radiuses centred around each stadium, depicted by the circles in Figure 11.1, considered as the impact (treatment) area.[4] We are initially interested in a simple comparison of the treatment and control areas in terms of selected output area property and neighbourhood characteristics. This will indicate where in the city stadia locate in general and provide

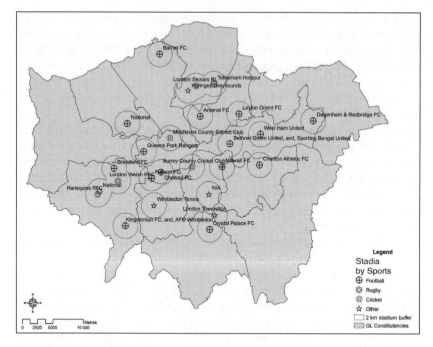

Figure 11.1   Location of London stadia

some prima facie evidence of a significant stadium impact in the surrounding neighbourhood. The results are presented in Table 11.1.

We observe that the difference between treatment and control area characteristics are statistically significant in most cases. In more detail, prices of properties within the 2-kilometre radius are higher, although smaller in terms of size. Properties in proximity to the stadia are also highly populated, as indicated by the average density. These findings are completely in line with the standard bid-rent models, as stadium locations are considerably closer to the city centre, as seen by the distance to the central business district statistic.

Regarding social composition the results are mixed. We find that areas proximate to the stadia are comprised of individuals on both a higher and a lower social grade. Holding an a priori belief that males might be more inclined to locate next to a stadium, we find no significant difference in the proportion of males between the two areas. Finally, taking the Key Stage 2 scores as a benchmark for the average social grade and the quality of public services in a neighbourhood, we can infer that treatment areas are worse off compared with more distant ones; a result that contrasts with the reported figures on property prices.

Table 11.1   Descriptive statistics

	Treatment area	Control area	Difference
Property price (£)	251 567.7	229 004.4	22 563.3[†]
	(147 351.7)	(106 348.9)	(1957.04)
Floor space (m²)	86.324	93.10	−6.78[†]
	(25.47)	(29.14)	(0.477)
Distance: central business	9.09	13.69	−4.601[†]
district (km)	(4.19)	(5.91)	(0.77)
Distance: station (km)	1.48	2.01	−1.33[†]
	(1.73)	(3.04)	(0.38)
Density (pop/ha)	131.53	90.74	40.79[†]
	(93.65)	(100.76)	(1.39)
Social grade: AB – higher/	0.28	0.26	0.016[†]
intermediate Managerial,	(0.143)	(0.122)	(0.002)
administrative,			
professional			
Social grade: E – on state	0.165	0.151	0.014[†]
benefit, Unemployed,	(0.09)	(0.082)	(0.001)
lowest grade workers			
Proportion of male	0.48	0.48	0.0001
population	(0.037)	(0.035)	(0.001)
School quality: Key Stage 2	49.40	51.05	−1.653[†]
score	(6.88)	(7.13)	(0.099)
Observations	7205	13 569	23 968

Notes:
Comparisons based on output area aggregates.
Observations for housing characteristics (Property price and Floor space) are 5072 (treatment), 13 569 (control), 18 641 (total) due to output areas with recorded census characteristics where no transactions took place during the observation periods.
† denotes significance at the 1 per cent level.
Standard deviations reported in brackets.

In an attempt to estimate marginal effects due to proximate stadium location, we estimate a number of semi-log models in our econometric methodology. We first estimate a relatively simple model, given by:

$$\log(P_{it}) = \alpha_0 + \alpha_1 D_i + \sum_n \beta_n X_{ni} + \sum_o \gamma_o S_{ito} + \sum_q \gamma_q L_{itq} + \sum_r \gamma_r N_{itr} + \sum_t \varphi_t + \varepsilon_{it}$$

$$(11.1)$$

where, D is a 5-kilometre stadium impact dummy defined based on the existing evidence in the stadium impact literature (Ahlfeldt and Maennig, 2010), X_n are 250-metre ring dummies around the stadium, S are structural

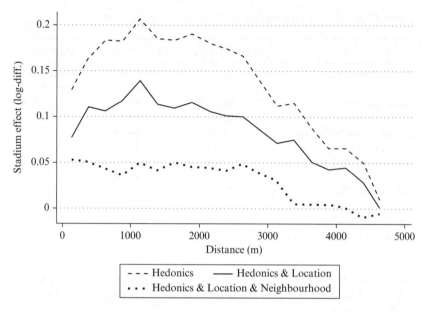

Figure 11.2   Stadium effect

characteristics of the property, L are location characteristics (largely considered to be exogenous), and N are neighbourhood characteristics. φ are year fixed effects and ε represents the error term.

Considering the generalization of the above specification which aggregates the impact of stadia, we re-estimate equation (11.1) by controlling for the varying effect of stadium type (football, rugby, cricket, other).

$$\log(P_{it}) = \alpha_0 + \alpha_1 D_i + \sum_n \sum_s \beta_{sn}(T_{si} \times X_{ni}) + \sum_o \gamma_o S_{ito} + \sum_q \gamma_q L_{itq}$$
$$+ \sum_r \gamma_r N_{itr} + \sum_t \varphi_t + \varepsilon_{it} \tag{11.2}$$

where, T_s are a set of dummies representing the functional type of the stadium.

The results based on estimation of both models can be viewed in Figures 11.2 and 11.3, respectively. Detailed results of both models are reported in the appendix.

Following the potential endogeneity of neighbourhood variables (for example, school quality), which might be reflecting families' self-selection effects based on unobserved preferences, Figure 11.2 presents three differ-

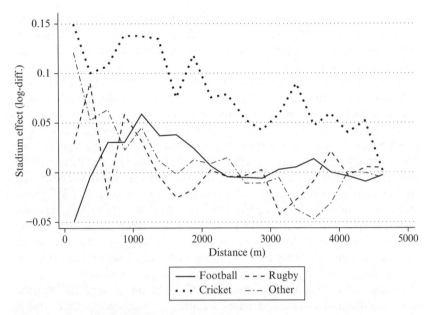

Figure 11.3   Stadium effect by sport

ent sets of results for equation (11.1). The dashed line represents a benchmark model of the distance-varying effect of the stadium on property
prices which only controls for structural amenities (S). The continuous
line then reports the estimates when we additionally control for location
characteristics (L). Finally, the dotted line plots the estimates when we
additionally control for these neighbourhood characteristics (N).

The results are quite informative. Overall, we observe that the effect of
the stadium decreases with distance. In more detail, our results suggest
that the impact increases the furthest away one locates from the stadium,
until it reaches a maximum at about 1 kilometre away, after which we
observe a smooth decay. The 1-kilometre peak can be justified when
considering a potential trade-off between willingness to locate close to
the stadium but at the same time be substantially distant so as to avoid
increased congestion and noise levels associated with fans during match
days. Furthermore, notice that each time additional controls are added
to the model the estimated effects deflate on a constant rate of about 0.5,
but remain statistically significant at the 1 per cent level. When controlling for neighbourhood characteristics though, properties beyond the
3.5-kilometre radius ring are unaffected by the presence of the stadium
(see Table 11.A1, column 3 in the appendix).

In Figure 11.3 we plot the estimated coefficients over the distance rings by breaking down the effect of the stadium and estimating the model specified in equation (11.2). The picture resulting from this exercise does not follow as smooth of a pattern as the one reported previously, where the effects vary considerably depending on the functionality of the stadium.

Interpreting this figure in conjunction with the estimated results provided in the appendix to this chapter, in Table 11.A1, column 4, the model suggests that the immediate proximate effects of a football stadium (up to 250 metres) are significantly negative, possibly due to a congestion or noise effect. Nonetheless, property prices start appreciating significantly 750 metres to 2 kilometres away, with no statistically significant effect thereafter. The evidence on rugby stadia, on the other hand, suggests that the stadium has a significant impact on property prices up to 1 kilometre away, with more distant properties (3.2 to 3.5 kilometre) being negatively affected. The latter pattern is more or less similar when considering various other stadia. Moreover, the effect of cricket grounds are rather impressive, being the only type of facility leading to a significant effect on prices almost throughout the entire distance range considered.

Finally note that the estimated coefficients on structural, location and neighbourhood characteristics are similar to those of other studies (Ahlfeldt and Kavetsos, 2013) and are not reported here for brevity.[5]

4   CONCLUDING REMARKS

In this chapter we offer results of a unique pooled analysis of 27 professional sports stadia in Greater London. Using 2000–2007 property transactions data from the Nationwide Building Society, which we merge with a variety of location and neighbourhood data, we are able to estimate the average effect on the treated properties.

Considering a maximum treatment area of 5 kilometres around each stadium, our findings support those of the existing literature suggesting that stadia have a positive impact on prices of proximate properties. We subsequently repeat our analysis based on the functionality type of the stadium. Results follow the same interpretation, although differ substantially in terms of their magnitude and persistence of the impact when considering more distant radiuses.

NOTES

1. We gratefully acknowledge the support of the Spatial Economics Research Centre and especially Stephen Gibbons and Felix Weinhardt, who provided invaluable help in

terms of data provision and preparation. We also wish to thank Giles Atkinson, Paul Cheshire, Ian Gordon, George MacKerron, Claire Mercer, Susana Mourato, Charles Palmer, Ferdinand Rauch, Kath Scanlon, Matthias Uepping, Servin Waights and Felix Weinhardt for useful suggestions.
2. Note that in a recent study examining the same hypothesis based on housing values instead of rents, Kiel et al. (2010) find that the presence of an NFL franchise has no significant effect.
3. Note that Paris was the favourite to win the bid (see Kavetsos, 2012, for appropriate sources justifying this claim).
4. At larger distance thresholds, our control would almost entirely exclude central London.
5. Full results are available from the authors upon request.

REFERENCES

Ahlfeldt, G.M. and Kavetsos, G. (2013), 'Form or function? The impact of new football stadia on property prices in London', *Journal of the Royal Statistical Society: Series A*, **176**, pt 4.

Ahlfeldt, G.M. and Maennig, W. (2009), 'Arenas, arena architecture and the impact of location desirability: the case of "Olympic arenas" in Prenzlauer Berg, Berlin', *Urban Studies*, **46** (7), 1343–62.

Ahlfeldt, G.M. and Maennig, W. (2010), 'Stadium architecture and urban development from the perspective of urban economics', *International Journal of Urban and Regional Research*, **34** (3), 629–46.

Ahlfeldt, G.M., Maennig, W. and Scholz, H. (2010), 'Expected external effects and voting: the case of the Munich Allianz-Arena', *Journal of Economics and Statistics*, **230** (1), 2–26.

Carlino, G. and Coulson, N. (2004), 'Compensation differentials and the social benefits of the NFL', *Journal of Urban Economics*, **56** (1), 25–50.

Coates, D. and Humphreys, B. (2006), 'Proximity benefits and voting on stadium and arena subsidies', *Journal of Urban Economics*, **59** (2), 285–99.

Dehring, C., Depken, C. and Ward, M. (2007), 'The impact of stadium announcements on residential property values: evidence from a natural experiment in Dallas-Fort Worth', *Contemporary Economic Policy*, **25** (4), 627–38.

Feng, X. and Humphreys, B. (2008), 'Assessing the economic impact of sports facilities on residential property values: a spatial hedonic approach. International Association of Sports Economists', Working Paper 0812, available at: http://ideas.repec.org/p/spe/wpaper/0812.html (accessed 15 April 2011).

Gibbons, S. (2004), 'The costs of urban property crime', *Economic Journal*, **114**, F441–F463.

Gibbons, S. and Machin, S. (2003), 'Valuing English primary schools', *Journal of Urban Economics*, **53** (2), 197–219.

Gibbons, S. and Machin, S. (2005), 'Valuing rail access using transport innovations', *Journal of Urban Economics*, **57** (1), 148–69.

Gibbons, S. and Machin, S. (2006), 'Paying for primary schools: admission constraints, school popularity or congestion?', *Economic Journal*, **116**, C77–C92.

Kavetsos, G. (2012), 'The impact of the London Olympics announcement on property prices', *Urban Studies*, **49**, 1453–70. http://papers.ssrn.com/sol3/papers.cfm?abstract_id=1552322.

Kiel, K.A., Matheson, V.A. and Sullivan, C. (2010), 'The effect of sports franchises on property values: the role of owners versus renters', College of the Holy Cross, Department of Economics Faculty Research Series, No. 10-01, available at: http://college.holycross.edu/RePEc/hcx/Kiel-Matheson_NFLStadiums.pdf (accessed 15 April 2011).

Siegfried, J. and Zimbalist, A. (2000), 'The economics of sports facilities and their communities', *Journal of Economic Perspectives*, **14** (3), 95–114.

Tomkins, J., Topham, N. and Ward, R. (1998), 'Noise versus access: the impact of an airport in an urban property market', *Urban Studies*, **35** (2), 243–58.

Tu, C. (2005), 'How does a new sports stadium affect housing values? The case of FedEx Field', *Land Economics*, **81** (3), 379–95.

APPENDIX: REGRESSION RESULTS

Table 11A.1   Regression results

	(1)	(2)	(3)	(4)
ds250m	0.130** (0.02)	0.077** (0.018)	0.064** (0.013)	
ds500m	0.165** (0.012)	0.111** (0.011)	0.059** (0.008)	
ds750m	0.184** (0.01)	0.107** (0.009)	0.047** (0.007)	
ds1000m	0.183** (0.009)	0.118** (0.008)	0.037** (0.006)	
ds1250m	0.207** (0.008)	0.140** (0.007)	0.048** (0.006)	
ds1500m	0.186** (0.008)	0.114** (0.007)	0.040** (0.006)	
ds1750m	0.184** (0.008)	0.110** (0.007)	0.047** (0.006)	
ds2000m	0.190** (0.008)	0.116** (0.007)	0.046** (0.006)	
ds2250m	0.181** (0.007)	0.107** (0.007)	0.048** (0.006)	
ds2500m	0.175** (0.007)	0.101** (0.007)	0.046** (0.006)	
ds2750m	0.167** (0.007)	0.101** (0.007)	0.052** (0.006)	
ds3000m	0.140** (0.007)	0.086** (0.007)	0.042** (0.006)	
ds3250m	0.112** (0.008)	0.072** (0.007)	0.036** (0.006)	
ds3500m	0.115** (0.008)	0.075** (0.007)	0.010^+ (0.006)	
ds3750m	0.088** (0.008)	0.052** (0.007)	0.005 (0.006)	
ds4000m	0.066** (0.008)	0.043** (0.007)	0.005 (0.006)	
ds4250m	0.066** (0.008)	0.045** (0.007)	0.003 (0.006)	
ds4500m	0.051** (0.008)	0.029** (0.007)	−0.008 (0.006)	
ds4750m	0.01 (0.008)	0.001 (0.007)	−0.007 (0.006)	
ds_base (0-5km)	0.013* (0.006)	−0.035** (0.005)	−0.018** (0.005)	
dfoot250m				−0.049* (0.02)
dfoot500m				−0.004 (0.013)
dfoot750m				0.030** (0.011)
dfoot1000m				0.030** (0.01)
dfoot1250m				0.058** (0.009)
dfoot1500m				0.037** (0.008)
dfoot1750m				0.038** (0.008)
dfoot2000m				0.024** (0.007)
dfoot2250m				0.007 (0.007)
dfoot2500m				−0.005 (0.007)
dfoot2750m				−0.005 (0.006)
dfoot3000m				−0.006 (0.006)
dfoot3250m				0.003 (0.006)
dfoot3500m				0.005 (0.006)
dfoot3750m				0.013* (0.006)
dfoot4000m				0.001 (0.006)
dfoot4250m				−0.004 (0.006)
dfoot4500m				−0.009 (0.006)
dfoot4750m				−0.003 (0.006)
dfoot_base (0–5km)				−0.002 (0.005)
drugby250m				0.029 (0.04)
drugby500m				0.091** (0.022)
drugby750m				−0.023 (0.016)

Table 11A.1   (continued)

	(1)	(2)	(3)	(4)
drugby1000m				0.058** (0.015)
drugby1250m				0.031* (0.014)
drugby1500m				−0.004 (0.016)
drugby1750m				−0.025⁺ (0.014)
drugby2000m				−0.017 (0.014)
drugby2250m				0.002 (0.013)
drugby2500m				−0.005 (0.013)
drugby2750m				−0.004 (0.012)
drugby3000m				0.002 (0.013)
drugby3250m				−0.043** (0.014)
drugby3500m				−0.028* (0.014)
drugby3750m				−0.009 (0.014)
drugby4000m				0.021⁺ (0.013)
drugby4250m				−0.003 (0.012)
drugby4500m				0.005 (0.011)
drugby4750m				0.005 (0.011)
drugby_base (0–5km)				0.117** (0.008)
dcricket250m				0.149 (0.118)
dcricket500m				0.100* (0.05)
dcricket750m				0.107** (0.035)
dcricket1000m				0.138** (0.028)
dcricket1250m				0.137** (0.021)
dcricket1500m				0.134** (0.022)
dcricket1750m				0.075** (0.024)
dcricket2000m				0.118** (0.021)
dcricket2250m				0.075** (0.017)
dcricket2500m				0.078** (0.019)
dcricket2750m				0.053** (0.018)
dcricket3000m				0.042** (0.016)
dcricket3250m				0.058** (0.016)
dcricket3500m				0.090** (0.016)
dcricket3750m				0.047** (0.016)
dcricket4000m				0.060** (0.016)
dcricket4250m				0.040** (0.015)
dcricket4500m				0.052** (0.013)
dcricket4750m				0.001 (0.013)
dcricket_base (0–5km)				0.160** (0.009)
dother250m				0.121** (0.034)
dother500m				0.052* (0.021)
dother750m				0.063** (0.015)
dother1000m				0.022⁺ (0.012)
dother1250m				0.045** (0.011)
dother1500m				0.011 (0.011)
dother1750m				−0.002 (0.01)

Table 11A.1   (continued)

	(1)	(2)	(3)	(4)
dother2000m				0.012 (0.01)
dother2250m				0.009 (0.01)
dother2500m				0.014 (0.01)
dother2750m				−0.011 (0.01)
dother3000m				−0.011 (0.01)
dother3250m				−0.006 (0.009)
dother3500m				−0.038** (0.009)
dother3750m				−0.047** (0.009)
dother4000m				−0.031** (0.009)
dother4250m				0.001 (0.009)
dother4500m				−0.001 (0.009)
dother4750m				−0.006 (0.009)
dother_base (0–5km)				−0.007 (0.007)
Structural char.	Yes	Yes	Yes	Yes
Location char.	No	Yes	Yes	Yes
Neighbourhood Char.	No	No	Yes	No
Year effects	Yes	Yes	Yes	Yes
Observations	66463	66442	66442	66442
R^2	0.72	0.77	0.86	0.78

Notes:
Regressions are OLS. Dependent variable is the natural logarithm of purchase price.
Columns 1, 2 and 3 are based on estimation of equation (11.1). Column 4 is based on estimation of equation (11.2).
Robust standard errors, clustered on postcode groups, are reported in parentheses.
** $p < 0.001$, * $p < 0.05$, + < 0.1.

12. Spain and the FIFA World Cup 2018/2022: a qualitative and quantitative analysis

José Baños and Plácido Rodríguez

1 INTRODUCTION

The Real Federación Española de Fútbol or RFEF (Royal Spanish Federation of Football) and the Federação Portuguesa de Futebol or FPF (Portugese Federation of Football) built the Iberian Bid to host the 2018/2022 FIFA World Cup. In order to arrange the documents for the bid, the RFEF and the FPF asked the Fundación Observatorio Económico del Deporte (FOED, University of Oviedo) and the Instituto Superior de Economia e Gestão de Lisboa (ISEG) respectively to write a report divided into two parts. In the first, a qualitative valuation of the Iberian Bid was carried out and in the second, a quantitative analysis was carried out in order to assess the impact of the event in Spain and Portugal in case the bid was chosen for the organization of the 2018/2022 FIFA World Cup.

This chapter corresponds to the reports made for the case of Spain and it is organized in the following way. In section 2, a review of the different economic impact studies made exclusively for football is described for the twenty-first century. In section 3, the qualitative report is presented based on a SWOT analysis which helped in identifying strengths, weaknesses, opportunities and threats that the FIFA World Cup would bring for Spain. Section 4 is about the quantitative report based on an input–output analysis, which allowed us to quantify the economic effects for Spain if it hosted the FIFA World Cup and the Confederations Cup. Finally, section 5 summarizes the main findings of the chapter as an executive document.

2   THE SPORTING EVENTS ECONOMIC IMPACT STUDIES

The economic study of a great sporting event must take into account a number of goods and services related to the organization of the event, the effect of it on employment, investment in stadiums and infrastructures, accommodation and meals, transport and the entertainment and leisure activities that accompany the event, such as previous and coexistent elements of the event, and a number of material and intangible results that can be present after the event.

These types of study analyze, on the one hand, the benefits that the cities, or the country, obtain as hosts and, on the other hand, the costs related to the organization. Regarding the benefits, it is necessary to distinguish between direct benefits, which are mainly translated in terms of production, employments and infrastructures, and indirect benefits, which are related to the image of the country and the different regions and local governments involved in the project. Regarding the costs, the most important thing is whether the origin of the funds is public or private.

Table 12.1 shows a sample of different studies about economic impact of different championships. The given references refer only to football since year 2000. In the table are the great sport events analysed, the bodies that entrusted the studies (if they existed) and the research institutions (or authors) that carried them out, in the case of FIFA Japan–Korea 2002, Germany 2006 and South Africa 2010; and the Euro Cups celebrated in Belgium and Holland 2000, Portugal 2004 and Austria and Switzerland 2008.

From Table 12.1 it can be concluded that, for the UEFA Euro 2000 organization, different ministries of the government of Holland entrusted a number of research organizations with the study; the German government asked a studies company to undertake the study, the Federal Chancellery of Austria asked a non-profit organization, whereas in Japan and Korea, Portugal and South Africa, the impact analysis were carried out by university researchers.

Table 12.2 summarizes some of the most relevant aspects of the cited studies.

In Table 12.2, the authors use different economic tools to measure the economic impact of the great football events. The most common is the input–out analysis although the computable general equilibrium, the cost–benefit analysis and the factor analysis are used too; the last two are used through surveys made of residents and non-residents in the case of Holland and *ex ante* and *ex post* surveys in that of Korea.

Table 12.1   Identification of the studies

	Belgium–Holland 2000	Korea–Japan 2002	Portugal 2004	Germany 2006	Austria–Switzerland 2008	South Africa 2010
Event	Final round of EuroCup of soccer in Holland	Final round of the FIFA World Cup in Korea	Final round of EuroCup of soccer in Portugal	Final round of the FIFA World Cup in Germany	Final round of EuroCup of soccer in Austria	Final round of the FIFA World Cup in South Africa
Study title	1) *Brood & spelen...*[1] 2) *Costs and Benefits of Major Sports Events. A Case Study of Euro 2000*[1]	'The impact of the World Cup on South Korea: comparison of pre- and post-games'[2]	'Avaliação do impacto económico do EURO2004'[3]	'The economic effects of the soccer World Cup in Germany with regard to different financing'[4]	*Economic Effects of the UEFA EURO 2008 in Austria*[5]	'The impact of hosting a major sport event on the South African economy'[6]
Promoting bodies	1) Ministry of Health, Well Being and Sports. 2) Ministry of Economy 3) Dutch Agency of Tourism 4) Home Office 5) Venue cities		Sociedade Portugal 2004	Home Office	Austrian Federal Chancellery/ Sport Division and the Austrian Economic Chamber	

Research institutions	MeerWaarde	School of Hospitality Business Management, Washington State University	Centro de Investigação sobre Economia Portuguesa (CISEP) – ISEG/UTL	GWS mbH	SpEA (Sports Econ Austria)	University of Pretoria
Other participant institutions	1) Diopter – Janssens en Van Bottenburg B.V. 2) Nederlands Research Instituut voor Toerisme 3) Sliepen Consultancy 4) TNC Inro 5) NIPO 6) Interview*NSS	Kyung Hee University, South Korea	1) Universidade Católica Portuguesa (Porto) 2) Universidade do Minho 3) Universidade do Algarve 4) Universidade de Coimbra		1) Economica Institute of Economic Research 2) Institute for Advances Studies, Vienna	

Notes:
1. Oldenboom (1999, 2006).
2. Kim et al. (2006).
3. CISEP (2004).
4. Ahlert (2001).
5. SpEA (2008).
6. Bohlmann and Heerden (2005).

205

Table 12.2   Objective, applied methodology and results obtained

Year	Belgium–Holland 2000	Korea–Japan 2002	Portugal 2004	Germany 2006	Austria–Switzerland 2008	South Africa 2010
Objective of politics	To create data bases to measure the costs and benefits of the EuroCup 2000	Perception of the local people about the impacts before and after the celebration of the FIFA World Cup	Impact of the event in the whole country	Impact of the event of the country	Quantify not only the effects of hosting the event, but its interaction in the economy of Austria	Examine the expenditure, *ex ante*, of hosting the FIFA World Cup
Objective of the study	1) Impact on the GDP, added value and employment 2) Costs and benefits 3) Financial and non-financial values 4) Tourism, nights per tourist, value of publicity, people support to the event, economic agents support	1) Analysis of the Benefit before and after the championship 2) Benefits from the cultural exchange 3) Natural resources and cultural development 4) Construction costs	1) Effects of the public funds 2) Local and regional impacts 3) Global evaluation of the event (economical, social, sport, cultural and of image	1) Impact on GDP 2) Regional Impacts	1) Impact on the whole economy (added value, employment) 2) Sectorial, regional and temporal impact	1) Impact on the national economy (GDP) 2) Impact on the employment
Methodology	Input–output analysis Cost–benefit analysis	Factorial Analysis MANOVA (*Multivariate analysis of variance*)	1) Multisectoral analysis (input–output model) 2) Calculation of financial flows	Analysis input–output	Analysis input–output	Computable general equilibrium (CGE)

		3) Valuation of the externalities of the event	1) National impacts 2) NUTS[1] 2 level impacts 3) Financial flows corresponding to each venue stadium		
Regions	4 venue cities and national impact	10 venue cities	10 regions of Germany	4 regions	
Actions developed by the study	1) Surveys 2) Telephone calls to five European countries to measure the image for promotional purposes 3) Telephone calls to the inhabitants of Holland	Surveys			
Non evaluated dimensions but cited in the reports	Future predisposition to host other events	Measuring the benefits for the image of the country	Extend the analysis to the frame of the cost–benefit analysis	Valuation of the 'qualitative effects'	1) Financial aspects. 2) Dynamic version of the model.

Note: 1. Acronym for the French *nomenclature d'unités territoriales statistiques*. The higher number (NUTS 1, NUTS 2, NUTS 3), the higher disaggregation.

3 QUALITATIVE REPORT

The qualitative report was based on the SWOT analysis methodology. A SWOT analysis consists of reflecting in a summary table or graphic, relevant information, in this case, about the organization of a big sporting event. On one side, the strengths and weaknesses are analyzed from an internal perspective and, on other side, the external aspects are evaluated as opportunities or threats.

The application of the SWOT analysis for the case of the Iberian Bid as organizers of the 2018/22 FIFA World Cup in Spain and Portugal can be explained using a matrix similar to the one in Table 12.3.

In Table 12.3, the strengths, weaknesses, opportunities and threats are divided into four categories: economic, tourism/trade, environmental and socio-cultural. The strategy to follow must increase the internal capacities of the RFEF and the FPF to possible factors (internal and external) that prevent the attainment of the proposed goals. So, Spain and Portugal had to take advantage of their strengths for the organization of these kind of events and, at the same time, be aware of the threats and weaknesses and to transform them into opportunities or minimize them. Table 12.4 must be analysed from this perspective.

A strategy S => O means the country must use an 'offensive strategy'. This is the optimal position for the RFEF, when the strengths are recognized by competitor countries, which allows it to highlight its own advantages with the aim of attracting potential voters to its bid in the final phase.

A strategy S => T means that the country must follow a 'defensive strategy'. The RFEF must use its strong skills to control and minimize the effects of the threats, which can consist of cultivating the loyalty of the supporters it already has.

A strategy W => O requires a 'strategy of reorientation'. In this case, there exist opportunities but the capacity to take advantage of them does not exist. The RFEF will have to modify its policies if it is to reach the programmed goals.

The strategy W => T means 'survival strategies'. This is where the RFEF does not have the necessary internal strengths to compete with its rivals. In this case it would be prudent to wait until the positive opportunities appear again.

Summarizing, the strategies to follow need to be built upon the strong points to strengthen the opportunities, control the threats and transform the weak points into opportunities. In this sense, it was considered that the major strength of the bid was the presidents of the RFEF and FPF, and the main threats were the strengths of some of the other rival bids, such as Russia.[1]

Table 12.3   SWOT analysis for the organization of an event

Strengths	Weaknesses
▶ Economic	▶ Economic
– Increase of the economic activity	– Increase the prices during the event
– Employment creation	▶ Tourism/trade
– Increase quality of life	– Decrease in the prestige of the country
– Reduced costs in stadiums and infrastructures already built	if the organization of the event is not accurate
▶ Tourism/trade	▶ Environmental
– Increase of the visibility of Spain as a tourist destination	– Bad environmental practices
– Increase of investments on touristic and commercial activities	– Higher pollution
– New opportunities of business	– Destruction of the heritage
▶ Environmental	– Traffic jams
– Improvement of the infrastructures for a sustainable development	▶ Social–cultural
– Preservation of the heritage	– Security decrease
– Protection of the environment	
– Positive impact of sport	
▶ Social-cultural	
– Experience organizing similar events	
– Local participation on the event	
– Enhance the traditional local values	
– Improvement of the image of the country	

Opportunities	Threats
▶ Economic	▶ Economic
– Use of underutilized resources (stadiums)	– The event can be an economic fiasco with great loss of money
– Greater development of the economic activity during and after the event.	▶ Tourism/trade
▶ Tourism/trade	– Losing image as a tourist destination would lead to losing future revenues
– Redefinition and consolidation of the image of Spain as a tourist destination	▶ Environmental
▶ Environmental	– Not to adopt good practices proceedings using the event window
– Consolidation of a good environmental policy	▶ Social–cultural
▶ Social-cultural	– To ignore the need to manage the feeling of belonging to the
– Possibility of increasing the feeling of national identity	community, in multi-ethnic societies.

Source: Fundación Observatorio Económico del Deporte (FOED).

Table 12.4 Definition of strategies using the SWOT analysis

	Strengths (S)	Weaknesses (W)
Opportunities (O)	Strategies: S => O	Strategies: W => O
Threats (T)	Strategies: S => T	Strategies: W =>T

Source: FOED.

4 QUANTITATIVE REPORT

This section shows the data used to analyze the economic impact of hosting the 2018/2022 FIFA World Cup,[2] and the results concerning the economic impact of tourism, the investments and the aggregated results as consequence of the organization of the 2018/2022 FIFA World Cup, for Spain.[3]

When this study was done in 2009 and 2010, only non-secure estimations could be made about the number of foreign visitors and the necessary investments for the event. That is why the authors have taken as a base of this study the results of the final phase of the FIFA World Cup organized in Germany in 2006. The FIFA World Cups in Japan–Korea 2002 and South Africa 2010 are considered less useful because they were in different continents.

In order to estimate the data used in this study,[4] we took into account the 500 000 (approximately) foreign visitors that went to France during the World Cup in 1998 and the 340 000 non-resident visitors that went to the World Cup in Germany in 2006.

As a consequence of this, and of the better climatic conditions in Spain and the development of activities associated with the World Cup (fan festivals, concerts, and so on), it has been estimated that 570 000 foreign visitors to Spain will attend the FIFA 2018/2022 World Cup. Of these, 420 000 are likely to go to Spain with tickets for the matches (included in this group are 20 000 media workers) and 150 000 will participate in the parallel activities which are supposed to contribute to the success of the World Cup in our country. The average length of stay is considered to be 8 days, and the expenditure estimated for each group is €320 per person/day (if we assume that the average price of a ticket is €100) for those that have bought tickets previously, and €220 per person/day for those who are not going to the stadium. Moreover, the number and the expenditure of other groups of participants in the World Cup have been calculated; groups like FIFA staff, soccer federations or the members of the teams are calculated to spend €1000 per person/day.[5]

4.1 Economic Impact of Tourism

The economic impact studies obtain the direct, indirect and induced effects of a sporting event. However, whereas the direct impact is calculated from the economic data of tourist expenditure and the investments made by the organizers of the competition, the indirect and induced effects need to be estimated using input–output (I–O) tables.

The direct, indirect and induced effects derived from tourist expenditure are quantified by showing the economic repercussion as gross value added (GVA) and employment generated, and breaking down economic activity into 16 branches of activity that are identified in Spanish regional accounts.

To measure the economic impact of tourism derived from the World Cup it is necessary to quantify, first, the internal tourist expenditure (in Spain), then the combined information about the number of tourists, their expenditure and the average stay. This information refers only to foreign visitors[6] going to Spain because of the World Cup.

An increase in internal tourist expenditure generates an increase in activity (direct effect) for the first suppliers of that demand (hotels, restaurants, and so on), which must increase their orders to other suppliers (food, beverages and the like). These, consequently, to satisfy the additional demand, will generate a second round of economic transactions as they will need to increase the number of orders to their suppliers, and so on (indirect effects).

The effects of internal tourist expenditure are not finished with the direct and indirect effects, as these generate an increase in household income via wages and salaries which are translated into a greater private consumption, thereby starting a new cycle of effects known as induced effects. The economic effects of tourism are summarized in Figure 12.1.

The economic effects generated by tourism in Spain, in terms of GVA, due to the organization of the 2018/2022 FIFA World Cup, are summarized in Table 12.5.

World Cup tourist expenditure based on an estimated number of visitors and the average expenditure and the average length of stay (days) of each visitor, has been valued at more than €767 net million. Tourists focus their expenditure on the hotel industry (representing 70 percent of the total), followed by trade and repairs (19 percent).

Taking the interior tourist expenditure sector, it has used the I–O table of Asturias of 2005 of intersectorial relations,[7] and by extension to the rest of the Autonomous Community of Asturias to estimate the impact on GVA. According to this, the indirect effects are distributed throughout the economic network, due to the investments that the other four

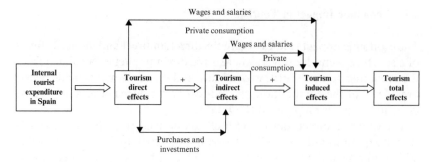

Source: FOED.

Figure 12.1 Economic impact of tourism

Table 12.5 Effects of the tourist expenditure on GVA: breakdown by branches of activity (€000)

Branch of Activity	Direct effects	Indirect effects	Induced effects	Total effects
1. Agriculture and fishing	–	18 028	3 173	21 200
2. Oil industries	–	3 341	1 019	4 360
3. Food, beverages and tobacco	–	23 606	3 582	27 188
4. Chemical industry	–	1 144	134	1 278
5. Other non-metallic mineral products	–	1 418	390	1 808
6. Metallurgy and metallic products	–	1 131	319	1 450
7. Metal transformation industry	–	2 684	626	3 310
8. Other manufacturer industries	–	3 632	1 490	5 122
9. Electric energy, gas and water	–	18 539	5 456	23 995
10. Construction	–	11 510	3 914	15 424
11. Trade and repairs	145 088	32 557	30 466	208 111
12. Hotel industry	537 373	3 569	20 955	561 897
13. Transport and communications	72 727	30 795	14 980	118 503
14. Financial and managing services	–	119 545	51 396	170 942
15. Education, health and social services	–	1 862	9 904	11 766
16. Other services	12 007	5 792	11 429	29 228
Total	767 195	279 154	159 233	1 205 582

Source: FOED.

branches have to make to satisfy their demand, highlighting the importance of financial and managing services (43 percent), trade and repairs (12 percent) and transport and communications (11 percent).

The induced effects, finally, would suggest the distribution of households' expenditure inside the country are again in financial and managing services (32 percent) and trade and repairs (19 percent), as well as in the hotel industry (13 percent).

The total effect tourist expenditure generated by the FIFA World Cup generates an estimated GVA of more than €1205 million (2010 prices).

Once the economic effects of tourism are estimated in terms of GVA, it is also interesting to know the repercussion on another important economic indicator, that is, employment. To do so, is necessary to use the relationship between GVA and employment derived from the I–O tables of Asturias of 2005, assuming that those proportions are the same for the region and the rest of Spain. The consequences of tourist expenditure on employment in Spain as a consequence of hosting the FIFA World Cup 2018/2022 are summarized in Table 12.6.

The effect on the direct employment due to touristic expenditures at the 2018/2022 World Cup is 18 674 people. The branch of activity that generated more employment in relative terms is the hotel industry (69 percent), followed by trade and repairs (24 percent) and transport and communications (5 percent).

On the other hand, the indirect effects are distributed mostly among the

Table 12.6   Effects of tourist expenditure on employment: break down by branches of activity (persons)

Branch of Activity	Direct effects	Indirect effects	Induced effects	Total effects
1. Agriculture and fishing	–	1 128	199	1326
2. Oil industries	–	85	26	111
3. Food, beverages and tobacco	–	320	49	369
4. Chemical industry	–	13	2	15
5. Other non-metallic mineral products	–	16	5	21
6. Metallurgy and metallic products	–	14	4	18
7. Metal transformation industry	–	45	11	56
8. Other manufacturer industries	–	85	35	120
9. Electric energy, gas and water	–	57	17	74
10. Construction	–	297	101	398
11. Trade and repairs	4 560	1 020	955	6 535
12. Hotel industry	12 926	86	504	13 516
13. Transport and communications	997	424	206	1627
14. Financial and managing services	–	1 344	578	1921
15. Education, health and social services	–	68	363	431
16. Other services	191	92	182	465
Total	18 674	5 095	3 234	27 003

Source: FOED.

financial and managing services (26 percent), agriculture and fishing (22 percent) and trade and repairs (20 percent). As regards induced effects, greater employment is produced in trade and repairs (30 percent), financial and managing services (18 percent) and the hotel industry (16 percent).

In total, the direct employment due to tourist expenditure motivated by the 2018/2022 FIFA World Cup is 27003 people.

4.2   Economic Impact of Investment

The investment made for the World Cup in Germany was €1400 million in construction of and repairing the stadiums, and €2700 million in infrastructure. In our study, we assume that all the venue stadiums will be built or remodeled in advance, except where a venue does not have the minimum capacity required in 2010 and enlargement is needed. Also, improvement repairs will be necessary in certain areas (mainly airports and trains), but are hard to quantify at the time of this report because it is not known which are the venue cities. Moreover, it will be necessary to arrange other temporary repairing infrastructure work, such as for the media and for cultural and recreational activities linked to the event.

As pointed out in the previous paragraph, we could estimate the amount for different investments, but it would be a risky exercise given the available information. Therefore, taking into account the current crisis situation that we expect to be extinguished for 2018/2022, a very prudent calculation of the event expenditure has been made, leading to a figure slightly higher than a sixth of the expenditure made by Germany in 2006. In our case, investment is estimated to be €538 million. The effect of this investment on the GVA is shown in Table 12.7.[8]

All direct impact is estimated to be in the construction sector. The economic sectors with more indirect impact on the GVA are construction, financial and managing services and other non-metallic mineral products, with 28 percent, 23 percent and 11 percent of the total effects, respectively.

The most important of the induced effects are financial and managing services (32 percent), trade and repairs (19 percent) and the hotel industry (13 percent).

The total effect of tourist expenditure due to the FIFA World Cup leads to an estimated GVA of slightly more of €1267 million, using 2010 prices.

Table 12.8 reports the effects of investment on employment.

The effect of investment for the 2018 World Cup on direct employment is 13945 more people. On the indirect effects side, the branch of activity that generates more employment in relative terms is construction (39

Table 12.7   Effects of investment on GVA (€000)

Branch of Activity	Direct effects	Indirect effects	Induced effects	Total effects
1. Agriculture and fishing	–	1 193	4 543	5 735
2. Oil industries	–	12 524	1 459	13 982
3. Food, beverages and tobacco	–	265	5 128	5 393
4. Chemical industry	–	3 494	192	3 686
5. Other non-metallic mineral products	–	55 908	559	56 467
6. Metallurgy and metallic products	–	29 539	457	29 996
7. Metal transformation industry	–	5 861	897	6 758
8. Other manufacturer industries	–	18 838	2 133	20 972
9. Electric energy, gas and water	–	10 356	7 812	18 168
10. Construction	538 378	139 588	5 604	683 570
11. Trade and repairs	–	45 392	43 622	89 014
12. Hotel industry	–	5 076	30 004	35 080
13. Transport and communications	–	54 140	21 450	75 589
14. Financial and managing services	–	116 428	73 592	190 020
15. Education, health and social services	–	112	14 181	14 293
16. Other services	–	2 256	16 364	18 621
Total	538 378	500 969	227 996	1 267 344

Source: FOED.

percent), followed by trade and repairs (15 percent) and financial and managing services (14 percent).

Furthermore, the induced effects are distributed mainly among trade and repairs (30 percent), financial and managing services (18 percent) and the hotel industry (16 percent).

In total, employment generated by expenditure on investment for the FIFA World Cup is 27 896 people.

4.3   Economic Impact of Tourism and Investment

In this section, the results of the two previous sections are brought together. The aggregated values of the total effect of the expenditure on tourism and investment on the GVA are reported in Figure 12.2, where it can be observed that the total effect of tourist expenditure and investment motivated by the FIFA World Cup generates a GVA, in terms of 2010 prices, estimated at almost €2473 million.

Figure 12.3 shows the total effect of tourist expenditure and investment on employment.

The effect on direct employment of tourist expenditure and investment

Table 12.8   Effects of the investments on the employment: breakdown by branches of activity (persons)

Branch of Activity	Direct effects	Indirect effects	Induced effects	Total effects
1. Agriculture and fishing	–	75	285	360
2. Oil industries	–	321	37	359
3. Food, beverages and tobacco	–	4	70	73
4. Chemical industry	–	41	2	43
5. Other non-metallic mineral products	–	648	6	655
6. Metallurgy and metallic products	–	371	6	377
7. Metal transformation industry	–	100	15	115
8. Other manufacturer industries	–	443	50	493
9. Electric energy, gas and water	–	32	24	56
10. Construction	13 945	3616	145	17 706
11. Trade and repairs	–	1428	1372	2800
12. Hotel industry	–	123	725	848
13. Transport and communications	–	748	296	1044
14. Financial and managing services	–	1314	830	2144
15. Education, health and social services	–	4	521	526
16. Other services	–	36	261	297
Total	13 945	9303	4648	27 896

Source: FOED.

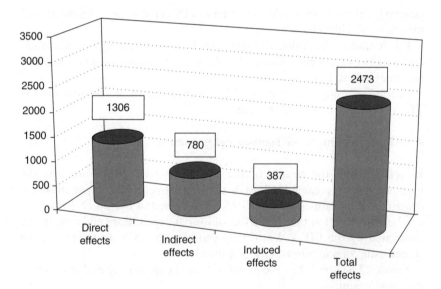

Figure 12.2   Total effects on GVA: breakdown by type of impact (€million)

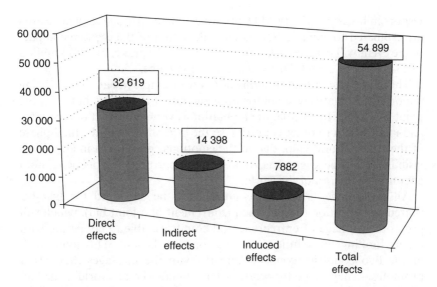

Figure 12.3   Total effects on the employment: breakdown by type of impact (persons)

on the 2018/2022 FIFA World Cup is 32 619 people. The branches of activity that generated most employment in relative terms was construction (43 percent) and the hotel industry (40 percent).

As regards indirect effects, construction (27 percent), financial and managing services (18 percent) and trade and repairs (17 percent) are the most important branches. In relation to the induced effects, the role of trade and repairs (30 percent), financial and managing services (18 percent) and the hotel industry (16 percent) are the most important.

The total effect of tourist expenditure and the investment from hosting the FIFA World Cup is 54 899 more employed workers.

5   CONCLUSION

From the qualitative analysis carried out here, it can be concluded that the organization of the final phase of the 2018/2022 FIFA World Cup is a great opportunity to improve the image of the country and spread 'brand Spain', consolidating the idea of the country as an organizer of great events, increasing its capacity as a tourist attraction and enhancing its identity and national esteem.

The FIFA World Cup in Spain and Portugal can host the most foreign visitors in history of the World Cup. An estimated 570 000 foreign visitors are estimated to come to Spain. The calculation of the economic impact of the event will generate a GVA, in terms of 2010 prices, of €2473 million (0.23 percent of 2009 GDP) and almost 54 899 jobs.

This economic impact in terms of GVA or employment, despite being important, is relatively small for the economy of a country, but from the point of view of the media, the reputation is very important of a country and image given to other countries, so the organization of the final phase of the FIFA World Cup, due to the emotional power and international visibility that the event has, is a great opportunity to publicize both countries to the rest of the world.

All these benefits for the countries will be enhanced for being a shared organization (despite the inconvenient of a joint bid), which will promote an image of entrepreneurial countries, able to cooperate with others looking for solutions for the common benefit. This joint work of the two countries connects directly with the messages that FIFA promotes: 'They excite the world', 'They build a better world'. The fact of being a shared project shows clearly the 'absence of racism' and the defense of 'fair play' as elements of mutual respect and cooperation. From the platform of the FIFA World Cup organizing countries, it is necessary to defend 'childhood rights' and the 'promotion of health'. But especially, it is a sporting competition, where the rules of fair play, teamwork, support for national teams and everything that football involves at a world level, with the biggest objective consisting in 'Develop the game'.

NOTES

1. FIFA had stipulated, before the election of the venues for the 2018 and 2022 World Cups, that one of them would be in Europe (apparently the one in 2018). The authors of this paper pointed out that 'the main rival would be Russia (for never having organized the event before and especially because of the economic power it could have, although having some weaknesses like the time frame of television broadcasts from Russia or the very high prices in Moscow). England would be the next choice to have into account and Belgium and Holland do not have any chance, which can be decisive in during the subsequent votes' (Rodríguez et al., 2010, p. 4).
2. The economic impact of the possible organization of the Confederations Cup in Spain and Portugal in 2017/2021 has been also estimated. The results of this study are available on request from the authors of this chapter.
3. In this field the literature is abundant, from the first analysis of the economic impact of an sporting event done for the Formula 1 Grand Prix in Adelaide made by Burns, et al. in 1986, until the publication about the economics of mega-sporting events coordinated by Maennig and Zimbalist that was published by Edward Elgar in 2012.
4. Based on different studies: Brauer and Brauer (undated), FIFA (2007), Maennig and

du Plessis (2007), Rahmann et al. (1997), Schily (2005) and several websites (see, for example, Wikipedia and www.todoslosmundiales.com in References).

5. The rest of the estimations of data used in this study are available on request from the authors of this chapter.
6. The expenditure of residents must not be included in the input–output analysis.
7. Other studies that use the input–output tables of Asturias to analyse the economic impact of sport are Aza et al. (2007) and Baños et al. (2012).
8. Figures are in net terms; that is, without VAT or other indirect taxes.

REFERENCES

Ahlert, G. (2001), 'The economic effects of the soccer World Cup in Germany with regard to different financing', *Economic Systems Research*, **13**, 109–27.

Aza, R., J. Baños, J.F. Canal, and P. Rodríguez (2007), 'The economic impact of football on the regional economy', *International Journal of Sport Management and Marketing*, **2** (5), 459–74.

Baños, J., F. Pujol and P. Rodríguez (2012), 'Economic impact analysis of hosting the World Speed Skating Championship in Gijón', *Estudios de Economía Aplicada*, **30** (2), 703–31.

Bohlmann, H. and J. Heerden (2005), 'The impact of hosting a major sport event on the South African economy', Working Paper Series, Department of Economics, University of Pretoria.

Brauer, S. and G. Brauer (undated), 'Sport and national reputation. The 2006 FIFA World Cup and Germany's image worldwide', available at: http://www.fifa.com/mm/document/afmarketing/marketing/83/31/80/sportverlagenglischtrackc hanges (accessed March 2010).

Burns, P., J. Hatch and T. Mules (1986), *The Adelaide Grand Prix: The Impact of a Special Event*, Adelaide: Centre for South Australian Economic Studies.

Centro de Investigação Sobre Economica Portuguesa (CISEP) (2004), 'Economic impact evaluation of hosting the final stage of the European Football Championship in Portugal', mimeo, Centro de Investigação Sobre Economia Portuguesa, Portugal.

Fédération internationale de football association (FIFA) (2007), *Informe sobre las Finanzas de la FIFA 2006*, Zurich: FIFA.

Kim, H., D. Gursoy and S. Lee (2006), 'The impact of the World Cup on South Korea: comparison of pre- and post-games', *Tourism Management*, **27**, 86–96.

Maennig, W. and S. du Plessis (2007), 'World cup 2010: South African economic perspectives and policy challenges informed by the experience of Germany 2006', *Contemporary Economic Policy*, **25** (4), 578–90.

Maennig, W. and A. Zimbalist (2012), *International Handbook on the Economics of Mega Sporting Events*, Cheltenham, UK and Northampton, MA, USA Edward Elgar.

Oldenboom, E. (1999), *Bread & Circuses: The Economic and Social Valuation of Major Sporting Events*, Amsterdam: MeerWaarde.

Oldenboom, E. (2006), *Cost and Benefits of Major Sport Events. A Case-study of Euro 2000*, Amsterdam: MeerWaarde Onderzoeksadvies.

Rahmann, B., W. Weber, Y. Groening, M. Kurscheidt, H.-G. Nepp and M. Pauli (1997), *Sozio-o'konomische Analyse der Fupbalt-Weltmeisterschaft 2006 in*

Deutschland (*Socio-economic Analysis of the Football World Cup 2006 in Germany*), Paderborn: Paderborn University.

Rodríguez, P., J. Baños and V. Puente (2010), 'Análisis del impacto económico para España, de la organización de la fase final de la Copa Mundial de la FIFA 2018. Documento ejecutivo', mimeo, Gijón: FOED.

Schily, O. (2005), 'Germany and the World Football Championship', opening speech of SportAcoord, 15 April, available at: http://wm2006.deutschland.de/ES/Content/ActualidadDelMundial/Discursos/2005/discurso-schily-inauguracion-de-sportaccord-2005.html (accessed March 2010).

SportsEconAustria (SpEA) (2008), *Economic Effects of the UEFA EURO 2008 in Austria*, Vienna: Institute for Sport Economics.

Wikipedia: http://es.wikipedia.org/wiki/Copa_Mundial_de_F%C3%BAtbol_de_2006 (accessed March 2010).

www.todoslosmundiales.com.ar/mundiales/2006alemania (accessed March 2010).

Epilogue

Plácido Rodríguez, Stefan Késenne and Jaume García

This book is the outcome of the VI Gijón Conference, held in Gijón (Spain) on 6 and 7 May 2011, at the auditorium of the Faculty of Trade, Tourism and Social Sciences Jovellanos of the University of Oviedo. The editors would like to thank the various authors for their contribution to this book, and Professor William Greene for writing the Prologue. The conference was organized by Professors Jaume García (Universitat Pompeu Fabra), Stefan Késenne (University of Antwerp and Leuven) and Plácido Rodríguez (University of Oviedo).

The Opening Ceremony of the Conference was presided by Dr Santiago García Granda (Vice-Rector for Research at the University of Oviedo) and Ms Paz Fernández Felgueroso (Mayor of the City of Gijón). Other speakers at the ceremony were Dr Herminio Sastre Andrés (Minister of Education of the Government of the Principality of Asturias), Dr Antonio Alvarez Pinilla (Director of Analysis and Innovation Department of Liberbank), Dr Rafael Perez Lorenzo (Dean, Faculty of Commerce and Tourism and Social Sciences Jovellanos) and Plácido Rodríguez Guerrero (Co-organizer of Congress)

Thirteen researchers from Europe, North America and South Korea presented papers at the conference. These authors were introduced by the following professors and researchers: Ángel Barajas, Jose A. Fraiz and Patricio Sánchez (University of Vigo); Pedro García del Barrio (International University of Catalonia); Ruud Koning (University of Groningen); Carlos Arias (University of Leon); Allan Wall, Antonio Alvarez, Cristina Muñiz, Levi Pérez, Luis Orea, Mary J. Suárez and Juan Prieto (University of Oviedo) and Victor Puente (Sport Economics Observatory Foundation). The editors would like to thank their contributions.

The organizers thank Cajastur-Liberbank; the Council of Education and Science of the Government of the Asturias; the Tourism Society of the Gijon municipal government; the University of Oviedo; the Department of Economics of the University of Oviedo; the Faculty of Trade, Tourism and Social Sciences Jovellanos of the University of Oviedo; and the Sport Economics Observatory Foundation, for financial support given for the conference. They also gratefully acknowledge financial support from the Spanish Sports Council, under grant 003/SAL30/11.

Index